SEXUAL HISTORY EVIDENCE AND THE RAPE TRIAL

Joanne Conaghan and Yvette Russell

BRISTOL
UNIVERSITY
PRESS

First published in Great Britain in 2023 by

Bristol University Press
University of Bristol
1–9 Old Park Hill
Bristol
BS2 8BB
UK
t: +44 (0)117 374 6645
e: bup-info@bristol.ac.uk

Details of international sales and distribution partners are available at bristoluniversitypress.co.uk

British Library Cataloguing in Publication Data
A catalogue record for this book is available from the British Library

ISBN 978-1-5292-0781-1 hardcover
ISBN 978-1-5292-0782-8 paperback
ISBN 978-1-5292-0785-9 ePub
ISBN 978-1-5292-0784-2 ePdf

Cover design: Nicky Borowiec
Front cover image: alamy/The Picture Art Collection

Contents

List of Cases

Australia

GP v R [2016] NSWCCA 150

Jackmain v R [2020] NSW 150

PJE v The Queen (High Court of Australia, No S8/1996; S154/1995, 9 September 1996, unreported)

R v Bernthaler (NSW, Court of Criminal Appeal, No 60394/93, 17 December 1993, unreported)

R v Burton [2013] NSWCCA 335

R v Morgan (1993) 20 NSWLR 543

R v PJE (NSW, Court of Criminal Appeal, No 60216/95, 9 October 1995, unreported)

R v Stanbrook (Supreme Court of Victoria, O'Bryan J, 10 November 1992, unreported)

R v Taylor [2009] NSWCCA 180

Canada

R v Ghomeshi 2016 ONCJ 155

Seaboyer v AG of Canada; Gayme v Same [1993] 1 LRC 464

England and Wales

In Re A (Children) (Conjoined Twins: Surgical Separation) [2001] 2 WLR 480

In Re F (Mental Patient: Sterilisation) [1990] 2 AC 1

A local authority v JB [2021] UKSC 52

DPP v Morgan (1976) AC 182

R v A (No 2) [2001] 1 UKHL 25

R v All-Hilly [2014] EWCA Crim 1614

R v AM [2008] EWCA Crim 818

R v Barker (1829) 3 Car & P 588

R v Bogie [1992] Crim L R 301

New Zealand

Republic of Ireland

People (DPP) v EH [2019] IECA 30
People (DPP) v GK (2007) 2 IR 92
People (DPP) v Walsh, extempore, Court of Criminal Appeal 18 July 2008

Scotland

Dickie v HM Advocate (1897) 24 R (J) 82
MacDonald v HMA [2020] HCJAC 21

United States

US v Dorsey 16 MJ 1 (CMA 1983)

List of Statutes

Australia

Criminal Law (Sexual Offences) Act 1978 (QLD)
Criminal Procedure Act 1986 (NSW)
Criminal Procedure Act 2009 (VIC)
Evidence Act 1906 (WA)
Evidence Act 1929 (SA)
Evidence Act 2001 (TAS)
Evidence (Miscellaneous Provisions) Act 1991 (ACT)
Sexual Offences (Evidence and Procedure) Act 1983 (NT)

Canada

Criminal Code (RSC 1985)

England and Wales

Contempt of Court Act 1981
Coroners and Justice Act 2009
Criminal Justice Act 1988
Criminal Justice Act 2003
Criminal Justice and Public Order Act 1994
Human Rights Act 1998
Offences against the Person Act 1828
Offences against the Person Act 1837
Offences against the Person Act 1861
Prisoners' Counsel Act 1836
Sexual Offences Act 1956
Sexual Offences (Amendment) Act 1976
Sexual Offences Act 2003
Substitution of Punishments of Death Act 1841
Youth Justice and Criminal Evidence Act 1999, ss 41–3

New Zealand

Evidence Act 2006
Evidence (Amendment) Act 1977
Sexual Violence Legislation Act 2021

Northern Ireland

Criminal Evidence (Northern Ireland) Order 1999

Republic of Ireland

Civil Legal Aid Act 1995
Criminal Justice (Victims of Crimes) Act 2017
Criminal Law (Rape) Act 1981
Criminal Law (Rape) Amendment Act 1990

Scotland

Criminal Procedure (Scotland) Act 1995
Sexual Offences (Procedure and Evidence) (Scotland) Act 2002

United States

Federal Rules of Evidence
See notes 66–70 of Chapter 4

About the Authors

Joanne Conaghan is Professor of Law at the University of Bristol and Fellow of the British Academy. She has published extensively on issues relating to law and gender, including in the fields of criminal justice and legal theory. She is author of *Law and Gender* (Oxford University Press, 2013).

Yvette Russell is Associate Professor in Law and Feminist Theory at the University of Bristol. She has published widely on feminist philosophy, law and sexual violence.

Acknowledgements

We would like to acknowledge the time and care of those colleagues who read over and commented on draft chapters of this book prior to its publication, in particular: Elisabeth McDonald, Ngaire Naffine, Gwen Seabourne and Olivia Smith. We would also like to acknowledge the support of Susan Leahy and Julia Quilter, who directed us to important literature in respect of the law in Ireland and Australia, which helped us with Chapter 4. Thanks as well to Nic Aaron, Jasmine Bundhoo and Megan Johnson for research assistance with Chapter 4. We are extremely grateful to Helen Davis, Grace Carroll and colleagues at Bristol University Press, who were consistently encouraging and patient while we worked on this book and did everything they could to support us to do our best work. We also benefitted greatly from the support and generosity of our colleagues at the University of Bristol Law School, and the rich and stimulating research environment of which we are so privileged to be part. Finally, a note of thanks to the legal feminist research community in the UK, who are doing difficult and painstaking research on sexual violence and law, for their encouragement while we worked on this book.

Introduction: Setting the Scene

Setting the scene: from Ched Evans to #MeToo

On 14 October 2016, four years after his initial conviction in 2012, Chedwyn Evans (known as 'Ched') was acquitted of rape in a retrial at Cardiff Crown Court after the admission of new evidence of the complainant's[1] sexual behaviour with other men. The verdict, and how it was reached, provoked intense, deeply diverging public responses. Evans' celebrity status as a professional footballer with Sheffield United FC, alongside the public support provided by his fiancée (and her millionaire father), drew the inevitable attention of the tabloid press, fuelling an apparently insatiable public appetite for stories of 'sleazy' behaviour by sports stars and other celebrities (Brown, 2016). Meanwhile, Evans' complainant had to be relocated repeatedly and to change her name after being relentlessly harassed and identified 'thousands of times' on social media (Morris, 2016a). The Evans saga – from first accusation, to conviction, incarceration, appeal and final acquittal – prompted an explosion of public commentary, speculation and (sometimes shallow) handwringing, at the heart of which lay, on any interpretation of the facts, a sordid tale of male sexual entitlement and female sexual degradation. As one headline after Evans' acquittal declared: 'There are no winners as rape case drags football down to its darkest depths' (Herbert, 2016).

Nearly a decade later, the Evans case remains an unresolved point of contestation within criminal justice scholarship and debate. Other celebrity cases have come and gone, displacing it in terms of notoriety and public

---

[1] 'Complainant' is the legal term used in England and Wales to refer to someone whose complaint of rape is heard in a criminal court. In Scotland, the term is 'complainer'. The complainant/complainer is neither a party to proceedings nor necessarily a victim of crime: her complaint has yet to be proven. In formal terms, she is 'merely' a witness, and as such, her input and control over proceedings, as well as her formal legal rights, are tenuous at best. The precarious position of the victim/witness in the rape trial is a focus throughout this book.

attention. The 2018 'Rugby Rape Trial' (as it is popularly known) – in which Irish rugby players, Paddy Jackson and Stuart Olding, were tried and acquitted of rape in a Belfast Crown Court – plumbed the murky depths of the misogynistic culture which repeatedly surfaces in elite male sport, shocking and riveting the highly conservative Northern Irish public in equal measure (Killean et al, 2021: 3–5). #MeToo is also a post-Evans phenomenon, shifting the public gaze from sports personalities to film and entertainment moguls. In 2020, producer, Harvey Weinstein, was convicted of rape and sexual assault after multiple women who had worked with him blew the whistle on his predatory sexual behaviour. His conviction was soon followed by that of Ghislaine Maxwell, daughter of Robert Maxwell, the deceased media mogul: in 2021, Maxwell was convicted of trafficking girls for sexual purposes on behalf of financier and convicted sex offender Jeffrey Epstein (also deceased).

Nearly every week heralds the emergence of new revelations of sexual transgressions by celebrities and other public figures. This endless media parade of impugned and/or disgraced public figures is playing out within the context of acute public concern about the effectiveness of criminal justice processes in combatting sexual violence. Over the last decade, the proportion of reported rapes resulting in a charge in England and Wales has fallen dramatically, producing an all-time low of 1.3 per cent in September 2021 (House of Commons Home Affairs Committee, 2022).[2] The overall picture is sufficiently bleak to have prompted the Victims Commissioner at the time, Dame Vera Baird QC, gloomily to pronounce that 'what we are witnessing is the de-criminalisation of rape' (Baird, 2020: 16). A damning report, commissioned by the Home Office and published in June 2021, concurred with Baird's view that the criminal justice system was failing victims of rape and sexual assault: 'The current situation is totally unacceptable, and the Government is determined to change it: We owe this to every victim and are extremely sorry that the system has reached this point' (Home Office, 2021: para 5).

Shocking reports about the length of time rape victims must wait before their case comes to court (Summers, 2022), along with calls from multiple quarters to address the depleted state of the criminal justice system,[3] ensure that the criminal justice response to sexual violence continues to remain at the forefront of public debate (Siddique, 2022). Moreover, this debate

---

[2] The most recent data, up to 30 September 2022, shows that while the volume of suspects being charged has risen slightly, there has been a corresponding decline in the rape conviction rate (Crown Prosecution Service, 2023).

[3] In September 2022, criminal barristers in England and Wales took the unprecedented step of engaging in strike action to halt further 'disintegration' of the criminal justice process (Sidhu, 2022). See also Siddique (2022).

is taking place against the backdrop of extensive reform of rape law and procedures as long expressed feminist concerns have steadily penetrated state agendas, prompting a transformative impetus which in the last few decades has swept the globe. Multiple jurisdictions have now reshaped their laws, practices and procedures governing the prosecution of rape and other sexual offences (McGlynn and Munro, 2010), while in the sphere of international law, a substantial normative infrastructure and jurisprudence has developed (Dowds, 2020). With all this fervent activity, one might expect to see something by way of results. Yet, if the figures in England and Wales are anything to go by, the effectiveness of rape law reforms in delivering justice for victims must surely be questioned.[4]

It is within a context of growing disillusionment with legal responses to sexual violence that we come to the use of sexual history evidence, that is, the introduction into trial proceedings in sexual offences cases of evidence of a complainant's sexual behaviour other than in relation to the incident which is the subject of the charge. Historically, as we shall see, such evidence was routinely invoked by the defence either to support a claim that the complainant had consented to sexual relations with the accused or to tarnish her character and, correspondingly, her credibility as a witness. The courtroom invocation of these 'twin myths' – that unchaste women are more likely to consent to intercourse and in any event are less worthy of belief[5] – has long been a focus of feminist concern about the way rape trials are conducted, producing a succession of legislative and judicial interventions to curb the improper use of evidence of a complainant's sexual history. In England and Wales, these efforts culminated in the enactment of a set of tightly drawn legal provisions in the Youth Justice and Criminal Evidence Act (YJCEA) 1999, the stated object of which was to restrict the use of sexual history evidence to those 'rare' occasions in which it was materially relevant. Yet, notwithstanding the apparently watertight protections the 1999 Act supposedly conferred, concerns continue to be expressed about the use of sexual history evidence in the rape trial, and in the aftermath of Evans' retrial (discussed at length later in this chapter), the nature, use, scope and legitimacy of sexual history evidence have become a renewed focus of academic and political debate, much of which we will track in the course of this book. Before launching directly into that formidable task, however,

---

[4]   As a review of rape cases carried out by HM Crown Prosecution Service Inspectorate in 2019 commented: 'If 58,657 allegations of rape were made in the year ending March 2019 but only 1,925 successful prosecutions for the offence followed, something must be wrong' (HMCPSI, 2019: 7).

[5]   The term 'twin myths' was first used judicially by McLachlin J in the landmark Canadian case, *Seaboyer v Attorney General & others intervening* [1993] 1 LRC 465, 475. See also *R v Evans* [2016] EWCA Crim 452, per Hallett J [44].

we begin with some brief reflections on the nature of our project and our reasons for pursuing it.

What is this book about?

What is sexual history evidence? Why and when is it believed to be relevant to a determination of whether a rape has occurred? Does the use of such evidence produce just outcomes in criminal cases? How effective has the law been in repressing its inappropriate use? How accurate is the view of many commentators that sexual history evidence is now only used exceptionally? How does its continued use sit in relation to broader problems with the criminal justice response to sexual violence? Who is the subject of sexual history evidence and what ideas of sexual agency and moral and legal responsibility underpin its relevance in the rape trial? What can sexual history evidence in the context of rape law and practice more broadly tell us about gender, justice and equality? These are some of the questions this book sets out to address. We do so in full awareness that the use of sexual history evidence is only one dimension of the much larger, multidimensional challenge that sexual violence presents for the criminal justice system, sitting alongside and intertwined with a range of other evidentiary contestations including access to a complainant's medical and digital records, the use of character evidence (both of complainants and defendants), and the extent to which criminal justice procedures should be adapted to take better account of the needs of vulnerable witnesses. At the same time, we believe that the (mis)use of sexual history evidence merits separate and sustained treatment precisely because it is so quintessentially expressive of wider criminal justice failings when it comes to responding to sexual violence. Attention to a complainant's sexual history places her sexual behaviour, rather than that of the accused, at the heart of forensic and legal enquiry, infusing the justice process from first report right through to final outcome. Reliance upon such evidence imbues the conceptual and normative architecture of rape law with a sexual imaginary in which sexual wrongdoing is primarily apprehended through the male gaze. Moreover, at its heart is the presumption that rape complainants, overwhelmingly women, lie about claims of sexual violation and that the law must and should enshrine protective mechanisms to guard against that mendacity.

Sexual history evidence shapes the contours and conditions of consent, delimits the harm which sexual assault is supposed to inflict, and inflects virtually all aspects of the sexual offences edifice with an onto-epistemology of gender or sex difference (this is notwithstanding efforts of many legal systems to 'gender-neutralise' sexual offences law).[6] In other words, the law

---

[6]   The term 'onto-epistemology' fuses the philosophical categories of ontology and epistemology to denote the intrinsic connectedness of questions of being and knowing, of how we experience the world and how we represent that world. We consider the onto-epistemological dimensions of sexual history evidence in depth in Chapter 7.

that governs sexual history evidence is profoundly infused with specific understandings of how men and women are and what they do, as well as being rigidly resistant to challenges to that received wisdom. The much-vaunted principle of sexual autonomy, the stated normative foundation of most progressive criminal justice responses to sexual violence, sits at best uneasily alongside an evidentiary regime in which a complainant's sexual past effectively fetters her freedom to choose when, where and with whom to have sexual relations. Sexual history evidence, as with the law of rape more generally, is, therefore, a profoundly gendered phenomenon and one which, we argue, must be situated and analysed as such.

Much ink, feminist and otherwise, has been spilt ruminating on when, if at all, a complainant's sexual history should properly feature in the rape trial process. This has prompted multiple jurisdictions to introduce legislation – often characterised as 'rape-shield laws' because their purpose is to shield rape complainants from intrusive or prejudicial questioning – to control or prohibit its use. That justice requires some restrictions on the use of such evidence has become increasingly recognised by lawmakers. Nevertheless, that a complainant's sexual history remains relevant in at least some cases to the determination of whether a rape has occurred is, in the well-rehearsed words of Lord Steyn, a 'matter of common sense'.[7] So entrenched is this perception of relevance in the collective legal and cultural psyche that the very idea that justice might better be served by excluding such evidence from the courtroom is met with either incredulity or derision.[8] We have moved beyond the bad old days, the enlightened narrative goes, in which a rape victim's prior sexual history was routinely raised to discredit her testimony and tarnish her reputation, but there remain instances in which the relevance of sexual history evidence to the determination of justice is beyond dispute. It is to accommodate those rare occasions (the narrative continues) that provision must be made, and while this may occasionally result in evidentiary abuses, we are fortunate that such instances are becoming increasingly infrequent.

We set out to problematise this narrative and its underpinning assumptions by relocating debate about the use of sexual history evidence within the frame of feminist theory and critique. While much has been said and written about how best to tackle the justice problems which the use of sexual history evidence in rape trials inescapably poses, the bleak reality, as we shall see, is that legislative interventions notwithstanding, a complainant's prior sexual behaviour continues to feature in criminal justice processes in ways which

---

[7]   *R v A (No 2)* [2001] UKHL 25 [31].

[8]   See, for example, the comments of popular online blogger 'The Secret Barrister' attacking Harriet Harman MP's proposal further to restrict the use of sexual history evidence in the wake of the Ched Evans trial as 'horrendously, stupidly dangerous' (Secret Barrister, 2017).

are unacceptable even by reference to the enlightened narrative. How do we explain the sheer irrepressibility of appeals to women's wayward sexuality? Feminist lawyers across the globe have gone some considerable way towards crafting workable legal lines between 'acceptable' and 'unacceptable' uses of complainant sexual history but have not, we argue, satisfactorily explained why those lines are repeatedly crossed in the courtroom. It is to the broader field of feminist theorisations of sexual violence and to feminist philosophy and psychoanalysis that we turn, both to explain this particular manifestation of the legal scrutiny of women's sexual conduct and to account for its wider functioning in a gendered social world in which sexual history evidence is one part of a broader toolbox of techniques deployed by the legal system to set the terms of sexual engagement within an epistemic and normative framework of masculine entitlement. By offering a feminist theoretical analysis of the legal phenomenon of complainant sexual history evidence, we hope to contribute to a reframing of the current legislative and policy dilemmas, endlessly recycled and seemingly never resolved.

The book adopts a multidisciplinary approach to the problem of sexual history evidence as emblematic of the broader problem of securing justice for victims of sexual violence. Our analysis combines feminist perspectives on history, law, social sciences and philosophy to generate new insights into how and why sexual history evidence continues to be used in the courtroom, its ubiquity in the popular and penal imaginary, and the problem this presents both for the criminal justice system and, more broadly, for law's capacity to recognise and redress sexual violence. We believe our analysis to be unique, not only in offering the first sustained book-length treatment of this pressing concern, but also in encompassing perspectives from law, social sciences and humanities within a single targeted analysis. Crucial to our approach is recognition that the problem of the misuse of sexual history evidence – indeed the problem of sexual violence in general – cannot be resolved by law alone but requires multidisciplinary, multifaceted engagement. Within this broad frame, we conceive sexual violence as a gendered harm, that is, a harm which is significantly mediated by notions of sex/gender. Notwithstanding that both men and women may be victims of sexual violence, our analysis is anchored in recognition of the fact that women remain far more likely to be victims of sexual violence than men and that, crucially, and regardless of the actual sex of the victim, sex/gender difference is integral to how sexual violence is apprehended, experienced and assessed.[9] We locate the

---

[9]   To foreground the gendered dimensions of sexual violence, we use the pronouns 'he' and 'she' for defendant/perpetrator and complainant/victim-survivor respectively. These pronouns should be understood not as factual designations of victim/perpetrator identity but as symbolic signifiers capturing the role and function of sexual difference in the phenomenon of sexual violence. This argument is further developed in Chapter 7; see also Russell, 2016.

use of sexual history evidence historically in relation to evolving legal and cultural conceptions of rape, plotting legal responses to the perception that it presents a justice problem. We also consider what current studies tell us about the use of sexual history evidence in the courtroom, interrogating the assertion frequently made in the public domain that sexual history evidence is now used only exceptionally. Applying ideas drawn from feminist theory and philosophy, this book challenges 'common sense' understandings of the relevance of sexual history evidence and explores the extent to which these dominant conceptions accord or deny agency to the rape victim. Our overall ambition is to show that concrete legal and policy problems around the use and/or restriction of sexual history evidence in the courtroom cannot be resolved without a much wider problematisation not only of social and cultural attitudes towards sexual behaviour (a persistent theme in much of the legal feminist literature), but also of the knowledge foundations which render these attitudes real and intelligible.

The primary jurisdictional focus is England and Wales, but the book also draws on comparative and historical material from other common law jurisdictions including Northern Ireland, the Republic of Ireland, Canada, Australia, New Zealand, the United States and Scotland.[10] Although our analysis is jurisdictionally grounded, we are confident that the insights generated by the application of feminist theory to this area are likely to have much wider cross-jurisdictional relevance.

At the end of this chapter, we present an outline of the structure and content of the rest of book. First though, with a view to providing a situated account of how the law currently operates, and the controversies it provokes, we take a closer look at the details of the *Evans* case and its aftermath.

Evans and its aftermath

On 29 May 2011, Ched Evans and his friend, Clayton McDonald, had sexual intercourse with an extremely intoxicated young woman in a hotel room, booked by Evans earlier in the day in McDonald's name. Evans and McDonald were both charged with rape, but only Evans was convicted, the jury accepting McDonald's account that he had consensual sexual intercourse with the complainant. Evans was sentenced to five years' imprisonment (leave to appeal being refused), serving two and a half

---

[10] While Scots law contains many elements of the common law tradition, it is generally described as a 'hybrid' system, in that much of the legal framework derives from the civil law (Roman) system. Scottish criminal law is much more common law influenced than Scottish civil law. For this reason, as well as its proximity to England and Wales, our primary jurisdiction, we include it in our discussion of the law of sexual history evidence, considered in more detail in Chapter 4.

years before his release in October 2014. In 2015, the Criminal Cases Review Commission (CCRC), to which Evans' case had been referred and which had 'fast tracked' the review of his case,[11] sent the case back to the Court of Appeal based on new information which was not raised at trial, and which in the CCRC's view could have added support to Evans' defence at trial.[12]

The new information heard by the Court of Appeal, and later by the Court at Evans' retrial, came from the testimony of two witnesses who claimed to have had sexual intercourse with the complainant. One witness testified to having sex with the complainant two days before the alleged rape, the other, two weeks after. Critically, both witnesses claimed that the complainant had been 'an enthusiastic participant' who 'directed her sexual partners to have sexual intercourse with her in particular positions including the "doggie position" and used a distinctive expression demanding intercourse with her harder'.[13] It must be said, and notwithstanding the ultimate jury verdict in Cardiff, there are a number of grounds for questioning the veracity of these accounts. Both witnesses had been interviewed at the time of Evans' initial conviction and neither statement included any reference to the events that they later described *after* they were approached by Evans' new legal team. Both witnesses were also part of the wider circle of Evans' friends and acquaintances and may well have been aware both of Evans' initial account of what had taken place and of the substantial reward offered by Evans' fiancée for information which might clear him. Indeed, the Court of Appeal acknowledged that legitimate questions might be raised about the credibility of the evidence, but nevertheless (and not wholly explicably) concluded that, for purposes of the appeal, the evidence was 'capable of belief'.[14]

In any event, the new evidence was significant because it chimed perfectly with Evans' account of events in his initial statement to the police in 2011. In particular, Evans had stated that he and the complainant had

---

[11] See further https://www.thejusticegap.com/ccrc-fast-tracking-ched-evans/ [Accessed 31 May 2023].

[12] The CCRC is an independent public body that reviews possible miscarriages of justice in the criminal courts of England, Wales and Northern Ireland and has the power to refer cases to the Court of Appeal where it finds that a conviction has a 'real possibility' of not being upheld. The CCRC does not publish its decisions, and there is no way for the public to obtain copies of them, absent the parties to relevant proceedings electing to share the reports. The authors' request to Evans' legal representatives for a copy of the full Statement of Reasons supporting the CCRC recommendation was declined.

[13] *R v Evans* [2016] EWCA Crim 452 per Hallett LJ [39]. The distinctive expression was "fuck me harder" in the first instance and "go harder" in the second ([24] and [35]).

[14] *Evans* [67].

consensual sexual intercourse "doggie style" and that she had encouraged him to "fuck her harder".[15] The new evidence, it was argued, suggested a pattern of behaviour on the part of the complainant which included getting very intoxicated, engaging in sexual intercourse with comparative strangers, taking the sexual lead and indulging in certain language and sexual practices.

How does the introduction of such evidence comply with a legal regime purporting to place tight limits on the use of sexual history evidence in the courtroom? The 17th-century jurist Matthew Hale famously declared that '[rape] is an accusation easily to be made and hard to be proved, and harder to be defended by the party accused, tho never so innocent' (Hale, 1800: 634), yielding a mantra that for nearly 400 years was habitually trotted out to justify the introduction of evidence attesting to a complainant's loose sexual morals into rape trials. The spectre of false accusations exerted a fearsome hold on the judicial imagination, and the result was a legal evidentiary regime steeped in scepticism regarding the testimony of female rape complainants (Temkin, 2002: chapter 4). Only in the closing decades of the 20th century were appeals to sexual history evidence seriously challenged by legislation in England and Wales. Initially, the Sexual Offences (Amendment) Act (SO(A)A) 1976 filtered its use by requiring leave from the court for its introduction.[16] Eventually, at the century's end, the YJCEA 1999 enacted further provisions to curb the use of complainant sexual history evidence by placing formal limits on the circumstances in which it might be judicially admitted.[17] The legislative ink was barely dry before these latest provisions were challenged on the ground that they violated a defendant's right to a fair trial. In *R v A (No 2)*,[18] the House of Lords held that legislative curbs on the use of sexual history evidence had to be read subject to an interpretative duty imposed on the courts by section 3 of the Human Rights Act 1998.[19] Specifically, the provisions should be read so as not to exclude evidence which would endanger the defendant's right to a fair trial.

---

[15] *Evans* [13].

[16] SO(A)A 1976, s 2 'Except with the leave of the judge, no evidence and no question in cross-examination shall be adduced or asked, by or on behalf of any defendant ... about any sexual experience of a complainant with a person other than the defendant.' Note the provision only applied to complainant sexual behaviour with other men; evidence of prior sexual behaviour with the defendant remained subject to the established rules governing the admission of such evidence.

[17] YJCEA 1999, ss 41–3.

[18] [2001] UKHL 25.

[19] HRA 1998, s 3(1): 'So far as it is possible to do so, primary legislation and subordinate legislation must be read and given effect in a way which is compatible with Convention rights.'

It is within this rather complicated regulatory regime that the *Evans* decision is located. The provisions of section 41 of the YJCEA 1999 formally mandate that where a defendant is charged with a sexual offence,[20] evidence about a complainant's 'sexual behaviour' may not be raised 'except with the leave of the court'.[21] Furthermore, leave may only be given when certain conditions are met.[22] Effectively, a court is empowered to allow sexual history evidence where it pertains to a relevant issue other than consent[23] and is not presented in order to impugn the credibility of the complainant.[24] Alternatively, a judge can allow the introduction of sexual history evidence relating to consent in a number of specified circumstances, one of which, as we shall see, was raised in *Evans*. In addition, where evidence is adduced relating to a complainant's sexual behaviour (whether or not pertaining to consent), it also has to be shown that the refusal of leave might result in rendering unsafe a conclusion otherwise reached by the jury or the court.[25] The intended effect of these provisions is to sew up tightly the circumstances in which sexual history evidence can be introduced, making no distinction between sexual behaviour with the accused and third parties, and imposing a particularly strict set of requirements in relation to the use of sexual history evidence to establish consent.

The evidence Evans' team sought to introduce pertained to consent. They relied on the 'similar fact' exception, that is, where

> the sexual behaviour of the complainant to which the evidence or question relates is alleged to have been … so similar … to any sexual behaviour of the complainant which … took place as part of the event which is the subject matter of the charge against the accused … that *the similarity cannot reasonably be explained as a coincidence.*[26]

---

[20] For purposes of brevity and simplicity, we refer to 'rape' and 'rape trials' when discussing the scope and operation of this legislation. However, it should be noted that YJCEA, as with many other rape-shield regimes, applies to a range of criminal offences, not just to rape. See YJCEA 1999, s 42(1)(d) and (2) and s 62, and generally Chapter 4.

[21] YJCEA 1999, s 41(1).

[22] Unlike the 1976 Act, the 1999 Act provisions apply to evidence of sexual behaviour both with the accused and third parties.

[23] YJCEA 1999, s 41(3)(a).

[24] YJCEA 1999, s 41(4) and except in so far as is necessary to enable the defendant to respond to any evidence of the complainant's sexual behaviour adduced by the prosecution (s 41(5)).

[25] YJCEA 1999, s 41(2)(b).

[26] YJCEA 1999, s 41(3)(c) (our emphasis).

The thrust of this provision introduced rather late in the legislative process[27] is to permit evidence of a complainant's sexual behaviour to support a defendant's account of events where the similarity between his account and the evidence sought to be introduced is apparently so marked as to go beyond mere coincidence. In this case, two other men attested that the complainant had behaved in a similar fashion with them to that described by Evans. This, it was argued, lent veracity to Evans' account of events and, were it not heard by the jury, might result in an unsafe verdict.

The Court of Appeal agreed. Hallett LJ emphasised that the test of admissibility under section 41(3)(c) was strict, requiring the defendant to 'overcome [a] high hurdle of relevance and similarity'.[28] At the same time, she cited with approval the comments of Lord Clyde in *R v A (No 2)* on the scope and meaning of section 41(3)(c), namely that '[i]t is only a similarity that is required, not an identity'; nor was there a need for the defendant to show that the similar conduct invoked was 'rare or bizarre ... so long as the particular conduct goes beyond the realm of what could reasonably be explained as a coincidence, it should suffice'.[29] This was important because one of the arguments advanced by the Crown in *Evans* was that the similar conduct upon which the defendant relied was 'commonplace' and not sufficiently unusual to transcend the bounds of coincidence.[30] In other words, no evidentiary conclusion could be drawn from the similarity of unexceptional accounts of sexual intercourse with the complainant proffered by three different men. To this end, the Crown sought to distance the facts in *Evans* from *R v T (Abdul)*,[31] at that time the primary legal authority supporting the application of section 41(3)(c). In *R v T*, in which the complainant was allegedly raped inside a children's climbing frame, defendant counsel wanted to cross-examine a complainant about previous sexual behaviour with the defendant inside the climbing frame. Holding the test of similarity had been met for purposes of s 41(3)(c), the Court of Appeal allowed the cross-examination to proceed. In *Evans*, the Crown sought to distinguish *R v T*, both because

---

[27] The so-called 'Romeo and Juliet' amendment, as it is sometimes known, relied on a member of the House of Lords offering an extraordinarily contrived hypothetical in which the complainant and the defendant re-enacted the balcony scene in *Romeo and Juliet* (Hansard, vol 597[2] col 45 [February 1999]).

[28] *Evans* [48].

[29] L Clyde in *A (No 2)* [131] cited by Hallett in *Evans* [51]. As McGlynn (2018: 218) points out, this rather flies in the face of the Parliamentary debates on the amendment in which the government made it clear that, to be admitted, the evidence must relate to behaviour 'so unusual that it would be wholly unreasonable to explain it as coincidental' (Hansard, col 1218 [23 March 1999]). 'Doggie-style' sex is certainly rather more commonplace than re-enacting the balcony scene in *Romeo and Juliet*.

[30] *Evans* [56].

[31] (2004) 2 Cr App R 32.

the events in that case were more unusual (an argument which the Court of Appeal unequivocally rejected[32]) and because *R v T* involved evidence of sexual behaviour with the defendant, not with other men.[33] It is this latter feature which is perhaps the most disturbing aspect of the *Evans* decision: it permits the introduction of evidence of sexual encounters with various men at various times and places to support an evidentiary conclusion that a woman consented to sex with a particular man at a particular time and place. This arguably was not envisaged when the amendment was introduced and, at the very least, creates a real and credible risk of opening the courtroom doors to a parade of former lovers and the subjection of the complainant to painful and intrusive cross-examination regarding her sexual conduct with other men. Witness tampering is also clearly a risk in this context.

These concerns are perhaps acknowledged by the Court of Appeal, Hallett LJ observing that 'we have reached this conclusion with a considerable degree of hesitation'.[34] She takes comfort from the fact that only in a 'rare' case will it be appropriate to indulge in forensic examination of the complainant's sexual behaviour with men other than the accused.[35] This rhetoric of rareness – which is somewhat out of accord with judicial insistence that the application of section 41(3)(c) does not require bizarre or unusual circumstances – is a dominant feature of commentaries defending the outcome in *Evans* as a proper application of existing law (Morris, 2016b). The Secret Barrister (2016) thus exhorts their many readers not to get too worked up about the *Evans* decision: 'A decision to allow evidence of sexual behaviour is rare' they observe, and 'that is the message we should be repeating loud and clear'. But is this correct? How can evidence of a complainant's prior sexual behaviour simultaneously qualify as 'fairly commonplace' *and* 'rare'?

Unsurprisingly, the outcome of Evans' retrial, and particularly the grounds on which his appeal relied, provoked widespread expressions of concern from feminist commentators and activists. Vera Baird – who among her many public roles was Solicitor-General in the Labour government from 2007 until 2010 – speculated that "[*Evans*] puts the law back 30 years", while Lisa Longstaff, speaking for Women Against Rape, considered the case to have driven a "coach and four through the supposed [legal]

---

[32] 'The flaw in Ms Laws' argument … is that she focused on there being nothing "unusual" about [the complainant's] alleged behaviour. The behaviour does not have to be unusual or bizarre; it has to be sufficiently similar that it cannot be explained reasonably as a coincidence' (*Evans* per Hallett LJ [73]). This rather ducks the issue because, of course, the more unusual or bizarre the alleged behaviour, the more unlikely the coincidence that different accounts concur.

[33] *Evans* [55].

[34] *Evans* [74].

[35] *Evans* [74].

protection" (Morris and Topping, 2016). Labour Member of Parliament (MP) Jess Phillips, leading a charge of 40 female MPs, sent a letter to the (then) Attorney General, Jeremy Wright, condemning the *Evans* decision as a 'dangerous precedent'.[36] Even Wright conceded that the case raised 'real concerns' which might require further legal reforms (Mason, 2016). By contrast, legal practitioners were far more sanguine and far less perturbed by the *Evans* verdict. The then Chair of the Criminal Bar, Francis FitzGibbon QC, complained that the verdict had elicited a "huge over-reaction" from women's rights campaigners, while her Deputy Chair, Angela Rafferty QC, echoed the Court of Appeal's judgment by reiterating that sexual history evidence was only legally permitted in "highly unusual circumstances" (Morris, 2016b).

There thus emerged two diametrically opposed accounts of *Evans*, the first seeking to contain the decision's impact by emphasising its exceptionality and limited applicability, the other worryingly alert to its expansive, precedent-setting character – the risk that it opened up rather than shut down opportunities to introduce evidence of a complainant's sexual history. Nearly a decade later, the jury is still out on the impact of *Evans*. Some commentators, such as Brewis and Jackson, while conceding that the case was 'unusual and challenging in equal measure' (2020: 71), do not think it raises particular cause for concern, nor that it provides a sound basis for further legislative reform. Other commentators, for example Thomason (2018), question the clarity and coherence of the Court of Appeal decision to allow the evidence, speculating that the courts are more likely to sweep the case under the rug rather than expand it further. This view is confirmed by Dent and Paul, who take the public furore provoked by *Evans* as an opportunity to defend the existing legislative framework, reasserting that the case is 'confined to the specific facts' and is 'much more likely to be the exception than the rule' (2017: 621). By contrast, McGlynn, perhaps the most vociferous critic of the *Evans* decision, calls for a 'wholesale review [of the legislative regime] starting from first principles' (2018: 228).[37]

It is difficult to gauge the actual impact of *Evans* on the ground. As with scholarly commentaries, empirical studies examining the use of sexual history evidence in the rape trial appear to come to very different conclusions depending on the perspective of those participating in the study. On the one hand, a survey of Independent Sexual Violence Advisors (ISVAs)[38] in 2017

---

[36] Labour MPs' letter to Jeremy Wright, Attorney General, 24 October 2016.

[37] See also McGlynn (2017) for an extended critique of the use of evidence of a complainant's sexual behaviour with third parties after *Evans*.

[38] ISVAs work locally with specialist agencies to provide specialist tailored support to victims of rape and sexual assault. Although they are generally funded by the Ministry of Justice, they are not in any sense legal representatives. We discuss the use of Independent Legal Representation (ILR) in other jurisdictions in Chapter 4.

lent weight to the claim that sexual history evidence continues to feature significantly in rape trials and that the processes prescribed by section 41 YJCEA are often not followed (LimeCulture, 2017). The view from the Criminal Bar, on the other hand, is rather different: Hoyano's survey of English criminal barristers in 2018 concluded that the existing statutory framework was broadly operating in the interests of justice, although strong views were expressed about its complexity and confusion-creating risks (Hoyano, 2018). One of the primary purposes of our book, pursued at length in Chapter 5, is to look more closely at what evidence we have on the use of sexual history evidence in the courtroom in order to test the confident belief of the legal establishment that the problem of the misuse of sexual history evidence in rape trials has been solved.

The dust may have settled on *Evans*, but the issues the case raised remain important, arguably extending beyond the courtroom to encompass the whole criminal justice response to sexual violence. Given what we know – and what we do not know – about the use of sexual history evidence in the courtroom, it can hardly be hyperbole to speculate that *Evans*-like arguments continue to feature in courtroom discourse. Moreover, in a context in which some rape complainants wait years for the resolution of their cases, face unprecedented demands from investigators for digital access to their private lives, and the overwhelming majority of whom report a negative, highly traumatic experience of the criminal justice process (House of Commons Home Affairs Committee, 2022), the quest for justice for victims of sexual violence has taken on a new and urgent saliency.

How this book proceeds

The chapters that follow fall within three broad groupings, the first of which attends to history, the second to law, and the third to philosophy and critical theory.

Chapters 2 and 3 set out to historicise the view that a complainant's sexual history may be relevant to the determination of a rape trial. To this end, Chapter 2 explores the evolution and development of conceptions of rape, from a property-type crime perpetrated against a (male) property holder, changing to an offence concerned with protecting women's chastity (viewed largely in terms of standards of morality/decency), and finally to the modern conception of rape as a violation of individual sexual autonomy. The chapter draws both on legal and non-legal materials to present a contextualised analysis of rape law in action from 1200, which is when the historical evidence begins to offer something resembling a concrete picture, to the present day. Chapter 3 traces the emergence of sexual history as a concept of evidentiary relevance and the form this has taken in relation to different conceptions of the harm/wrong in rape. This helps us to see both why a complainant's sexual history came to be regarded as relevant to determining whether an offence had occurred and the varying ideas of what is meant by sexual history for these purposes. The historical and cultural contingency of rape as a crime is also highlighted, and law's alignment with culturally male perspectives of female sexuality is exposed and analysed. By the end of Chapter 3, the reader will have a better understanding of what is meant by sexual history evidence as well as its doctrinal and fundamentally gendered roots. This lays the grounds for consideration of legal and policy efforts to restrict its use in rape trials.

Chapters 4 and 5 shift the focus to contemporary law and criminal justice practice. Chapter 4 assesses the contemporary legal framework governing the use of sexual history evidence in rape trials. Although the primary focus remains England and Wales, to assist critical analysis, the chapter draws upon the experience of other common law jurisdictions, notably Ireland, Scotland, Canada, Australia, New Zealand and the United States, highlighting how different approaches to the problem have prevailed at different times and in different jurisdictional contexts. The (in)effectiveness of these legal reforms is assessed against their primary policy aim, that is, to prevent the inappropriate use of irrelevant and prejudicial sexual history evidence (usually but not exclusively by defence counsel), thereby striking a fair balance between the defendant's right to a fair trial and a complainant's right to justice as a victim of a criminal offence. The chapter highlights the difficulties reformers face in drawing a clear line between 'legitimate' and 'illegitimate' uses of sexual history evidence and the irrepressibility of narratives in trial discourse which promote the use of sexual history evidence in problematic ways. The limits of criminal justice, its normative underpinnings, and their historical and cultural specificity are also highlighted to demonstrate (and critique) the modes of and justifications for weighting the balance of justice so heavily in favour of the defendant.

The evaluation of the legal framework in Chapter 4 reveals both the strengths and limitations of 'rape-shield laws', that is, laws introduced to limit the use of a complainant's sexual history in rape trials. In Chapter 5, and against the background of the assessment conducted in Chapter 4, the claim which reverberated around the legal and political establishment after *Evans* that sexual history evidence is only rarely or exceptionally considered in rape trials is re-examined. Again, focusing primarily on empirical studies conducted in England and Wales, but drawing also on overseas studies, the chapter summarises significant past studies of sexual history evidence (for example, Adler (1987) and Lees (1996)), identifies and details the various contemporary studies, from Kelly et al (2006) to Smith (2018) and Daly (2022), highlighting the methods applied, scope, limitations and gaps in current knowledge, to present as comprehensive picture as possible of the extent of the problem contemporaneously. Chapter 5 is critical in establishing the persistence of problems with sexual history evidence notwithstanding legal reforms, staunchly problematising claims that this kind of evidence features only exceptionally in rape trials.

Chapters 6 and 7 take a philosophical turn, with Chapter 6 focusing on epistemology and Chapter 7 drawing upon feminist philosophical and psychoanalytic theory to explore notions of agency and subjectivity. Chapter 6 probes basic assumptions underpinning claims of relevance and their allegedly logical and 'common sense' character. Drawing on perspectives from feminist theories of knowledge, the chapter asks: How do we *know* that sexual history is relevant, and what counts as 'knowledge' for these purposes? The chapter argues that the predominant way in which knowledge is generated and validated in law is problematic because it is based on the idea that what we know corresponds with what is real and, more importantly, that what is real is separate or independent from what we know. This representation/reality dichotomy, which is at the heart of modernist conceptions of knowledge, objectivity and truth, has been the focus of extensive critique by feminist and other critical scholars on the grounds that it enables the presentation of the knowledge of the powerful as objective and impartial when in fact it is subjective and interest-laden. Taking this critique of objective knowledge, the chapter shows how claims of relevance in a sexual history context are reliant on generalised assumptions and beliefs about women's sexual behaviour which, upon examination, are often highly contestable. Cases such as *Evans*, and other key cases in the legal canon, are deployed to support the arguments made here. The chapter concludes by asking whether it is possible to be confident about claims of relevance of sexual history in the absence of a satisfactory process for interrogating the underpinning generalisations and assumptions upon which such claims are made.

Chapter 7 engages with a common feminist critique of rape law, namely that it reflects the perspective of the (male) perpetrator rather than the (female) victim. We explore the construction of subjectivities in rape law discourse, with a particular focus on the role and function of sexual history evidence as a subjectivity erasing and constituting tool. We understand subjectivity for these purposes to signify the cultural construction of particular roles, positions and forms of consciousness which are materially, symbolically or discursively supported, inter alia, by law. Within the context of the rape trial, we focus on unpacking the subjectivities of both the defendant and the complainant, considering the impact of the introduction of sexual history evidence on the construction of subjectivity and also on the types of stories prosecution and defence lawyers are able to tell about the defendant and complainant. Central to our analysis in this chapter is a distinction between legal subjectivity and what we term 'sexuate subjectivity'. This distinction is important because it helps us illustrate how subjectivity is always historically, culturally and political imbued and allows us to map the ways in which sexual history evidence intercedes and mobilises different forms of subjectivity during the rape trial which impacts those party to the trial in different ways. In broad terms, we argue sexual history evidence is a useful and extraordinarily effective specular tool in the rape trial that functions to redirect the court's attention away from the defendant while simultaneously activating a particular understanding of feminine subjectivity, which helps to undercut a linear story of violation a prosecutor might be trying to tell.

In Chapter 8, we draw together our analysis to reflect on the question: What is to be done about sexual history evidence? We situate the contribution of this book very much within a broader canon of critical social justice and feminist scholarship, and in this conclusion we show how our work on the rape trial and on sexual history evidence sits within that broader body of research. How we approach answering the question just posed depends very much on what we think 'justice' means, and how that meaning relates (or does not) to law and legal reform mechanisms. While we are sceptical of law's capacity and ability to 'solve' the problems associated with sexual violence, we see some promise in a normatively embedded approach to law that matches the aspirations of the imaginary domain (Cornell, 1995), through which we continue to envision and strive for the equality and social justice we want to see. To this end, we gather the most promising options open to law and policy makers as we see them, and reflect on avenues for further thought and research. Ultimately, doing the difficult and painstaking work that thoughtful research on sexual violence requires demands both dexterity and reflexivity in respect of the commitments we make to each other and ourselves, whether through or with the law or outside it, as well as to the horizons of possibility for the future.

2

A History of Rape Law in Action

Why history?

The 18th-century jurist William Blackstone famously said: 'It is better that ten guilty persons escape than one innocent suffer' (Blackstone, 1803, IV.27). This is just one example of how the contemporary criminal trial is expressive of value judgements which, while made long ago, have since assumed the status of fundamental principles in modern criminal justice. Few criminal law scholars would deny that their territory is deeply normatively imbued. Indeed, much criminal law scholarship today is preoccupied with normative enquiry into the moral rationales for criminalising individual acts (Wertheimer, 2003; Duff, 2018; Green, 2020).

From where does the normative content of criminal law come, and how does it acquire weight and validity? This is first and foremost a historical question. As Alan Norrie argues, the normative contours of contemporary criminal law were 'formed in a particular historical epoch [which Norrie identifies with 18th-century Enlightenment thought] and derived their characteristic shape from fundamental features of the social relations of that epoch' (Norrie, 2014: 10). Lacey too emphasises the historical dimensions of criminal law, showing how conceptions of the criminal subject have varied over time and space so that ascriptions of criminal responsibility are best understood, not abstractly but contextually, in relation to 'broader social, cultural, political and economic developments' (Lacey, 2016: vii). By historicising and contextualising criminal law, Norrie and Lacey highlight the specificity of the ideas and perceptions of human relations which underpin modern criminal justice. Importantly, their work reveals not only that criminal law is normatively imbued, but also that the terms of normative engagement are historically derived, governed by conceptions of human nature, social relations and the role, functions and legitimacy of the state, which are now so well embedded in the criminal justice infrastructure as to appear beyond contest. 'At the core of the philosophy behind criminal law', Norrie comments, 'is a moral individualism which proclaims that for the state to intervene against the individual, it must have a good and clear licence to do so' (Norrie, 2014: 13). Both Norrie and Lacey set out to represent the liberal individualism of criminal law – the unchallenged and essentially unchallengeable foundation of the criminal justice edifice – as a social and historical construct which derives its weight and validity from the 'ideas, interests and institutions' (Lacey, 2016) that shaped its formation and development. Lindsay Farmer also advocates an approach to criminal law, and to matters of criminalisation, other than in terms of abstractly framed normative contestation: 'Instead of beginning by asking what principle or principles should guide us … I ask what I see as the *prior question* of how it is that questions … have come to be framed in these terms' (Farmer, 2016: 1).

It is this 'prior question' of how a complainant's prior sexual behaviour came to be regarded as relevant to the determination of a defendant's guilt or innocence that interests us here. How did sexual history evidence come to be a feature in rape trials? When did the question of its relevance assume the status of 'common sense'? How has knowledge and assessment of sexual behaviour for these purposes been formed and validated? In this and the following chapter, we seek to contextualise the norms and practices governing the use of complainant sexual history evidence within the broader history of rape law and practice. In Chapter 2, drawing upon legal and non-legal materials, we present a contextualised analysis of rape law in action from 1200 AD to the present day, focusing primarily on the evolution and operationalisation of rape law in what is now the jurisdiction of England and Wales. In Chapter 3, we trace the emergence of sexual history as a concept of evidentiary relevance in the rape trial and the norms and procedures developed to embed and regulate its use. Together, the two chapters ground the concept of complainant sexual history evidence in the conditions which led to its production as an object of knowledge and focus of concern in relation to criminal justice responses to sexual violence.

The historical development of rape law

Rape law has a long history. Its first known written iteration is in the Babylonian Code of Hammurabi (circa 1750 BC) which prescribed death for forcing 'the betrothed wife of another' to have sexual intercourse (Gold and Wyatt, 1978: 696). Rape also features in the Old Testament, and in Greek and Roman law. It is from the latter that the modern term 'rape', adapted from the Latin *rapere* (to seize or carry off), derives. In each of these contexts, rape was conceived as a private wrong, entailing the improper use of, or injury to, a woman over whom a man (usually a husband or father) had formal governance.[1] The seriousness of the violation varied, depending on a woman's social status and sexual virtue (or lack thereof). Prostitutes, for example, could not be raped in Roman law (Nguyen, 2006: 86). Chastity was highly prized in ancient cultures, and as, once lost, it could not be restored, to ravish a virgin, particularly from a good family, was to inflict a serious harm upon the household. The biblical Book of Deuteronomy states:

> If a man find a damsel that is a virgin, which is not betrothed, and lay hold on her, and lie with her, and they be found; then the man that lay with her shall give unto the damsel's father fifty shekels of silver, and she shall be his wife; because he hath humbled her, he may not put her away all his days. (22:28–9)

By contrast, where a man 'lies' with another man's wife, it is prescribed that both parties be put to death regardless of whether the woman consented to her defilement (22:22).[2] Here we see plainly the close alignment of rape law with social, cultural and religious norms regarding men's access to and control over women's sexuality. This is a feature which characterises rape law throughout the course of its development from ancient to modern times.

In its British, Anglo-American and colonial incarnations, rape law derives from English common law. In pre-Conquest times, to ravish a 'virgin sole' attracted 'judgment of life and member' (T.E., 1632: 378),[3] a penalty said to have been reduced by William I to castration and blinding. In the late 13th century, during the reign of Edward I, the penalty for rape is reported to have been relaxed further,[4] but because 'the mitigation of the old law … brought forth many enormities' (T.E., 1632: 381), within a decade rape was once again made a capital offence[5] and remained so until 1841 when the maximum penalty was reduced to transportation for life.[6]

---

[1] Rape became a public wrong in late Roman law under Emperor Constantine (Brundage, 1990: 107).

[2] In the case of a 'betrothed damsel', a concession is made where she is forced but only if the rape is perpetrated in a place where her cries will not be heard (Deuteronomy 22:23–6).

[3] T.E.'s *Lawes Resolutions of Women's Rights* was published anonymously in 1632. Here the author cites Bracton, a 13th-century text describing the law as it stood in King Athelstan's reign in the 10th century. According to Groot, while rape *was* a serious crime pre-Conquest, it was 'emendable', that is, it could be resolved by paying reparations to the victim (Groot, 1988: 324).

[4] Chapter 13, Statute of Westminster II (1275).

[5] Chapter 34, Westminster II (1285). The extent to which these penalties were actually inflicted and their application other than to traditional *raptus* (that is, abduction) is very difficult to assess.

[6] Substitution of Punishments of Death Act 1841, amending Offences against the Person Act 1828, s 16.

The concept of rape in medieval times was both broader and narrower than today. From the Roman concept of *raptus* came the notion of carrying off, that is, abducting a woman, a crime likely to be motivated by greed (for the woman's wealth) as by lust.[7] Increasingly, however, *raptus* also came to encompass forcible sexual intercourse, whether or not accompanied by abduction. The precise scope and application of this latter notion remained in legal doubt well into the early modern era. In the 13th century, Bracton continued to conceive the crime narrowly in terms of ravishing virgins. Yet Groot's examination of late 12th-century plea rolls suggests that rape complaints could be brought by women of sexual experience, for example wives and widows (1988: 325).

One of the difficulties with reading texts from this time – legal and non-legal – is that it is not always clear which notion of *raptus* is being invoked.[8] Both excited public concern but for different reasons. Abduction was conceived predominantly in property terms, that is, as a wrong perpetrated upon the man in whose charge a woman and her wealth were legally placed. Brundage reports that the 'practice of seizing and making off with heiresses plagued medieval society' (1990: 148). Certainly, it was the repeated focus of legislative intervention by English monarchs (Kelly, 1997; Hawkes, 2007). The fact that a woman agreed to her abduction was not strictly relevant to establishing the offence; the wrong to male authority was no less as a result of her collusion.[9]

Raptu mulieris, on the other hand, was concerned with forcible sexual violation, and, for this reason, the victim's consent or more precisely, lack, was formally pivotal. This conception of rape is much closer to our modern understanding. T.E. describes it as 'libidinous rape … a hideous, hateful kind of whoredom … when a woman is enforced violently to sustain the fury of brutish concupiscence' (1632: 377). Over time, *raptu mulieris* came to be regarded as the more serious manifestation of *raptus*.[10] Increasingly too, it was conceived as a wrong against the person of the woman herself. As Groot notes, as early as the late 12th century (and possibly earlier), women were regarded as legally competent to pursue a rape complaint – in formal terms, an 'appeal' – in English law. This suggests legal acceptance of the idea that the rape victim herself

---

[7] '[W]herein avarice is as great an agent as carnality' (T.E., 1632: 383).

[8] On the legal confusions this created, see Kelly (1997).

[9] According to Brundage, the ancient Greeks viewed seduction as more serious than forcible rape because it interfered with a woman's proper feelings of loyalty and fidelity to her father/husband (1990: 14).

[10] During the reign of Elizabeth I, rape was made non-clergiable, signifying a crime of the utmost gravity. (The doctrine of 'benefit of clergy' allowed clergymen accused of a crime to be outside the jurisdiction of the secular courts.)

had sustained a kind of harm which warranted public condemnation (1988: 330).

By the early modern period, these two understandings of rape were being formally differentiated in legal texts. Hawkins' *Treatise of the Pleas of the Crown*, published in the early 18th century, states that '[o]ffences against women made felonies by statute are of two kinds. 1 Rape. 2 Forcible Marriage.' He proceeds to define rape as 'unlawful carnal knowledge of a woman by force and against her will' (Hawkins, 1716: 108). Matthew Hale, whose famous *Historia Placitorum Coronae* was published just two decades after Hawkins' treatise, provides a more precise definition: 'Rape is the carnal knowledge of any woman above the age of ten years against her will, and of a woman-child under the age of ten years with or against her will' (Hale, 1800: 628).[11] It is notable that Hawkins, but not Hale, includes the words 'by force' in his definition of rape. Blackstone, writing in the late 18th century, also refers to force,[12] and it is his definition which subsequently shaped the development of rape law in the United States, in which force became treated as a separate legal requirement, distinct from and additional to lack of consent for purposes of establishing the offence.[13] Like Hawkins and Hale, Blackstone clearly distinguished rape from abduction and/or forcible marriage (Blackstone, 1803, IV.15: 207), and, increasingly, the attention of jurists shifted to consideration of the precise ingredients of rape as an act of violent carnality. T.E., for example, speculates about what might constitute 'force', suggesting that a man must 'overcome a woman, hand to hand, by length and breadth of his own sinews' (1632: 395–6). He thus equates force with the complete physical subjugation of the victim by the body of her rapist.

Another question attracting close juristic attention was what precisely was required, in terms of the sexual act, to establish the offence. According to Hale, 'the least penetration makes it rape', dismissing Coke's intimation that rape also requires ejaculation (*emissio seminis*) as 'mistaken' (Hale, 1800: 628).[14]

---

[11]   Although written in the 17th century (Hale died in 1676), Hale's great work was published only posthumously in 1736. An enactment prohibiting sex with a child under ten, with or without consent, was introduced in 1576 during the reign of Elizabeth I. The age of sexual consent for girls was raised to 12 in 1861. By 1885, it had been set at 16, as it continues, for both girls and boys, in all parts of Britain today.

[12]   Blackstone defines *raptu mulierus* as 'carnal knowledge of a woman *forcibly* and against her will' (1803, IV.15: 209).

[13]   On the 'peculiar' development of US rape law, see Berger (1977), noting that the legal emphasis on force led some states to adopt an additional requirement that the victim 'resist to the utmost' for rape to occur (8). Thus, somewhat paradoxically, the practical application of the requirement that the defendant use force was to focus further attention on the conduct of the victim.

[14]   In fact, Coke writes that emission is 'evidence' of rape, and it is not entirely clear that he requires it, though that is how Hale interprets Coke's statement (Coke, 1629, III:10:59).

Anna Clark (1987: 62) suggests that the emission requirement was largely a late 18th-century juristic invention, stoked by the increasingly scientific approach to legal evidentiary questions. However, Coke's *Institutes* were published in the first half of the 17th century, suggesting a somewhat earlier genesis. What is clear is that notwithstanding Hale's pronouncement, most 18th-century jurists endorsed the emission requirement (see, for example, Jacob, 1729; Viner, 1741, 18: 153). This placed a heavy evidentiary burden on victims so that even clear evidence of violent penetration did not always suffice to convict a rapist (Durston, 2007: 144–5). The emission requirement was eventually abolished by section 18 of the Offences against the Person Act 1828, and it is perhaps no coincidence that in the period immediately thereafter, rape convictions began to rise (Clark, 1987; Wiener, 2004).

While these understandings of law were being refined by learned jurists, popular and cultural understandings of rape conveyed a more ambivalent picture. Catty (1999: 39–41) draws attention to the way in which cultural representations of rape in the early modern period resonated with romantic ideals of courtship and heroism.[15] Even in so-called 'normal' sexual encounters, men were expected aggressively to initiate, and women reluctantly to submit to, sex. Therefore, a man's persistence in the face of a woman's unwillingness could easily be construed as part of the accepted ritual of courtship and sexual conquest (Catty, 1999: 39). According to Bowers, a structural depiction of sexual encounters in terms of (male) pursuit and (female) response is a significant feature of literary works in the late 17th and 18th century, a period which, she also maintains, saw the cultural cementing of a distinction between rape and seduction ('force or fraud') as a means of gauging moral responsibility in the context of non-marital sexual encounters (2011: 20–4). Both seduction and rape, Bowers argues, acknowledge the coercive nature of sexual encounters, conceived as a natural consequence of men's sexually aggressive impulse. However, in seduction, a woman's weakness in succumbing to the force of male desire implicates her in her undoing, whereas, in rape, her vigorous and visible resistance exonerates her – though she is no less undone for her efforts (Bowers, 2011: 8–9). The line between rape and seduction thus relies less on the level of force deployed by the man and more on the level of resistance offered by the woman, with the moral pendulum hovering uncertainly, depending on how the encounter is classified. Inevitably, these constructions of sexual responsibility surfaced in the legal process, informing juristic analyses of rape law in this period (King, 1998: chapter 3).

---

[15] See also King's analysis of 17th-century ballads and plays which often represented female reluctance as part of the courtship ritual (1998: 88–95).

In addition, because two legal understandings of rape were in circulation, only one of which, *raptu mulieris*, was concerned with whether the woman (as opposed to her male guardian) had given consent, the significance of a victim's lack of consent was not always appreciated even in legal proceedings. Hawkes' analysis of rape depositions in the late 14th century finds that in so far as consent features in witness statements at all, it relates to the consent of the victim's male kin, not of the woman herself (2007: 130).[16] Moreover, the legal notion of consent differed in significant ways from how we think of it today. In modern law, consent signifies an internal state of mind which law seeks to establish by factual enquiry. In medieval and early modern law, however, lack of consent was formally dependent on the presence of certain external signs and manifestations, for example visible injuries and dishevelment – 'showing her wrong, her garments torn' (T.E., 1632: 393). If the rape victim became pregnant, this was treated as proof of consent on the basis of a widely held belief that women's sexual pleasure was necessary for conception to occur (T.E., 1632: 395).[17] There was even some legal debate as to whether a woman's submission under threat of death or serious injury counted as consent, thereby precluding a finding that rape had taken place, although the body of opinion appears to have been against this for, as T.E. opines, 'consent must be voluntary' (1632: 395).[18]

The temporal dimensions of consent were also differently conceived. Early modern law recognised that consent could be granted retrospectively by the victim, thus barring her claim, although this did not prevent a suit on the part of her husband or father (Hale, 1800: 632).[19] The granting of consent after the fact could also pave the way for a formal union between the victim and her rapist, and for some families this was regarded as the best solution to an otherwise hopeless turn of events. Hufton remarks that 'society viewed with resignation a girl who was soiled merchandise

---

[16] Hawkes finds that 'women's consent was only ever foregrounded in indictments involving single women (2007: 131); interestingly, these were only a small proportion of victims, the majority, certainly in terms of initiating indictments, being wives (2007: 121).

[17] 'If at the time of the supposed rape, the woman conceives a child, there is no rape for none can conceive without consent' (T.E., 1632: 395). Both Hawkins (1716: 108) and Hale (1800: 631) question whether conception does provide conclusive evidence of consent. By the 19th century, the belief that conception could not follow from rape had been 'completely exploded' (Roscoe, 1846: 860).

[18] Hale (1800: 631) also discusses this point, concluding that submission on a threat of death is not consent.

[19] Hawkes details the efforts of successive English monarchs in the 13th and 14th centuries to prevent consent after the fact from paving the way for a successful elopement/abduction, by barring the woman and/or her abductor from inheriting her property. By the time of Hale, this concern to discourage after-the-fact consent appears to have been confined to abduction rather than *raptus mulieris*.

marrying the man who had thus devalued her' (1995: 267), and pressure was sometimes placed on the raped woman to agree to marriage, if only to save the rapist from the gallows (particularly if he came from a respectable background) (Hufton, 1995: 267).[20] Recognising this different temporality also allows us better to understand why a husband could not be guilty of raping his wife, 'for by their mutual matrimonial consent and contract, the wife has given herself up in this kind unto her husband which she cannot retract' (Hale, 1800: 629). This is a formal idea of consent, akin to a contractual agreement (as Hale himself points out); it is not intended to allude to a wife's internal state of mind.

The fact that consent could be granted irrevocably by a wife and retrospectively by a rape victim, and that marriage to the rapist was regarded as an appropriate response to violation in at least some circumstances, is indicative of a strong concern underpinning rape law in this period to protect a woman's chastity and reputation. The harm which rape law sought to avoid was the 'hideous hateful kind of whoredom' which a man's 'brutal concupiscence' inflicted upon an otherwise virtuous woman (T.E., 1632: 377). A wife's chastity was in no way threatened by a rapacious husband. Similarly, the reputation of a violated maiden could be restored by marrying the violator. Fletcher (1995: 3–29) confirms that a preoccupation with female chastity was a hallmark of the early modern period, in which notions of honour and virtue were actively and explicitly gendered. Indeed, the setting of stricter sexual and moral standards for women than for men, Fletcher argues, was in part attributable to widely shared masculine anxiety about women's sexual potency, justifying the exercise of male authority to control and contain female sexuality (Fletcher, 1995: 58). In other words, it was precisely because women were perceived to be sexually (and morally) irresolute that men had to govern them, in part by promoting a model of virtuous female behaviour in which any exercise of female sexual agency was viewed as wanton and deviant. According to prevailing sexual narratives, reluctant submission or vigorous resistance were the only responses permitted to women in sexual encounters, and the former only sanctioned in relation to courtship and marriage (Bowers, 2011: 20–4). The prevalence of such beliefs during a period in which modern rape law was taking shape inevitably influenced the way in which the law was operationalised, including the kinds of victims who could expect some form of justice. It is to these matters that we now turn.

---

[20] Laws varied across Europe as to the extent to which marriage could formally mitigate the offence (Hufton, 1995). In England, as we have seen, a rape appeal could still be brought by the girl's family, though they would be unlikely to take this course of action if they were actively seeking marriage to save their daughter's reputation.

Rape law in (historical) action

It has long been a juristic practice to cast rape as among the most serious offences. Hale famously decried it as a 'most detestable crime' (1800: 635). Coke called it 'hainous' (III.XI: 60), and T.E., as we have seen, pronounced it to be 'hideous and hateful'. Yet, a strikingly consistent feature of the history of rape law is that notwithstanding the seriousness with which jurists purported to view the crime, rape was rarely prosecuted and even more rarely resulted in conviction. This is certainly true of English law and appears to have been the case in Europe more widely, certainly during the early modern period (Hufton, 1995: 264–7; Walker, 2013a). Our historical knowledge has been greatly enhanced by a multitude of recent studies, analysing original court documents, legislative enactments, legal treatises, newspapers and literary and cultural representations, spanning a period from the late Middle Ages to the present day. Although inevitably limited by what material has survived, as well as by its contextualisation and interpretation, the historical picture to emerge is an all too familiar one of significant underreporting, limited prosecutions and a woefully low conviction rate. This is not to assert a history of rape as static and unchanging: trends clearly vary across time and space as to the incidence of prosecutions, profile of victims, content and conduct of the legal process, and the results that process yielded. Nevertheless, our survey of the studies suggests that it is difficult to argue with Wiener's conclusion that 'for centuries, rape figured only slightly in the workings of English criminal justice' (2004: 77).

Two aspects stand out in particular: the first is the relatively low number of rape cases in extant legal documents (especially when compared to violent crime more generally); the second is the paucity of convictions and/or reluctance to inflict the full rigours of the law on those convicted of the offence.

Take Groot's (1988) analysis of early eyre rolls,[21] dating from 1194 to 1216, spanning the reigns of Richard I and John. He identifies 95 cases of rape, none of which yielded a conviction. At that time, rape accusations were laid through a form of private prosecution known as an 'appeal', initiated by an 'appellor', either the rape victim or her male kin.[22] Groot (1988: 324) speculates that the lack of convictions may be explained by a preference on the part of victims' families to resolve matters privately, whether through the

---

[21] Eyre rolls were pleas presented to itinerant royal justices managing most criminal business on behalf of the Crown.

[22] The appeal process later gave way to a bill of indictment issued by a grand jury for a felony, but the responsibility for bringing the offence to the attention of the authorities, and, to a significant extent, leading and paying for the prosecution, continued to lie with the victim.

payment of reparations or by marriage to the perpetrator.[23] Kittel's survey of eyre records dating from 1202 to 1276 confirms the low numbers of rape cases, with only 142 rapes as compared to 3,492 homicides in her sample (1982: 112). Kittel notes that a substantial proportion of women (56 per cent) discontinued their prosecutions, and only a few resulted in conviction: she posits a rape conviction rate of only 6 per cent, observing that in none of these cases did the convicted offender suffer the prescribed penalty – at that time, castration and blinding (Kittel, 1982: 110). Inevitably such calculations should be approached cautiously. As Kittel acknowledges, her sample is small, historical records were often incomplete, and the wrong to the victim may have been assuaged in other ways, for example via monetary compensation.[24] Nevertheless, taken together, Groot's and Kittel's studies offer some evidence for thinking that in the late medieval period rape victims fared poorly in the criminal courts.

The early modern period provides us with considerably more surviving legal material, much of which has been mined by legal historians, often in conjunction with non-legal sources such as news reports and fictional and theatrical depictions of rape (see, for example, King, 1998; Catty, 1999; Walker, 2013c). Nazife Bashar's (1983) pioneering research focuses on rape cases from the assizes and quarter sessions, covering parts of the South East and North East of England from 1550 to 1700. Bashar's study was among the first to expose a gap between the formal legal perception of rape as a serious crime and the reality of few prosecutions and convictions. In Sussex, for example, during the reign of Elizabeth I (1558–1603), the records show 100 cases of larceny, 150 burglaries, 100 homicides and only 14 rapes (Bashar, 1983: 33). Similar patterns emerge in other county records, and Bashar's findings are replicated in other studies of the period.[25] Overall, Bashar found that rape constituted less than 1 per cent of all indictments in the Home Counties Circuit between 1558 and 1700. One could of course conclude that the lack of prosecutions for rape reflected a crime that was rarely committed. Bashar (1983: 34) doubts this, pointing out, not unreasonably, that 48 rapes in Sussex and only 21 in Hertfordshire over a 150-year period is too few to credibly reflect the number of rapes

---

[23] This is notwithstanding that rape had ceased to be an 'emendable' offence, that is, a felony subject to private resolution, after the Conquest (Groot, 1988: 26–7).

[24] Kittel mentions at least 18 cases where a concord (a money settlement) was agreed (1982: 108) and at least two which resulted in the victim marrying the rapist (1982: 107).

[25] Cockburn's study of the incidence of crime between 1558 and 1625, based on the records of the Home Circuit Assize, found that only 50 of 7,544 persons were charged with rape (1977: 58). Similarly, Sharpe (1983), looking at Assize and Quarter session records in Essex from 1620 to 1680, identified only 36 rape cases in total, producing seven convictions (six of whom were hanged) (Sharpe, 1983: 63).

perpetrated.[26] Again, as with the medieval studies, Bashar found that few of those prosecuted were convicted. Thus, of 274 rape cases recorded in five home counties between 1558 and 1700, 45 men were found guilty, and of that 45, 31 were hanged, the rest receiving lesser sentences (Bashar, 1983: 35).

Antony Simpson (1984) and Anna Clark (1987) have both carried out fairly extensive studies of rape cases in 18th- and early 19th-century England. Both conclude that this was a critical period in terms of shaping the development of formal legal processes around rape, crystallising in a set of gender-inflected legal norms which we examine in some detail in the next chapter. Bashar's study had shown that towards the end of the 17th century, the number of prosecutions and convictions for rape declined (1983: 35), causing her to speculate that as rape transitioned from a crime against male authority to a physical assault upon women, a patriarchally imbued legal system became less invested in addressing it (1983: 42). Taking up the tale at this somewhat low point for gender justice, Simpson's research spans the period between 1730 and 1830, focusing mainly, though not exclusively, on Old Bailey cases. His figures show, for example, that of 183 prosecutions for rape in the Old Bailey between 1730 and 1790, only 31 yielded a conviction and, of those convicted, less than half were executed (Simpson, 2004: 55). He calculates that the conviction rate for rape in the Old Bailey in the whole period from 1730 to 1830 was only 17 per cent, low in comparison to other capital crimes such as burglary (56 per cent) and robbery (35 per cent) (Simpson, 1986: 109). Simpson's figures also show that as the 18th century progressed, the proportion of convictions resulting from prosecutions declined further still (2004: 55–6), supporting his claim that during this period, legal innovations added to the procedural and evidentiary burden already faced by prosecutrices. A similar picture of a legal system largely indifferent to the sexual assault of women emerges from Clark's (1987) study of over 1,000 sexual assault cases between 1770 and 1845, encompassing London and the North East, and supplemented by other material such as magistrates' minutes books, newspaper reports and charity records. Clark highlights the greater

---

[26] Porter approaches the evidence more sceptically: 'We have absolutely no way of knowing with tolerable accuracy how much sexual violence went on … two, four, or six centuries ago' (1986: 220). He concludes that the low incidence of rape prosecutions could equally be viewed as an indication that certain kinds of rape (what he describes as 'the "street-crime" … assault upon strangers' (Porter, 1986: 221)) were less frequent than they are in modern times. In reaching this conclusion, Porter erroneously assumes that stranger rapes typify modern rape, which multiple, cross-jurisdictional studies have shown is not the case. Porter applies his own limited understanding of rape in 1986 to analyse material about rape from a much earlier period, a salutary lesson on the risks of bringing assumptions about the present to bear on the past.

likelihood of conviction in the case of attempted rape,[27] a finding consistent with Simpson's study (2004: 67), and that of Beattie (1986). Beattie found that in Surrey, between 1660 and 1800, 18 cases of rape and 33 cases of attempted rape were brought, with conviction rates of 15 and 64 per cent respectively (1986: 411). Unlike rape, which was a capital felony, attempted rape was an indictable misdemeanour attracting a lower penalty such as a fine, short prison sentence, flogging, period in the stocks, or some combination thereof (King, 1998: 25; Durston, 2007: 146). Problematically, it was not possible at this time to charge a defendant simultaneously with rape *and/or* attempted rape (Simpson, 2004: 64–7), although a man acquitted of rape could later be charged with attempted rape, and this did occasionally occur (Durston, 2007: 145–6). The larger number of attempted rape cases, and their comparative success, may evidence a strategic preference to prosecute for attempted rape rather than rape itself (King, 1998: 56), with the added benefit that such an allegation did not require a victim publicly to admit her loss of chastity (Clark, 1987: 47).[28]

Both Simpson and Clark identify a new trend in rape cases from the early 19th century, with more cases coming to court. Clark (1987: 60) tells us that in the North East Circuit, 54 per cent of rape accusations made by women over 12 came to trial between 1800 and 1829 compared to only 33 per cent between 1770 and 1799. According to Simpson (1984: 818), rape prosecutions rose nationally from about 18 per year between 1811 and 1820, to 26 a year between 1821 and 1828, and 36 a year between 1829 and 1830. In explaining the rise in prosecutions, Clark (1987) acknowledges efficiency gains in the criminal justice system, in particular diminished levels of corruption. She also notes the favourable impact on rape cases of the abolition of the emission requirement in 1828 (Clark, 1987: 60). Clark's main contention, however, is that the increased legal attention on sexual assault in this period expressed a growing middle-class concern to control working women's access to public space in the context of the threat to social and moral order posed by mass industrialisation (1987: 2–4). Certainly, the late 1830s saw the rise in prosecutions gradually translating into more convictions: rape convictions rose from six in 1837, seven in 1838, 17 in 1839, and 18 in

---

27   'While only 7% (Old Bailey sessions 1770–99) to 13% (North-East Assizes, 1770–1800) of men accused of raping adult women were found guilty, juries convicted about a quarter [Middlesex sessions 1770–75, 1780–85, 1790–95] of assailants accused of attempted violation' (Clark, 1987: 49).

28   Prosecuting attempted rape was also less costly and could be tried in the quarter sessions not the assizes, making court attendance more convenient and less intrusive (King, 1998: 56). Beattie (1986: 130) notes a greater tendency to 'down charge' rape in urban rather than in rural areas, speculating that in rural areas women were more likely to be supported by friends and family.

1840, an upward trend which, according to Wiener (2004: 87–8), continued throughout the 19th century, and which he attributes to the development of a genuine public concern to ensure that sexual assault was properly addressed in the courts. To assess 19th-century trends in rape prosecutions and convictions, Wiener (2004: 77) looked at a sample of Old Bailey trial reports (174 in total), reports of rape trials (about 800) in *The Times* between 1790 and 1905, and sample reports from other newspapers, along with various official documents of cases from other parts of England, Scotland and Wales, producing an analysis which supports the contention that as the 19th century progressed, sexual assault garnered greater public and political attention. In 1841, for example, in the course of a Parliamentary debate on the scope of the death penalty, the negative impact of executions on the rape conviction rate was repeatedly stressed as a reason for removing rape from the list of capital offences.[29] Wiener (2004: 91–2) also stresses the significance of legal changes making rape easier to prosecute, highlighting not just the abolition of the emission requirement (previously discussed) and the removal of rape from the list of capital offences, but also the introduction of an ability to convict on a lesser charge (for example, assault), freeing jurors from the stark choice of convicting for rape or not at all.[30]

At this point, we have some sense of historical patterns of rape law in action, generally characterised by low rates of prosecution and conviction from the earliest surviving written records, dipping deepest during the course of the 18th century, and picking up again as the 19th century progressed. What about the women whose experiences formed these patterns? Were there particular types or profiles of victims who were more or less likely to invoke the legal system successfully? In answering this question, we are inevitably dependent on the quality and content of legal records and associated material: there is not always sufficient information in the depositions, indictments, court or media reports to produce a clear picture of the person bringing the complaint. Groot (1988) notes that few of the appellors whose cases he scrutinised are recorded as married and a number identified by reference to their mother not their father. From this, he concludes that late 12th-century rape appellors were typically unmarried, poor (there is rarely any mention of a surety pledge) and likely to come from female-headed households (Groot, 1988: 328). This supports his hypothesis that women with male protectors resolved their grievances privately rather than through the courts (Groot, 1988: 329).[31]

---

[29] Parliamentary Debates, 3rd S, 57 (1841), pp 51–2; Wiener (2004: 87).

[30] Offences against the Person Act 1837, s 11.

[31] The civil action for trespass did not emerge until the mid-13th century, so there would have been no formal way for aggrieved families to secure damages through the courts in the late 12th or early 13th centuries (Groot, 1988: 332).

Bashar's (1983) analysis of 16th- and 17th-century rape cases flags the victim's age as a factor in patterns of prosecution. She notes an overall preponderance of cases in which the victim was under 18 but also observes that as the 17th century progressed, more adult women brought prosecutions, though without any positive impact on the number of convictions (Bashar, 1983: 37). The relatively young victim profile leads Bashar to conclude that convictions of those who raped children were easier to secure, a finding confirmed by other studies and for other periods (see, for example, Sharpe, 1983; Clarke, 1987; Walker, 2013a).[32] She conjectures that the higher rate of success enjoyed by young victims is indicative of a strong legal concern to protect virginity, conceived as the property of a girl's father (Bashar, 1983: 42). The significance Bashar attaches to virginity does not, however, fully resonate with other studies. For example, many of the cases looked at by Groot make no explicit mention of virginity, and 'no appeal of rape was nullified because of this omission' (1988: 325). Moreover, Hawkes' (2007) analysis of 132 rape indictments in the late 14th century shows that a clear majority of cases involved the rape of wives by men other than their husbands.[33] King suggests that Bashar's conclusion that virginity was critical to a successful rape appeal relies on a linguistic misinterpretation of the term 'defloravit', which Bashar assumes to mean 'deflower' but, according to King, was also used as a general term for 'ravish' (1998: 11).[34] Interestingly, Simpson (1986) makes a link between virginity and the apparently high incidence of child victims, accounting for the sexual vulnerability of children in terms of the prevalence of a popularly held belief that sex with a virgin could cure venereal disease. In fact, the higher conviction rate can be explained by a range of factors, including that, for children under ten, there was no need to prove lack of consent. Most scholars also agree that throughout the periods under study, the rape of a child was regarded as more morally heinous than the rape of an adult

---

[32] Walker's (2013a: 133) analysis reveals that of trials reported in the *Old Bailey Proceedings* in the late 17th century, half of those for the rape of girls aged ten or 11 produced convictions, with the same rate for children under ten whose consent was immaterial. This was double the conviction rate for victims aged 14 or older. According to Clark, 'in London out of 15 men tried at the Old Bailey for rape between 1770–1799 for rape on girls under 13, five were found guilty and sentenced to death and four were remanded for trial on a charge of assault with intent to commit rape' (1987: 48). By contrast, in the same court in the same period, 'out of 43 men tried for rape of females over 12, only three were found guilty' (Clark, 1987: 58).

[33] It is not always clear in these studies of the premodern period whether the cases reviewed concern forced sexual violation or abduction (with or without the woman's consent), further complicating the issue of what significance to assign to virginity as well as determining the profile of rape victims (see further Hawkes, 2007: 123–9).

[34] King's point is another reminder of the risks of reading present meanings into past texts.

woman,[35] although that may in part be a legacy of the value which early common law *did* bestow upon virginity (Bracton, 1210–68: 415). That said, even prosecuting child rape was not without its difficulties. Some legal doubts were expressed about the competency of children to swear the oath or give reliable evidence, and some jurists took the view that very small children could not be penetrated.[36]

A more detailed picture of the profile of rape victims engaging with the legal system emerges from King's (1998) study of 52 Ely and Northern Circuit depositions between 1640 and 1750 and a further 29 depositions from the Northern Assizes between 1780 and 1800. She identifies the prosecuting women as of 'middling' social status (for example, wives or daughters of skilled workmen), some of whom were maidservants or otherwise employed, and the majority (two thirds) of whom were single (King, 1998: 66–7).[37] The assaults which were the subject of the depositions usually occurred in the daytime when women were working, often outside, sometimes in their own home, and only rarely was the perpetrator a complete stranger (King, 1998: 70–1). As King observes, these were mainly 'opportunistic assaults on a female acquaintance' (1998: 72). Clark's (1987) more extensive analysis of cases in London and the North East yields similar results. Her analysis of rape cases tried at the Old Bailey between 1770 and 1799 reveals only 27 per cent of cases involved encounters with strangers (Clark, 1987: 138). Clark's study also confirms women's vulnerability to rape while working outside or walking to and from work,[38] although, like King, she comes across a number of rapes taking place in women's homes, including the rape of servants by fellow servants or masters (Clark, 1987: 28). According to Simpson, around half of the cases he examined involved assaults by a fellow worker or a member of the victim's household, from which he concludes that the female domestic servant was 'the typical rape victim of her time' (2004: 48). Interestingly, Clark (1987) found a significant difference between the proportion of rape cases brought against masters in London (20 per cent) as opposed to the South East more widely (9 per cent). This may have been because female servants in urban areas were likely to be isolated and more vulnerable than those in smaller, more tightly knit communities who could

---

[35] Clark describes such cases as 'excit[ing] almost universal revulsion' (1987: 48).

[36] See extended discussion of the juristic treatment of child rape cases in the 17th and 18th centuries by King (1998: 41–56); see also Walker (2013b) discussing the monstrous child rapist, inter alia, highlighting the serious physical consequences which could follow the rape of a small child, including death due to injury sustained, as another reason it was viewed as so heinous (2013b: 19).

[37] Two thirds of the women in King's study were between ten and 25 years of age (1998: 67).

[38] '43% of rapists chose victims who were travelling across the lonely moors or fields, typically from home to work' (Clark, 1987: 25).

draw upon the resources of that community for some measure of support. In any event, Clark's figures contrast markedly with King's (1998): only four of the cases in King's sample of 83 involved allegations by a servant against a master (King, 1998: 71).[39] The likelihood, however, is that female servants *were* vulnerable to assault by unscrupulous masters but struggled to bring a credible claim because of their lower social status. As Clark cynically observes, 'masters seemed to believe that they had a right to their servants' or apprentices' sexual favours', yet 'no master was punished for rape in the 18th century records I examined' (1987: 40–1). In so far as the combined weight of historical studies produces a 'typical' profile, it is one in which the prosecutrix and accused tended to be of broadly similar social standing. Prosecutions initiated by low status women against men of a high standing, as in the case of domestic servant Ann Bond, who successfully prosecuted her rich master, Francis Charteris, in 1730, were the exception, and no doubt explains the lasting notoriety of this particular case (for extended discussion, see Simpson, 2004).

Clark, King and Simpson all identify the vulnerability to sexual assault of ordinary working women. However, their studies also attest to women's willingness to challenge their abusers notwithstanding the obstacles, social and legal, which lay in their path. King, in particular, is struck by the 'dominance of the one story of an ordinary single woman surprised by rape as she goes about her everyday blameless routines' (1998: 74). She suggests that this narrative dominates because it had the best chance of being well received by the courts, with assaults which failed to conform to this dominant stereotype rarely surfacing (King, 1998: 80–2). Clark (1987) is less convinced that the courts regarded the sexual abuse of working women sympathetically, as King suggests, pointing to the low rate of convictions as clear evidence of a lack of public concern, certainly in the late 18th century (Clark, 1987: 43). Even when a public and political concern with sexual assault did emerge during the 19th century, Clark accounts for it largely as a social control mechanism to discipline the working class and entrench a new gendered order better suited to the needs of an industrialised society. In this way, the Victorian doctrine of 'separate spheres', confining women to the private sphere of home and family and fuelling a middle-class ideal of chaste and dutiful femininity, increasingly operated as a norm against which the behaviour (and particularly sexual behaviour) of all women was measured. In contrast to the early modern conception of women as sexually voracious (Fletcher, 1995), the Victorian period is notable for cementing a new narrative – which Harvey (1994) identifies as emerging in the 18th

---

[39] Similarly, Hawkes' (2007: 127) examination of late 14th-century indictments found none which stated that a master had raped a servant.

century – of female *asexuality*, essentially a conception of women as naturally lacking sexual desire, while at the same time labelling women who displayed a sexual appetite as deviant (Edwards, 1981: 23–6).

Clark's link between rape law and industrialisation goes some way to explain patterns of prosecution and conviction in the 18th and 19th centuries as well as the regional variations in victim profile previously noted. More generally, her analysis demonstrates the value and importance of looking at the operation of law in its wider social, cultural and political context. As Walker (2013c), among others, has stressed, the history of rape law in action is not linear; nor is it solely or simply explained through the lens of patriarchal and/or misogynistic attitudes subsisting through time and space, uninflected by the conditions in which they operate. Particular cultural understandings of gender and sexuality did undoubtedly shape the development and application of rape law, from late medieval notions of women as men's intellectual, physical and moral inferior, their worth gauged by their association with and value to specific men (Fletcher, 1995: 69–77; Wiesner-Hanks, 2008: 18), to the emergence in the early modern period of representations of masculinity and femininity at odds, in which sexuality was increasingly conceived in terms of powerplay and challenge to authority (Bowers, 2011), and the sphere of sexual deviance (of the heterosexual sort) contained so narrowly as to render the line between rape and 'ordinary' sex difficult to draw. As we have seen, broader changes in law, and specifically the legal process, also had an influence. Wiener (2004: 84) points to the negative impact on rape convictions of the greater use of legal counsel by criminal defendants from the late 18th century onwards, but he also argues that the formalisation of rules of evidence and procedure in the 19th century broadly benefitted the prosecution (Wiener, 2004: 89–95). As we turn to consider more closely the emergence of a legal regime governing the admissibility of a complainant's sexual history in the rape trial in the next chapter, it is important to keep this broader context of rape law in historical action to the fore. First, though we briefly consider rape law in action today.

Modern rape law

Until the late 20th century, the definition of rape in English law continued to be governed by the common law. During the 19th century, it was typically classified as an 'offence against the person' (see, for example, section 48 of the Offences against the Person Act 1861) alongside homicide, assault and other crimes of violence, but as the 20th century progressed, rape became subsumed within the newly emerging category of 'sexual offences', reflected in its inclusion in the first Sexual Offences Act (SOA) 1956 enacted in England and Wales (Farmer, 2016: 280–5). In the 1956 Act, all references to rape, as in previous statutory enactments, formally incorporated the common law definition articulated by Hale and refined in later judicial pronouncements. In *DPP v Morgan*,[40] a case which preceded but also partly triggered the legislative reforms of late 20th- and early 21st-century rape law, Lord Hailsham predictably turned to these longstanding authorities to define the offence:

> First amongst these authorities I would cite the traditional definition of rape as enshrined in paragraph 2871 of the current Archbold, *Criminal Pleading, Evidence & Practice*, 38th ed. (1973): 'Rape consists in having unlawful sexual intercourse with a woman without her consent by force, fear or fraud'[41] for which are cited as authorities 1 East's *Pleas of the Crown* 434 and 1 *Hale's Pleas of the Crown* 627.

Thus, the parameters of the offence, as delineated by 17th- and 18th-century jurists, continued, relatively unaltered, into the last quarter of the 20th century, when the common law definition was at last superseded by an explicit statutory articulation in SO(A)A 1976 which, as originally enacted, stated:

> For the purposes of section 1 of the Sexual Offences Act 1956 (which relates to rape) a man commits rape if – (a) he has unlawful sexual intercourse with a woman who at the time of the intercourse does not consent to it; and (b) at that time he knows that she does not consent to the intercourse or he is reckless as to whether she consents to it.

Notwithstanding that the formal parameters of the offence remained relatively unchanged for over three centuries, 20th-century rape victims nevertheless faced legal challenges not encountered by their early modern counterparts. The issue contested in *Morgan*, namely what was required by way of criminal intention or *mens rea* (literally translated as 'guilty mind') to commit the crime of rape, is a good example. As Lacey (2016) and others have shown, the contemporary criminal law concept of *mens rea* is of comparatively recent origins, grafted on to an older conception of felonious intent which presumed that an actor intended the natural consequences of his acts. A forensic focus on the accused's internal state of mind was not a feature of 18th-century criminal trials, a concern with

---

[40] (1976) AC 182.
[41] The inclusion of the words 'fear or fraud' reflects developments in 19th- and early 20th-century case law; see especially *R v Camplin* [1845] 1 Cox CC 220, *R v Case* [1850] ER 169, *R v Flattery* [1877] 2 QBD 410, and *R v Williams* [1923] I KBD 340, discussed in Edwards (1981: 38–40).

subjective intent emerging during the 19th century as a character-based conception of criminal responsibility increasingly gave way to a capacity-oriented approach (Lacey, 2016). The decision of the House of Lords in *Morgan*, determining that a defendant who honestly though unreasonably believed that a woman was consenting to sex was not guilty of her rape, was a quintessential expression of the capacity-based approach, the idea that responsibility flows from what we consciously choose to do or refrain from doing (Lacey, 2016: 27). Will or intention thus becomes critical to determining whether a criminal offence has been committed, creating the very concrete possibility of non-consensual sexual intercourse with a woman which is *not* rape because the defendant lacked the necessary intention when he engaged in the relevant act. In this sense, *Morgan*, while controversial in appearing to ride roughshod over a woman's lack of consent, aligned with the doctrinal consensus of the time.[42] Nevertheless, the public outcry the decision provoked led the Home Secretary to set up an Advisory Group, chaired by Baroness Heilbron, 'to give urgent consideration to the law of rape in light of recent public concern' (Heilbron, 1976: para 2). The Group reported within a matter of months, recommending, inter alia and for the first time, that rape complainants be accorded anonymity for purposes of press and media reporting and that restrictions be placed on the introduction of complainant sexual history in the courtroom.[43] The Report did *not* recommend the reversal of *Morgan*, which, it concluded, was consistent with the relevant legal principles pertaining to criminal culpability (Heilbron, 1976: para 81). Rape victims had to wait another 28 years until the SOA 2003 finally introduced a requirement that the defendant's belief in a victim's consent must be honestly *and* reasonably held.[44]

Public concern about the criminal justice approach to rape continued after Heilbron. By the 1980s, feminist activism was fuelling the production of compelling empirical evidence documenting the multiple ways in which the criminal justice system was failing rape victims, from first report through to final resolution of the complaint (McGlynn, 2010a). Highlighted concerns included low levels of reporting, declining conviction rates, police mishandling of investigations, ill-treatment of complainants, the traumatic impact on victims of the trial itself, and the general saturation of virtually every aspect of the criminal justice process with sexist and misogynistic

---

[42] Although both Temkin (2002: 118–19) and Naffine (2019: 18–19) argue that the question as to the required *mens rea* for rape was more open-ended than was credited by academic commentators of the time.

[43] Both these measures were enacted in the SO(A)A 1976, although, interestingly, the Act also extended anonymity rights to defendants, which Heilbron explicitly rejected. The defendant's right to anonymity was repealed by the Criminal Justice Act 1988.

[44] See discussion of the SOA 2003 immediately following.

practices and attitudes.[45] Pressure for reform gathered pace and, aided by a change in government to one more sympathetic to sexual violence concerns, finally generated a swathe of changes in the law and practice of rape law in England and Wales in the 1990s and early 2000s.[46]

An increasing focus of legislative attention was the improper use of evidence of a complainant's prior sexual history, prompting, as we have seen in Chapter 1, limited legislative changes in the SO(A)A 1976, followed by more radical reform in the YJCEA 1999.[47] The period also saw further changes to the legal definition of rape, including the judicial abolition in the early 1990s of the marital rape exemption[48] and the expansion of rape in the Criminal Justice and Public Order Act 1994 to include penile penetration of the anus, thereby encompassing rape of a man.[49] Further changes in the 1994 Act included the abolition of the notorious 'corroboration' warning which judges were required to give in rape trials. The gist of the corroboration requirement, which we will explore further in Chapter 3, lay in a judicial warning to juries of the dangers inherent in convicting a defendant of rape on the uncorroborated testimony of the victim, presenting judges with ample opportunity for invoking highly prejudicial and sexist stereotypes of women, as well as confusing juries as to the burden of proof required to convict.[50]

By the early 2000s, sexual offences had assumed centre stage in Home Office law reform policy. A committee was set up, reporting in 2000 (Home Office, 2000), and, in 2003, further significant changes were introduced. In particular, the SOA 2003 offered the most explicit statutory elaboration of rape to date: '1 (1) A person (A) commits an offence if – (a) he intentionally penetrates the vagina, anus or mouth of another person (B) with his penis, (b) B does not consent to the penetration, and (c) A does not reasonably believe that B consents.' Under this new articulation, the concept of recklessness, previously enshrined in the 1976 Act, was abandoned in favour of reasonable belief in consent. A general definition of consent was

---

[45] Notable studies of the period include Chambers and Millar (1983); Blair (1985); Adler (1987); Lees (1996); Harris and Grace (1999); Gregory and Lees (1999); HMCPSI (2002). See further Chapter 5.

[46] For an excellent overview of these reforms, see McGlynn (2010a) (England and Wales) and Cowan (2010) (Scotland).

[47] For detailed discussion of the YJCEA 1999, see Chapter 4.

[48] *R v R* [1992] 1 AC 599.

[49] Before 1994, what we now understand as male rape was legally classified as 'buggery'. The 1994 Act expanded the range of rape victims to include both sexes, but the category of 'rapist' continued to be confined to men. See generally Temkin (2002: 67–70).

[50] See generally Temkin (2002: 255–67). The requirement for judges to give a corroboration warning in sexual offences cases was abolished by the Criminal Justice and Public Order Act 1994, s 32(1)(b). See further Chapter 3.

introduced,[51] and evidentiary presumptions favouring consent in prescribed circumstances were created.[52] The term 'sexual intercourse' used in the SOA 1976 was dropped in favour of an anatomical formulation so that for the first time English legislation was explicit about the need for a penis to commit rape.[53] More broadly, the Act engaged in the wholesale restructuring of sexual offences law, creating four core categories: rape (section 1), assault by penetration (section 2), sexual assault (section 3) and causing a person to engage in sexual activity without their consent (section 4). The adoption of this fourfold model evidenced a legislative conception of sexual offences in which rape is not only distinguished from other acts of sexual violation but is located at the top of the sexual offences' hierarchy.

Conclusion

Reading rape law historically, and with an eye to the wider context, allows us to see how deeply enmeshed legal principles and practices are in the ideas and contestations, challenges and conditions of their time of production. An important feature of our study is to apply such a historical lens to track the emergence of legal norms and practices around the use of a complainant's sexual history as evidence in a rape trial, to understand the context and interrogate the conditions in which assumptions about the relevance and probative value of a women's prior sexual behaviour emerged and took hold, and, most importantly, to assess the extent to which, in the light of subsequent changes, those assumptions should continue to compel our regard. It is to these issues that we now turn directly.

---

[51] SOA 2003, s 74: 'A person consents if he agrees by choice and has the freedom and capacity to make that choice.'

[52] SOA 2003, ss 75 and 76. For full discussion of the changes made to rape law, see Temkin and Ashworth (2004).

[53] See also SOA 2003, s 78, defining 'sexual', and s 79, defining 'penetration'. Previous statutory elaborations incorporated the penis requirement implicitly by using gender-specific language ('man', 'woman' and so on).

3

Emergence of a Legal Regime Governing the Use of Sexual History Evidence

Introduction: Hale's legacy

Matthew Hale is often maligned for visiting upon women in perpetuity a legal regime ill-disposed towards the rape victim (see, for example, Geis, 1978). In fact, Hale adopted a more liberal approach to rape law than many of his contemporaries. As we saw in Chapter 2, Hale rejected the emission requirement long before it was finally abandoned and was sceptical of the claim that conception evidenced a woman's consent to sex. True, wives have Hale to thank for crafting the legal rationale supporting the marital rape exemption. Nevertheless, his most lasting contribution to the legal treatment of rape surely arises from his remarks about the need for caution when assessing the credibility of a rape complainant.

Hale did not invent the idea that rape victims should not be trusted. It was not uncommon, even in the 17th century, for men accused of rape to attribute a malign motive to their accuser.[1] Certainly, by the time Hale's treatise was published in 1736, challenging the motives and veracity of the rape prosecutrix was a recognised defence tactic (Simpson, 1986; Edelstein, 1998).[2]

---

[1] For example, Walker, commenting on the conduct of rape trials in the Star Chamber in the 17th century, notes a tendency to attribute political motives to rape accusations: 'In rape narratives produced in that court, men frequently portrayed the women who accused them as malicious, revenge-seeking harpies who "plotted, practiced and conspired" with like-minded confederates to bring about the "utter overthrowe and distruccon" of hapless male victims' (1998: 4).

[2] See also Simpson's discussion of the notorious Charteris case in 1730: 'His defense took the usual tack in such cases of attempting to impugn the virtue and motives of the complainant and she was specifically accused of compliance, theft, prostitution and extortion' (2004: 33).

39

Hale's comments would have resonated with a legal and popular culture already well attuned to the idea that women lacked moral fibre and were prone to dissemble, particularly about matters of sex (Fletcher, 1995: 69–77). Nevertheless, it would be wrong to view Hale's remarks solely in terms of the misogynistic attitudes of the time. As Laurie Edelstein acknowledges, Hale was genuinely concerned to ensure that those accused of serious crimes received a fair trial (Edelstein, 1998: 355–6), repeatedly expressing the view that justice should err on the side of the innocent: 'It is better that five guilty persons should escape unpunished than one innocent person should die' (Hale, 1800: 39.289).

Yet, such a juristic preoccupation with countering the risks of false accusations of rape does not appear to have extended to other crimes or certainly not to the same extent. Hay's analysis of malicious prosecution cases in the 18th century shows, rather, a lack of judicial and public concern about false accusations other than of rape (1989: 377–8). Nor is there any evidence to suggest that rape was more frequently the subject of false accusation than other offences and, indeed, given the many obstacles impeding the prosecution of rape and the slim likelihood of a successful outcome, good reasons for thinking it was not (Edelstein, 1998). Regardless of these realities, however, rape appears to have become fixed in the 18th-century legal and popular imagination as a crime peculiarly susceptible to false accusations. The particularities of that perception as it became manifest in rape trial rules and procedures are largely derived from Hale's admonitions.

Here is what Hale says:

> The party ravished may give evidence upon oath and in law as a competent witness; but the credibility of her testimony and how far she is to be believed, must be left to the jury … For instance, if the witness be of good fame, if she presently discovered the offence and made pursuit after the offender, showed circumstances and signs of injury … of the place wherein the fact was done was remote from people … if the offender fled for it; these and the like are concurring evidences to give greater probability to her testimony … But on the other side, if she concealed the injury for any considerable time after she had an opportunity to complain, if the place where the fact was supposed to be committed were near to inhabitants … and she made no outcry … *these and the like circumstances carry a strong presumption that her testimony is false or feigned.* (633, our emphasis)

Hale spends some time discussing the testimony of children before going on to inscribe those famous lines which have since echoed in courtrooms around the globe:

It is true rape is a most detestable crime and therefore ought severely and impartially to be punished ... but it must be remembered that it is an accusation easily to be made and hard to be proved, and harder to be defended by the party accused though never so innocent. (635)

Hale illustrates his point by giving an account of a series of rape cases over which he presided in which the accusation (he opines) was manifestly false and maliciously motivated, concluding his discussion as follows:

I only mention these instances, that we may be the more cautious upon trials of offenses of this nature ... the heinousness of the offense many times transporting the judge and jury with so much indignation, that they are over hastily carried to the conviction of the person accused thereof, by the *confident testimony of sometimes malicious and false witnesses*. (36, our emphasis)

We have repeated Hale's comments at length to place them in context. As we have sought to emphasise, context is important. And in truth, in terms of the times, there is nothing too remarkable about what he said. What is remarkable is the way in which these central paragraphs regarding the truthfulness or otherwise of a rape victim's testimony have travelled down the ages, from treatise to treatise, virtually verbatim, to craft and embed the procedural and evidentiary rules governing the rape trial (see, for example, Blackstone, 1803, IV:15:III; East, 1803: 445; Archbold, 1822: 260).[3] Their combined effect is to construct a specific imaginary of the 'genuine' rape victim, setting the standards for and criteria against which the veracity of all rape victims' testimony has since been assessed. Beyond legal definitions of the specificities of the offence, Hale's words graft upon the legal process an additional set of conditions which must be satisfied before the defendant's guilt can be affirmed, conditions which place the character and conduct of the victim at the heart of the forensic enquiry. Let's look at the legal legacy Hale's remarks have bequeathed.

Late complaints

It must first be acknowledged that some of the factors to which Hale draws attention were already routinely included in formal legal expositions of the time. Take, for example, the enjoinder upon the rape victim to 'presently discover' the offence, that is, to bring it to the attention of the authorities

---

[3] Until at least the 1970s, Hale's cautionary statement was read out verbatim in rape trials in many US states (Simpson, 1986: 109).

in good time and, preferably, as soon as possible. This requirement considerably predates Hale and likely derived from a general obligation in medieval law to raise a 'hue and cry' on witnessing a crime, transmuting, in the case of rape, to a specific injunction upon the victim to 'goe straight away and with hue and cry complaine to the goode men of the next town' (T.E., 1632: 392–3).[4] Hawkins, writing in 1716, asserts: 'It is a strong but not conclusive presumption against a woman that she made no complaint within a reasonable time after the fact' (108). It is Hale, however, who makes explicit the link between failing to report rape in good time and the likelihood that the complaint is false or malicious: 'Otherwise it carries a presumption that the suit was but malicious and feigned' (Hale, 1800: 632). Blackstone echoes Hale's concern, explaining the legal requirement to report 'immediately' as precisely 'in order to prevent malicious accusations', adding that 'the jury will rarely give credence to a stale complaint' (1803, IV.15.III).

The belief that late complaints of rape are likely to be false has since secured deep roots in the investigative and trial process (Temkin, 2002: 189–90). It is only in recent years, as the psychological effects of serious trauma have become better understood, that the 'common sense' rationality of the assumption has begun to be questioned (Temkin, 2002: 190). In England and Wales, the requirement that rape complaints be made 'as soon as could be reasonably expected' persisted as a feature of the rape trial until formally abandoned in 2009.[5] No temporal restrictions currently govern the reporting of rape in England and Wales. Indeed, the presumption against late complaints is increasingly presented in legal and policy discourse as one of a number of pernicious 'rape myths' – false or stereotypical beliefs about rape which 'serve to deny, downplay or justify sexually aggressive behaviour that men commit against women' (Gerger et al, 2007: 423). That said, there is evidence that, even in the 21st century, defence lawyers continue to draw attention to a late complaint to cast doubt on the truthfulness of a rape victim's account (Smith, 2018: 65–6).[6] Jury simulation studies suggest that juries may also interpret delayed reporting to the detriment of a complainant's credibility (Ellison and Munro, 2009b: 209–10).

---

[4] According to Hale, the law did not prescribe a fixed time for notifying the authorities, and it was left to the 'discretion of the court', although the Statute of Westminster had formerly prescribed 40 days. He concludes: 'Long delay of prosecution in such cases of rape always carries a presumption of malicious prosecution' (1800: 632–3).

[5] Coroners and Justice Act 2009, s 112.

[6] Interestingly, a New Zealand study found that defence lawyers are more likely to use a late complaint to challenge the credibility of a witness today than in the 1950s. The researchers suggest this may be explained by the fact that more cases of late reports are making it through to trial (Zydervelt et al, 2017).

Corroboration warnings

The adoption of a sceptical stance to late complaints is just one example of the way in which Hale's rape imaginary has operated to discredit victims who fail to conduct themselves as Hale, and the generations of judges coming after him, imagined they should. This is the beginning of the inscription of the 'real rape' stereotype into the legal fabric, the normative privileging of a particular rape encounter in which victimhood is conceived as unequivocal or not at all (Stevenson, 2000). It is vital to recognise the role of historically embedded and culturally derived juristic utterances, both in constructing the real rape paradigm and according it authority in the context of a wider framework of norms and practices predicated upon a belief in the high likelihood of false rape reports. Because Hale's concerns were already widely shared within a legal world resolutely male in outlook and experience, they quickly crystallised into a formal judicial practice to issue a warning at the commencement of rape trials about the risk of convicting the defendant with no corroborating evidence other than the victim's testimony. Often directly quoting Hale himself – 'it must be remembered that [rape] is an accusation easily to be made ' – corroboration warnings about the danger of convicting on the evidence of the rape complainant alone became standard throughout the common law world, often accompanied by judicial generalisations about the female tendency to fantasise or deceive (Lees, 1996: 111–12; Temkin, 2002: 256–8).[7] The requirement to issue a corroboration warning was not a feature of other offences where no independent witnesses to the crime might be found (for example, robbery), and it is difficult to account for it other than in terms of the influence of cultural assumptions about women's moral weakness and sexually perfidious tendencies.[8] Ultimately, it is women's nature or, more precisely, historically specific, male-propagated

---

[7] See, for example, Salmon LJ in *R v Henry & Manning* (1969) 53 Cr App R 150, explaining the corroboration warning in the following terms:

> What the judge has to do is to use clear and simple language that will without any doubt convey to the jury that in cases of alleged sexual offences it is really dangerous to convict on the evidence of the woman or girl alone. This is dangerous because human experience has shown that in these courts girls and women do sometimes tell an entirely false story which is very easy to fabricate, but extremely difficult to refute. Such stories are fabricated for all sorts of reasons, which I need not now enumerate, and sometimes for no reason at all. (153)

[8] Other 'types of witness' to whom corroboration concerns have traditionally been raised include accomplices of the accused testifying for the prosecution and children giving sworn evidence (Dennis, 2020: 15.039).

beliefs about women's nature[9] which best explains why rape victims as a class were designated within the category of 'presumptively unreliable' witnesses so that a failure to issue a warning was regarded as sufficient grounds for appealing a conviction (Temkin, 2002: 256). It was only in 1994[10] that the requirement to issue a corroboration warning was formally abolished in England and Wales,[11] with the Court of Appeal in *R v Makanjuola*[12] later ruling that a warning might still be given where there existed actual evidence to doubt the credibility of a particular witness. It is difficult to gauge the application and effectiveness of the *Makanjuola* ruling as there is a dearth of empirical evidence on the current use of corroboration warnings in England and Wales. However, on the basis of interviews conducted with judges and defence barristers in the early 2000s, Temkin and Krahé speculate that corroboration warnings are still being given outside the *Makanjuola* restrictions in some sexual offence cases (2008: 43–145). Similarly, Susan Leahy's (2014) analysis of the rules governing the use of corroboration warnings in sexual offences cases in England and Ireland suggests that trial judges continue to exercise a considerable degree of latitude on the question of whether to issue corroboration warnings, prompting Leahy to press for further restrictions on their use. There is no doubt that we have come a long way from the legally entrenched suspicion of rape victims' credibility which Hale's remarks launched and the standard use of corroboration warnings in rape trials represented. Nevertheless, as Smith's (2018) detailed study of rape trials in North East England shows, complainant credibility continues to be the organising concept around which most rape trials are conducted, in which context, and notwithstanding a range of policy-ordained strategies to minimise appeals to rape myths in the courtroom (2018: 77–80), a juristic legacy of suspicion infuses the assessment of evidence. This becomes more apparent as we consider the evidential relevance of a complainant's character.

---

[9] Literary studies show that the early modern period coincided with an enhanced intellectual and literary focus on women's nature, often generating quite polarised positions regarding women's virtues and vices (Woodbridge, 1986). See also Wiesner-Hanks (2008) tracing the relation between the 'Debate about Women' and changes in women's position under law (17–51).

[10] Criminal Justice and Public Order Act 1994, s 32(1)(b).

[11] Corroboration remains a requirement in Scotland albeit within a set of fairly complex rules about corroboration more generally. For discussion of their impact upon rape trials, see Cowan (2019). For a comparative study of the regulation of corroboration in sexual offence trials, see Lewis (2006).

[12] [1995] 3 All ER 730.

Complainant character

Hale is explicit about the relevance of a rape victim's general character to assessing the credibility of her account: the witness, he says, should be 'of good fame' (1800: 633). One must therefore assume it was a factor influencing the initiation and outcome of rape prosecutions at the time Hale was writing – in the mid to late 17th century. Interestingly, it does not feature significantly in studies of earlier periods: there is little evidence, for example, of consideration of a victim's character in Groot's (1988)[13] examination of late 12th-century eyre rolls. Nor does it really emerge as important in Bashar's (1983) analysis of assize records from the 16th and 17th centuries, a period encompassing Hale's life and legal practice. Indeed, Bashar observes that 'surprisingly little is made of the victim's past sexual history', and, in so far as it is mentioned, it tends to relate to a complainant's past sexual relations with the accused, not to 'her general standard of "virtue"' (1983: 38–9).

There is limited trace of a concern with a rape complainant's character in legal treatises published before Hale's *Historia Placitorum Coronae* appeared in 1736. T.E. (1632) does not consider the character of the rape victim other than in attributing to Bracton the claim that 'it is a good plea to say that before the rape supposed he kept the plaintiff and bed her as his concubine', adding that 'it was no plea to say she was another man's concubine or harlot' (1632: 395). T.E.'s focus on concubinage resonates with the findings of Groot and Bashar in their examination of legal records. Hawkins (1716), writing after Hale had died but before his work was published, also refers to the 'ancient' law whereby it was 'said to be no rape to force a man's own concubine' (1716: 108) but attributes no evidentiary or legal significance to a rape victim's general character. In fact, declares Hawkins, 'nor is it any excuse ... that she was a common strumpet; for she is still under the protection of the law and may be forced' (1716: 395). The assertion that a 'common strumpet' can invoke the protection of the law aligns with T.E.'s claim that a man cannot rape his own concubine but can be liable for raping someone else's, reflecting a legal concern with men's rights of sexual access to women rather than with the moral character of the women themselves.

Interestingly, Hale also refers to the view in Bracton that a man cannot rape his concubine but only to doubt it: 'But this is no exception at this day, it may be an evidence of an assent, but it is not necessary that it should be so, for the woman may forsake that unlawful course of life' (1800: 628–9). At first glance, these comments appear inconsistent with Hale's emphasis on the importance of the rape complainant's good character, but in fact they are

---

[13] Groot (1988) mentions one case in which the defendant was acquitted after lodging a plea that 'the appellor had been his concubine before and after the event' (329).

not. They merely allow for the possibility of character reform. This emerges more clearly in Blackstone's remarks on a similar theme:

> The civil law seems to suppose a prostitute or common harlot incapable of any injuries of this kind: not allowing any punishment for violating the chastity of her, who has indeed no chastity at all, or at least has no regard to it. But the law of England does not judge so hardly of offenders, as to cut off all opportunity of retreat even from common strumpets, and to treat them as never capable of amendment. It therefore holds it to be felony to force even a concubine or harlot; because the woman may have forsaken that unlawful course of life. (1803, IV:15)

Blackstone's comments hold out the possibility, at least in theory, that a woman's poor sexual reputation may be rehabilitated by visibly relinquishing her wrongful ways. In this way, the formal articulation of the offence that he, along with Hale and other jurists, seeks to delineate remains intact: rape is forcible sexual intercourse *against a woman's will*. At the same time, her prior sexual history does not cease to be irrelevant, but instead of pertaining to the question of who is entitled to access her sexually, it is redirected towards a consideration of whether her accusation is credible.

This shift in the legal and evidentiary significance of a rape complainant's prior sexual history probably occurred gradually as the legal definition of rape became refined around the notion of forced sexual intercourse. In the medieval period, when competing ideas of rape abounded and *raptus* was broadly viewed through the lens of property rights, the character of the rape victim and her complicity or otherwise in the disputed events were of less importance than the threat her ravishment posed to the interests of her male kin. As Dunn observes: 'Women were measured not by their own qualities but by the power and status of their male relatives' (2012: 52). Chastity, of course, was important but as a measure of a man's worth not a woman's character. For the same reason, a woman's account of events, and its veracity or otherwise, was not necessarily the primary forensic focus. We have seen how the issue of consent featured unevenly in early rape cases, and, as often as not, it was the consent of the male guardian rather than the woman herself that was asserted in pleadings (Hawkes, 2007). As this broader understanding of rape in terms of *raptus* or abduction gave way to a modern understanding of rape as sexual violence, the weight of a woman's account of events inevitably increased. With greater reliance necessarily being placed on her testimony, concerns about convicting men on the word of a woman alone emerged more forcefully. In other words, the shift in the legal meaning of rape during the early modern period generated conditions which prompted closer legal scrutiny of women's accounts of sexual violation within a social and cultural context in which men's authority over women went largely unquestioned

(Fletcher, 1995). It is in this context that the complainant's character, including her prior sexual experience, assumed particular significance.

The rape trial at the end of the 18th century

At the time Hale was writing and practising law (the 17th century), character testimony would have been a common feature of criminal trials. However, it was generally the defendant's character, not the victim's, which was the evidentiary focus. In her analysis of conceptions of criminal responsibility, Lacey highlights the importance of character assessment in the disposition of criminal justice prior to the 19th century (2016: 61–2). Perceptions of an accused's status or reputation, she explains, were often critical to determinations of their guilt or innocence (Lacey, 2016: 136–8). Lacey proceeds to trace the historical decline of character-based criminal responsibility in favour of an understanding grounded in capacity, that is, in the actions and choices of morally autonomous human agents (2016: 139–45). It is the capacity-based model, she posits, which now grounds criminal law theory (30–2), although (as she points out) it has only ever been partially and unevenly realised in criminal justice practice.[14] What is striking about Lacey's (2016) analysis for our purposes is that just as a character-based approach to the attribution of responsibility to defendants began to wane, it assumed greater significance in the assessment of witness testimony in rape trials.

We have already seen how changes in the nature and conception of rape as a criminal offence encouraged a juristic focus on the character and credibility of the rape complainant. The rising preoccupation with complainant character also coincided with the transformation of the criminal trial from a judge-led to adversarial model (Cairns, 1998). When Blackstone published his *Commentaries* in the mid-18th century, rape was a capital felony tried at the assizes, or in London, at the Old Bailey. Yet, notwithstanding the serious consequences that a felony conviction unleashed, these were not criminal trials as we understand them today. They were, for example, extraordinarily brief, Beattie (1991: 222) speculating that trials generally lasted no more than half an hour. Many of the rights and principles we regard as fundamental to a fair trial, for example the right of the accused to be represented by legal counsel[15] or presumed innocent until proven

---

[14] For detailed elaboration of Lacey's models of criminal responsibility, see Lacey (2016: chapter 2); for her historical analysis, see Lacey (2016: chapter 5).

[15] An accused's right to be represented by legal counsel was not fully realised until the Prisoners' Counsel Act 1836 (establishing professional counsel as a right and allowing counsel to address the jury on the accused's behalf). See 6 & 7 Will 4, c 114 and generally Cairns (1998: 3–6); Beattie (1991: 250–8). For Cairns, this signals the formal acceptance in English criminal law of the adversarial trial (1998: 2–3).

guilty,[16] were at best embryonic. Furthermore, the disposition of criminal cases occurred within a hugely decentralised infrastructure of victim-initiated prosecutions, filtered by discretionary, magistrate-led local processes (Beattie, 1986). As Lacey concludes: 'The criminal law of the late eighteenth century was not fully legalized ... findings of criminal liability turned on moral, conventional, and pragmatic considerations as much as on legal standards' (2016: 111–12).

As a felony, an accusation of rape would first come to the attention of a local magistrate, who would determine whether the case should be sent to the assizes or the charge dismissed for want of evidence.[17] Alternatively, the magistrate might opt to try the case himself on a lesser charge – attempted rape or common assault, for example (Wiener, 2004: 80). Even after a case was sent for trial, it faced the further filter of the grand jury who decided whether there was a case to answer (Beattie, 1986: 318). Moreover, as we saw in Chapter 2, if and when a rape case was finally heard, the chances of conviction were poor. As Durston summarises: 'Magistrates were reluctant to commit men accused of the crime [of rape] for trial, grand juries often refused to indict them when they did, and, if indicted, petty juries were frequently unwilling to convict them' (Durston, 2005: 168). Bearing in mind that at this time, the impetus to bring prosecutions, as with felonies in general, still lay largely with the victim herself (or her family), and that the process was expensive – including the cost of court fees and, often, the additional expense of a doctor's examination (Durston, 2005: 177) – it is little surprise that rape victims struggled to secure any kind of formal justice. However, even more significant, in terms of affecting the conduct and outcome of trial proceedings, was the growing use of defence counsel from the mid-18th century onwards.

In medieval law, assistance of counsel at trial to persons accused of felonies was not permitted.[18] By the late Middle Ages, this harsh position had been tempered to allow legal representation of felony defendants on a point of law, but, in general, defence lawyers were not a significant part of felony trials until the late 18th century. Even the use of counsel by the prosecution

---

[16] See Farmer (2018) arguing that the presumption of innocence is a 20th-century creation, cemented by the House of Lords in the case of *Woolmington v DPP* [1935] AC 462.

[17] According to laws enacted in the 16th century, magistrates were bound to send all felony complaints to trial (Beattie, 1986: 270). However, by the 18th century, magistrates were increasingly assuming the power to filter out weak cases, the formal position notwithstanding (Beattie, 1986: 274).

[18] Such a rule might seem strange if not egregious to modern sensibilities, but it fitted within a contemporary conception of the trial as a truth-seeking process in which two 'unprepared amateurs' (the prosecutrix and accused) were compelled to confront each other's testimony in open court (Beattie, 1986: 271–2).

was far from commonplace (Beattie, 1986: 353–5). As the 18th century progressed and particularly from the 1730s onwards, the situation changed. Judges became increasingly willing to allow defence counsel to participate in the trial process, particularly in the examination and cross-examination of witnesses (Beattie, 1991). It was also more common for lawyers to appear for both sides. By the end of the 18th century, the presence of legal counsel was having a marked impact on the conduct of criminal trials (Beattie, 1986: 362–76; Cairns, 1998: 30–2). This prompted, among other things, the formalisation of rules and procedures governing the introduction and exclusion of evidence (Beattie, 1991: 232–4).

Historians are agreed that judicial relaxation of the rules governing the use of counsel by the accused – a process culminating in the enactment of the 1836 Act – intensified the focus on witness character and credibility in the rape trial environment. The presence of defence counsel further 'legalised' trial discourse, encouraging the citation of case precedents and the deployment of skilled techniques of cross-examination (Clark, 1987: 54; Wiener, 2004: 84). The changing significance of cross-examination is particularly important here. Prior to the late 18th century, the judge was often the only trained lawyer in the courtroom and led on the examination of witnesses (Langbein, 1996: 1199). Once legal counsel started to examine and cross-examine witnesses, the trial assumed a different character: courtroom culture became more competitive, and the skill with which defence counsel demolishes a witness's testimony became the focus of professional and public admiration (Beattie, 1991). Increasingly, cross-examination came to replace the oath as the approved way of getting to the truth of the matter (Langbein, 1996: 1168), constituting the epistemological heart of the adversarial model.

Consequently, a gamut of effective rhetorical techniques, many of which we would now recognise as rape myths, entered the frame of formal legal consideration in rape trials, for example the suggestion that the victim invited the assault, or in some sense enjoyed it (Walker, 2013c: 140–1). Inevitably, this added to the stress and intensity of the rape complainant's trial experience. Women were already quite unused to speaking about sexual matters in any circumstances and certainly not in a public forum (Clark, 1987: 55). The quasi-theatrical atmosphere of the courtroom did little to cultivate an environment in which female complainants felt able effectively to articulate their traumatic experiences (Durston, 2007: 169).

Viewed through the lens of contemporary criminal justice norms, according a right to legal representation to accused felons must be regarded as a positive development. More open to contention, however, is the institutionalisation of this right within a highly combative courtroom culture, one which while popular at the time of its emergence is arguably less in tune with modern views about how to elicit best evidence, particularly from vulnerable witnesses.[19] Before defence counsel became commonplace in criminal trials, the judge's role in examining and cross-examining witnesses was essentially conceived in terms of truth-seeking. Defence lawyers, however, did not see themselves as truth-seekers but as client advocates. It was their commitment to representing the rights and interests of their clients which fostered the competitive environment in which the trial became reconfigured as a battle of legal wits (Beattie, 1991: 233–4). Over time, cultural and legal perceptions adjusted to embrace this 'new' imaginary of criminal justice, which is why today we tend to apprehend it as transhistorical.

The judicial development of evidentiary rules on sexual history evidence in 19th-century rape trials

By the beginning of the 19th century, allegations of rape had become increasingly structured around issues of chastity and unchastity, making the credibility and character of the rape complainant central to the conduct and disposition of the rape trial (Durston, 2007: 154).[20] The idea of rape in operation was concerned not with 'the violation of a woman's body but the theft of her virtue' (Clark, 1987: 128). This essentially moral understanding is echoed in legal texts of the time. For example, East, in his *Treatise of the Pleas of the Crown*, pronounces rape to be 'a brutal attack on the honour and chastity of the weaker sex' (1803: 436).

Yet, as the pressure to introduce evidence of a complainant's sexual history into trial proceedings mounted, so, inevitably, did judges' concern to place some evidentiary limits on what could fairly be considered. In the analysis which follows, we trace the evolution of evidentiary rules governing the introduction of a complainant's sexual history evidence in rape trials during the course of the 19th century. This was a critical period of evidentiary norm creation, coinciding with the crystallisation of the criminal trial as an adversarial process (Langbein, 1996; Cairns, 1998). It fell to judges to ensure that the interests of justice were protected in the trial environment. How then did they perceive the introduction of evidence of a complainant's prior sexual history? To what extent did they seek to suppress or moderate its use? What kinds of justice considerations did judges call upon to navigate this new evidentiary terrain?

---

[19] See, for example, challenges to the traditional advocacy approach in favour of a 'best evidence' model in which witness testimony and cross-examination are viewed as a mode of eliciting the truth of an allegation (Henderson, 2016).

[20] This is notwithstanding that, as Clark (1987) and Wiener (2004) both observe, the early 19th century also witnessed a marked growth in public concern about the perceived prevalence of sexual assault.

In *R v Hodgson* (1812),[21] a 16-year-old girl was allegedly raped by the defendant on a country road.[22] At the Yorkshire summer assizes, prisoner's counsel (as defence counsel was then described) sought to cross-examine the complainant ('prosecutrix'), Miss Halliday, about her prior sexual behaviour. Specifically, they sought to ask "whether she had not before had connections with other persons? and whether she had not before had connection with a particular person? (named)".[23] The judge, Baron Wood, whom Wiener (2004: 95) suggests was known to be sympathetic to female witnesses, upheld the prosecution's objection that Miss Halliday was not obliged to answer the questions put. Moreover, he upheld a similar objection to defence counsel's request to call witnesses who could attest "that the girl had been caught in bed about a year before ... with a young man" (Wiener, 2004: 95). The defendant was found guilty and the judgment upheld on appeal.

On what ground was the admission of evidence refused in *Hodgson*? One can discern two considerations from the brief formal report of the trial: first a concern, expressed by Baron Wood, that the complainant should not be compelled "to criminate and disgrace herself";[24] and second a concern, voiced by the prosecution, that questions pertaining to a prior sexual encounter with someone other than the accused 'was not connected with the present charge as [the prosecution] could not come prepared to answer them'.[25] Thus, the justice considerations called into play to preclude the evidence encompassed both the complainant's right not to incriminate herself when giving testimony and ensuring that the prosecution was not unduly burdened in the case it was required to make. Strikingly, the defendant's interests did not explicitly feature in the court report.

A slightly different approach is taken in *R v Clarke* (1817).[26] In this case, an indictment for assault with intent to commit rape, the defence sought to tarnish the complainant's character by questioning not only her chastity but her honesty.[27] The judge, Holroyd J, affirmed that 'in the case of ... rape, evidence that the woman had a bad character previous to the supposed commission of the offence is admissible'.[28] Therefore, the defence was

---

[21] (1812) Russell & Ryan 211.
[22] Additional factual details drawn from Wiener's analysis of contemporaneous newspaper reports (2004: 95).
[23] *Hodgson*, 211.
[24] *Hodgson*, 211.
[25] *Hodgson*, 212.
[26] (1817) 2 Starkie 241.
[27] Accusing the prosecutrix of theft or dishonesty was not an uncommon defence strategy in rape trials of the period (Clark, 1987: 66); see also Simpson's (2004) discussion of the Charteris case.
[28] *Clarke*, 242.

permitted to cross-examine the complainant, a Mrs Webb, about alleged prior acts of theft. However, Holroyd J also allowed the prosecution to introduce witnesses to attest to the fact of Mrs Webb's subsequent return to an honest path. As to the evidence pertaining to her chastity (or alleged lack thereof), the judge sought to draw a clear line between 'particular' and 'general' evidence, that is, between the facts of specific sexual encounters with persons other than the defendant (which Holroyd J ruled against) and 'general' evidence of the complainant's unchaste reputation (essentially how her character was publicly perceived). The latter Holroyd J permitted on the ground that '[general] evidence has been held to be admissible in all cases where character is an issue' and that '[i]n the case of an indictment for a rape, evidence that the woman had a bad character previous to the supposed commission of the offence is admissible'.[29] In his *Summary of the Law Relative to Pleading and Evidence in Criminal Cases*, published in 1822, Archbold presents *Hodgson* and *Clarke* as authority for the following propositions:

> Upon an indictment for rape, the defendant may give general evidence for want of chastity or he may prove that she had before been criminally connected to him [a reference to unlawful fornication] but not that she had been criminally connected with others ... and the same upon an indictment with an attempt to commit a rape. (Archbold, 1822: 69)

R v Barker (1829)[30] further affirmed the emerging distinction between general and particular evidence, the judge permitting defendant counsel to put questions to the complainant about walking the streets "with a woman reputed to be a common prostitute"[31] while reaffirming his reluctance to admit evidence 'of particular acts of criminality in the prosecutrix'.[32]

Matters took a different turn in *R v Robins* (1843).[33] According to Wiener, lawyers were not entirely comfortable with the line of argument kickstarted by *Hodgson*, and defence counsel increasingly sought inventive ways to circumvent it (2004: 96–8). In *Robins*, the complainant, Miss Robins, was

---

[29] *Clarke*, 244.

[30] 3 Car & P 588 (1829).

[31] *Barker*, 590.

[32] *Barker*, 590. In fact, the questions put to the complainant straddled a somewhat fine line between 'general' and 'particular' acts: "Were you not on – [since the time of the alleged offence] walking in the High Street, at Oxford, to look out for men?" "Were you not on – [since the time of the alleged offence] walking in High Street, with a woman reputed to be a common prostitute?" The complainant denied these claims, and the defendant was convicted. Wiener cites other examples where defence counsel pushed the line between general and particular evidence to barely credible lengths (2004: 97).

[33] (1843) 2 Moody & Robinson 512.

asked in cross-examination whether she had had 'connection' with men other than the defendant. On her denial, the defence asked the judge whether they could call witnesses to show that she had lied. Clearly, this line of enquiry hovered dangerously on the periphery of particularity. Nevertheless, Coleridge J (in consultation with Erskine J) allowed the witnesses to be called, stating that '[i]t is not immaterial to the question whether the prosecutrix has had this connection against her consent, to shew that she has permitted other men to have connection with her, which on her cross-examination she has denied'.[34] The defendant was subsequently acquitted.[35]

Robins, reported in the briefest of terms, is interesting for a number of reasons. First, it is noteworthy that prosecution and defence counsel both drew on developing case law to support their arguments, evidencing the growing grip of principles of precedent in legal argumentation. The prosecution invoked *Hodgson* as authority for excluding evidence of the complainant's 'connection' with other men, the defence citing *Barker* and a later case, *Martin*,[36] to support its inclusion. In fact, neither *Barker* nor *Martin* fully justify the position advocated by the defence, and the *Robins* decision must therefore be taken as expanding, albeit conditionally (and as we shall see, temporarily), the scope of permissible sexual history evidence. A second reason why *Robins* is interesting is that Coleridge J justifies the introduction of the evidence by referencing its relevance to the issue of whether or not the complainant *consented* to sex with the defendant. Unlike, for example, *Hodgson*, in which the purpose of raising the complainant's sexual history was to tarnish her reputation and therefore her credibility, *Robins* explicitly foregrounds the question of consent in deliberating the admissibility of sexual history evidence.

This linkage of consent with prior sexual behaviour continues to emerge in *R v Holmes* (1871).[37] The facts are like *Robins* in that the complainant was asked in cross-examination about a prior sexual encounter with another man – which she denied – prompting the prosecution to call the man in question, Sharp, to contradict her denial. The Court refused to allow Sharp to give testimony, partly because a case heard at the Liverpool Assizes the previous year[38] had refused to follow *Robins*. The question of the admissibility of Sharp's evidence went to the Court for Crown Case Reserved (CCCR), with the defence, invoking *Robins*, making the case for admissibility on

---

[34] *Robins*, 513.

[35] According to Wiener (2004: 98), Miss Robins was the defendant's 13-year-old daughter.

[36] *R v Martin* (1834) C & P 562 in which the judge agreed that the complainant could be asked whether the defendant had intercourse with her with her consent before the time of the alleged offence.

[37] (1871) Law Rep 1 CC 334.

[38] *R v Cockcroft* (1870) 11 Cox CC 410.

the basis that the evidence bore directly and materially upon the question of whether the complainant had consented to sex with the defendant. Remarkably, the CCCR were unanimous in upholding the exclusion of the evidence, Kelly CB explaining the Court's reasoning in the following terms: 'If such evidence as that here proposed were admitted, the whole history of the prosecutrix's life might be gone into; if a charge might be made as to one man, it might be made as to fifty, and that without notice to the prosecutrix.'[39] Reviewing the developing case law from *Hodgson* onwards, Kelly CB declared *Robins* to be 'in opposition to the whole current of authority'.[40] He distinguished *Martin* as the disputed evidence in that case related to prior sexual behaviour with the defendant, which, Kelly CB concluded, 'is undoubtedly admissible, for it has a direct bearing upon the question of consent'.[41] The other judges had less to say but broadly fell in with Kelly CB's position. Byles J reasserted the formal legal position that 'rape may be committed upon a prostitute'[42] as reason to exclude evidence of connections with other men, while Pigott B simply remarked that the proposed evidence was 'not relevant to the issue; and its admission might lead to great injustice'.[43] Hannen J adopted a formalistic approach, insisting on the authority of *Hodgson*, although he also expressed the view that Sharp's testimony should be excluded because 'the prosecutrix cannot come prepared to try all the issues that would be thus raised'.[44] Only one judge, Lush J, admitted to any degree of equivocation before coming to the conclusion 'that the evidence on question was too remote from the issue'.[45]

Looking at these judgments, there emerges an assortment of judicial reasons for excluding evidence of a complainant's prior sexual behaviour with men other than the defendant. First and foremost is the lack of relevance to the issue of consent which Kelly CB stated explicitly and Lush J obliquely. Additionally, however, the judges clearly view the question of whether and what evidence should be introduced as an issue which encompasses the justice interests of both the defendant *and* the complainant – indeed requires a balancing thereof. The firmer grip of norms of legal precedence is also in play, enabling the judges both to distinguish *Martin* (as a case in which the proposed evidence pertained to prior sexual behaviour between the complainant and the defendant) and dismiss *Robins* as inconsistent with established authorities.

---

[39] *Holmes*, 336.
[40] *Holmes*, 337.
[41] *Holmes*, 337.
[42] *Holmes*, 337.
[43] *Holmes*, 337.
[44] *Holmes*, 338.
[45] *Holmes*, 338.

By 1887, the legal position appeared close to settled, with *R v Riley*[46] confirming that prior sexual behaviour with the defendant should be treated differently from prior sexual behaviour with other men. While the former was thought to be plainly material and relevant, the latter was not. Coleridge CJ, quashing the trial court conviction in *Riley*, commented as follows:

> The question in issue being whether or not a criminal attempt has been made upon her by A., evidence that she has previously had connection with B. and C. is obviously not in point ... But to reject evidence of her having had connection with the particular person charged with the offence is a wholly different matter because such evidence is in point as *making it so much the more likely that she consented* on the occasion charged in the indictment.[47]

Interestingly, while Coleridge CJ foregrounds relevance to consent as the primary reason for including (or excluding) complainant sexual history evidence, he also expresses concerns about the use of such evidence, including the unfairness to and hardship on the complainant[48] and the fact that 'the results of admitting such evidence [of sexual behaviour with men other than the defendant] would be to deprive an unchaste woman of any protection against assaults of this nature'.[49] He thus reiterates the formal view that the offence turns not on the chastity or otherwise of the complainant but on the presence or absence of her consent. At the same time, and as Stephen J is quick to point out, this does not preclude the introduction of general evidence 'that a woman was a common prostitute'[50] because that goes to the issue of her character and therefore the credibility of her account rather than to the presence or absence of consent as such.

The final case to consider in this short trawl through 19th-century law reports is *Dickie v HM Advocate* (1897),[51] a Scottish case which neatly

---

[46] (1887) QBD 481.

[47] *Riley*, 484 (our emphasis). See also Pollock B agreeing:

> It is clear that evidence of the woman having had connection with other men would not be relevant, but where the only question is whether she consented to what was done by the prisoner, I am clearly of opinion that evidence of her having previously allowed him to have connection with her is relevant to the issue. (484)

[48] *Riley*, 483.

[49] *Riley*, 484.

[50] *Riley*, 485.

[51] 24 R(J) 82.

captures the doctrinal position at the end of the 19th century. Once again upholding the relevance of evidence of prior sexual behaviour with the defendant – particularly when close in time to the alleged act – as well as permitting general attacks on the complainant's character for want of chastity, the Court was nevertheless clear that 'evidence of individual acts of unchastity with other men'[52] was not permissible. His Lordship continued: 'I am not aware that such evidence has ever been allowed, and indeed it could only be allowed upon the footing that a female who yields her person to one man will presumably do so to any man – a proposition which is quite untenable.'[53] The only situation in which the Court was prepared to tolerate the possible introduction of evidence of sex with other men was where it was very close in time to the alleged rape. Lord Adam puts it thus:

> [I]t is not competent to prove specific acts of connection with other men, unless such acts are so closely connected with the crime charged as to form, as Lord Neaves puts it, part of the *res gestae*, by which I understand him to mean that they would or might furnish evidence tending to account for the physical condition and appearance of the woman.[54]

As we shall see, this glimmer of exceptionalism, captured in the notion of close temporal, spatial or physical connection, was to widen during the 20th century.

Evaluating the use of complainant sexual history evidence in 19th-century law and practice

At the close of the 19th century, the English and Scottish courts had developed a reasonably clear approach to the introduction of complainant sexual history evidence, distinguishing prior sexual behaviour involving the defendant (which was generally admissible) from prior sexual behaviour with other men (which, other than taking the form of general evidence of a complainant's bad character or reputation, was not admissible). It is somewhat ironic then to discover that the evidence introduced in *Evans*[55] in 2016 would not have been formally permitted in a late 19th-century British courtroom.

---

[52] *Dickie*, 84 per Lord Justice Clerk.
[53] *Dickie*, 84 per Lord Justice Clerk.
[54] *Dickie*, 86.
[55] [2016] EWCA Crim 452.

This is not to suggest that the formal legal position was always followed. Indeed, historical studies suggest otherwise. Clark's analysis of the transcripts of Old Bailey trials shows that evidence pertaining to complainants' chastity or otherwise significantly determined the outcome of rape trials in 18th-century London, in particular by casting doubt on their general character and therefore credibility.[56] In the 19th century, as the question of consent assumed an increasingly central role in legal and public discourse around rape, evidence of unchastity continued to be invoked, increasingly to undermine any allegation that a sexual encounter had been non-consensual. As we have seen, skilled defence counsel persisted in ferreting out new ways to circumvent the distinction drawn between general and particular evidence of prior sexual behaviour. In this, they met with little resistance – judges, juries, newspapers and moral campaigners all being aligned in adopting a highly judgmental approach to wanton femininity. Thus, in practice, Clark argues, what determined a woman's consent 'was not whether or not she said yes or no to a particular act, but whether she conducted herself as the sexual property of husband or father, or as common property of all men' (Clark, 1987: 72). In other words, and notwithstanding the formal position that even a 'common strumpet' could be raped, prior sexual experience (or the taint thereof) commonly served to evidence the fact of consent. Citing newspaper reports to illustrate public attitudes here,[57] Clark recounts an extract from *The Times*:

> In Derby, two 'labouring lads sprang out from behind a hedge' and one 'assisted' the other in 'violating' Harriet Hartshorne according to the newspaper account. The reporter admitted that the men assisted each other in the question but questioned 'whether it was a rape at all' since the prosecutrix 'had by no means a good character' and her sister 'a very loose character indeed'. (1987: 73)

Even the 'loose character' of a complainant's family member was enough to raise questions about whether a rape had in fact been perpetrated.

While Wiener (2004) broadly affirms the significance of chastity in rape discourse of the time, he questions the bleak picture of 19th-century criminal justice painted by Clark. Wiener argues that the doctrinal crystallisation of rape as non-consensual sex,[58] alongside the development

---

[56] 'In half of the trials … [examined] … impugning a woman's character sufficed to gain accused men a verdict of not guilty' (Clark, 1987: 57).

[57] Clark relies on newspaper reports and other unofficial sources to elicit a picture of 19th-century rape trials because by that time the practice of publishing public transcripts of sexual crimes had been largely discontinued, presumably on grounds of their morally offensive content (see generally Clark, 1987: 16–17).

[58] See in particular *R v Camplin* (1845) 1 Cox 22, discussed by Wiener (2004: 111–12).

of formal rules governing the introduction of sexual history evidence at trials, delivered tangible benefits, making it 'less onerous than it had ever been to prosecute and convict for rape' (2004: 89). Certainly, as we have seen in Chapter 2, the number of rape prosecutions and convictions did rise in the 19th century, particularly after the removal of rape from the list of capital crimes in 1841. However, as Wiener acknowledges, this did not diminish the importance of sexual history evidence in rape trials but simply strengthened the position of victims who could produce unimpeachable evidence of their chastity. A chaste woman, even if poor, unmarried or otherwise unprotected by social or familial privilege, was, Wiener points out, in a better position in the 19th century to pursue a rape complaint than hitherto (Wiener, 2004: 92). The Victorian preoccupation with female sexual virtue thus worked to place some restrictions on 'men's sexual freedom' as 'more and more women became "out of bounds" for sexual aggression' (Wiener, 2004: 93): 'In general, the "character" discourse so popular in the nineteenth century enhanced, for women who could meet its heightened behaviorial demands, their moral authority as against men, making women's evidence count for somewhat more, and men's (against women's) for somewhat less than previously' (93).

It is small comfort to know that women who successfully rebuffed the slurs on their reputation which adversarial logic decreed to be cast occasionally received some measure of justice. However, the price paid for such minimal gains was heavy indeed, as the result of according greater weight to female sexual virtue was to continue to entrench in law an operative conception of rape turning not on whether a woman's consent had actually been given but on whether a man's access to sex with that woman conformed with prevailing norms of male sexual entitlement. This operative conception, while plainly not in line with the formal legal position, was nevertheless embedded in criminal justice practice. Critically, what enabled the co-existence of two contradictory ideas of rape, one manifest (that is, in compliance with the official legal conception), the other operative (how a concept is operationalised in practice), is the judicial linkage of a complainant's sexual history with the fact of consent.[59] This allowed rape law to embrace a crime in which women's choice was formally pivotal, while at the same time maintaining men's access to sex on their own terms, as the evidentiary relevance of a complainant's prior sexual history gradually shifted from raising questions about the credibility or truthfulness of her testimony to being factually probative of her consent to sex with the defendant. This direct linkage of a complainant's prior sexual behaviour (particularly with the

---

[59] On the distinction between 'manifest' and 'operative' concepts of rape, see Hänel (2018).

defendant himself) and the fact of consent is most explicitly made in *Riley* in which the court assert that the fact that the complainant and defendant have previously 'connected' make it much more likely that she consented to sex on the occasion in question. This is an argument from propensity, an argument which attempts to resolve factual uncertainty through the application of principles of probability, the underpinning assumption being that a prior, presumably consensual sexual connection with the defendant makes it more probable that the complainant has consented on this occasion. While, formally, this same logic is rejected in relation to a complainant's sexual connections with other people, the practical effect of exposing a complainant's less than chaste prior history was to encourage the application of the same logic wherever unchastity was in evidence. Certainly, historical studies suggest that few efforts were made to scrutinise the precise nature of the evidentiary claims being made or their probative value. In an analysis of late 19th-century rape trials involving underage complainants, Lammasniemi (2020) shows that notwithstanding public and political concern to strengthen and clarify the law so that it better protected women and girls from the widely perceived threat of sexual danger, the nuance and sophistication of the evolving legislative and doctrinal framework did not materialise in the everyday trial experience.[60] Even in cases in which the complainant was underage – where, technically, consent was irrelevant to the commission of the crime – evidence of the complainant's bad character or sexual precocity was frequently raised: 'Girls who were suspected to have had sexual encounters with men were considered unreliable witnesses and their past sexual history – real or suspected – was discussed openly in trials' (Lammasniemi, 2020: 258). Lammasniemi's study shows how far the law in practice diverged from the law in the books, even at the 19th century's close.

Crystallising the common law in the 20th century

The doctrinal scaffolding constructed by the courts in the 19th century set the formal parameters for the introduction of complainant sexual history evidence for much of the 20th century. The common law permitted such evidence insofar as it was relevant to a fact in issue (usually consent) and/or to the credibility of the complainant's testimony (Dennis, 2020: 15-006). Within this general framework, various types of evidence were more or less likely to be deemed admissible. Evidence of previous sexual intimacy between the complainant and the accused was almost always deemed

---

[60] See also Wiener: 'For decades, the precise line between proper and improper questioning remained vague and could move one way or the other according to the skill of defense and prosecution counsels, and the inclinations of particular judges ... everyday court practices were always subject to variation' (2004: 100).

relevant, particularly where the defence argued that intercourse had been consensual: 'The rationale was that if the complainant had previously had consensual sex with the accused, the probability of further intercourse, also with consent, increased' (Roberts and Zuckerman, 2010: 616). By contrast, evidence of specific sexual encounters with other men was not *generally* deemed to be admissible, although it could be allowed in certain limited circumstances, the embryonic exception in *Dickie* (which held that a sexual connection with someone other than the defendant might be relevant where it was 'so closely connected with the crime charged as to form part of the *res gestae*'[61]) opening up new avenues for circumventing the settled position.

In this regard, judicial reasoning built upon and subtly expanded the old law admitting the relevance of evidence that the complainant was a common prostitute. In particular, in *R v Krausz* (1973), the Court of Appeal not only reaffirmed the admissibility of evidence that the complainant was a prostitute but also suggested that mere evidence of promiscuity, whether or not, strictly speaking, amounting to prostitution, was admissible insofar as it evidenced that the complainant 'was in the habit of submitting her body to different men indiscriminately, whether for pay or not'.[62] In taking this position, the Court in *Krausz* envisaged no conflict with well-established authorities supporting the exclusion of evidence of 'particular acts of sexual intercourse with other men',[63] Stephenson LJ offering the following account of how the law stood:

> It is settled law that she who complains of rape or attempted rape can be cross-examined about (1) her general reputation and moral character, (2) sexual intercourse between herself and the defendant on other occasions, and (3) sexual intercourse between herself and other men; and that evidence can be called to contradict her on (1) and (2) but that no evidence can be called to contradict her denials of (3).[64]

This is effectively a reiteration of the *Robins* position over a century earlier.

The issues raised in *Krausz* are, interestingly, not dissimilar to those raised in *Evans* (although *Krausz* was decided before the use of complainant sexual history evidence was statutorily restricted). Maintaining that the complainant had consented to sexual intercourse (notwithstanding evidence that the defendant had been violent towards her, resulting in a separate

---

[61] (1897) 24 R (J) 82.
[62] *R v Krausz* (1973) 57 Cr App R 466 at 474 per Stephenson LJ.
[63] *Krausz*, 475.
[64] *Krausz*, 472.

conviction for assault occasioning actual bodily harm),[65] defence counsel sought to introduce a witness (an acquaintance of the defendant's) who could attest to a sexual encounter with the complainant similar to that recounted by the defendant; specifically who could confirm that, after consensual sex had occurred, the complainant asked for payment. The trial judge, assuming himself bound by authority not to allow evidence of specific sexual encounters with other men, excluded the testimony. The Court of Appeal quashed the defendant's conviction, ruling that the evidence should have been introduced on the grounds that the evidence was relevant to the question of whether the complainant was a prostitute and, in so far as it provided support for that argument proffered by the defence, it was admissible.[66] The judicial distinction between general evidence of a complainant's immoral character or loose reputation (traditionally permitted) and evidence of particular sexual encounters with men other than the accused had effectively collapsed.

We saw in Chapter 2 that, in the aftermath of the outcry provoked by the *Morgan* decision, rape law in England and Wales was subject to legislative reform. The changes introduced by the SO(A)A 1976 included the first statutory restrictions on the use of sexual history evidence, section 2 providing that in a rape trial 'no evidence and no question in cross-examination shall be adduced or asked at the trial, by or on behalf of any defendant at the trial, about any sexual experience of a complainant with a person other than that defendant' except with the leave of the judge, in other words, at the judge's discretion. In practice, as we shall see in Chapter 5, this provision did little to limit the use of sexual history evidence, Zsuzsanna Adler's study of rape trials at the Old Bailey in the late 1970s revealing that sexual history evidence continued to be introduced in most rape trials (Adler, 1987). Evidence from Adler's study and the subsequent work of Sue Lees (1996), among others, lent strong support to the case for tightening the regulation of sexual history evidence in the debate leading up to the passing of the YJCEA 1999.[67]

One concern raised by the introduction of section 2 of the 1976 Act was its effect on the previous common law position. Although it was agreed in principle that leave could not be given by a judge where the evidence sought to be introduced did not meet the common law requirements of relevance, the wide interpretation and application of section 2 in *R v Viola*,[68] which was

---

[65] There was also considerable corroborating testimony including that of two witnesses living in the building where the complainant claimed she had been raped.

[66] The Court of Appeal relied on an earlier trial court decision, *R v Bashir* (1970) 54 Cr App R 1, which had held to that effect.

[67] For detailed consideration of the current legal regime, see Chapter 4.

[68] [1982] 1 WLR 1138.

followed and confirmed in a series of subsequent Court of Appeal cases,[69] further eroded the common law position. In *Viola*, the trial judge had ruled that evidence of the complainant's alleged sexual behaviour with other men could not be introduced to support a defence claim of consent. On appeal, the judge's decision was overturned, the Court of Appeal holding that the evidence did go to the issue of consent and should have been allowed. The Court appear to have been influenced here by the temporal proximity of the sexual behaviour the defence sought to introduce and the alleged rape. This included (1) evidence suggesting that the complainant had entertained[70] two men at her home earlier on the evening that the rape was said to have occurred, (2) evidence that she had sexual intercourse with her boyfriend the day after the alleged rape and (3) evidence that on the morning after the alleged rape there was a naked man in the complainant's flat. Interestingly, the Court did not think that the evidence pertaining to the complainant's boyfriend met the test of relevance and would have happily followed the trial court on that issue alone. The other evidence, they ruled, should have been admitted:

> It seems to us that the presence of the two men in the maisonette prior to the incident in question and the presence of the naked man in the maisonette immediately after the event are matters which went to the question of consent and were matters which could not be regarded as so trivial or of so little relevance as for the judge to be able to say that he was satisfied that no injustice would be done to the appellant by their exclusion from the evidence.[71]

Looking back at *Viola*, it is difficult to see how this evidence was relevant other than to support the proposition that a woman who has (allegedly) consented to sex with other men is more likely to have consented to sex with the defendant. This is the first of the now discredited 'twin myths' historically associated with the use of sexual history evidence. One can only speculate because, as is often the case, the Court of Appeal do not give grounds to support their relevance claim; they merely assert it. Equally bemusing is the fact that the Court place more evidentiary weight on the merest hints that the complainant had engaged in sexual behaviour with unidentified other men than on having sexual intercourse with her boyfriend even though the events took place within the same three-day time frame. What precisely was the thinking here? There was significant evidence to support the complainant's account of events, including the fact that she had sustained physical injury

---

[69] See especially *Redguard* [1991] Crim L R 213; *Bogie* [1992] Crim L R 301.
[70] Including, it was alleged, 'making sexual advances', essentially flirting with them both (per Lane CJ, 1144).
[71] *Viola*, 1144–5.

and that the defendant had changed his story, at first denying he had sexual intercourse with the complainant and then admitting it while claiming it was consensual. There is a definite whiff of judicial disapproval of (what is perceived to be) female promiscuity in *Viola*, echoed in subsequent cases such as *R v Bogie*,[72] where the case of a homeless woman, who accepted a bed for the night with a slight acquaintance and had the temerity to say no to sexual intercourse, invited the following appellate observations:

> It was a remarkable case because, from the facts, it was hard to imagine a case where a complainant had gone further in being prepared to have sexual intercourse but at the last minute, according to her, said "No". Of course, she was entitled to do that, but it might be difficult for the appellant. She was prepared to spend the night with a man in a deserted house, to take off all her clothes except her bra and to put on a scanty shirt and get into bed with a man who was wearing nothing but underpants. It perhaps was not entirely surprising that in those circumstances sexual intercourse had taken place.[73]

Bogie followed *Viola* in emphasising that notwithstanding that section 2 of the 1976 Act was introduced to afford a modicum of protection to complainants, the test to be applied was whether failing to admit the evidence would result in unfairness to the defendant, framed in terms of whether the jury would reasonably have taken a different view had the evidence been introduced.[74] Most significantly, as McColgan (1996: 282), among others, has noted, the Court's assertion, without more, that evidence of specific sexual encounters with specific third parties is relevant to the issue of consent, flies in the face of the carefully crafted position laid out by Coleridge CJ in *Riley*.[75] The glimmer of exceptionalism presaged in *Dickie*[76] and extended in *Krausz*[77] had by *Viola*[78] erased the established norm structure almost entirely.

Conclusion

This chapter has tracked the emergence of the legal regime governing the use of sexual history evidence in English common law. Against the backdrop of a historical analysis of rape law in the previous chapter, we

---

[72] [1992] Crim L R 301 (CA).
[73] *Bogie*, 303.
[74] Further clarified by Lane CJ in *Brown* (1989) 89 Cr App R 97 (CA), 109.
[75] (1887) QBD 481.
[76] (1897) 24 R (J) 82.
[77] (1973) 57 Cr App R 466.
[78] [1982] 1 WLR 1138.

began by exploring the earliest criminal law and evidence treatises, with a particular focus on the writings of Matthew Hale, popularly associated with the genesis of rape law's failings. We saw how Hale's work set the tone and substance for the development of an array of common law rules governing the conduct of the rape trial, all of which derived from a formally inscribed legal suspicion of the testimony of rape complainants. The rules governing the use of sexual history evidence sat within this broader framework but were also the result of a distinct line of case law which developed in the 19th century and coincided with the development of adversarial criminal justice and the cementing of precedent.

There is no doubt that adversarial trial practices provided an ideal forum for incorporating and embedding commonly circulating cultural assumptions about female sexuality into legal norms and processes. At the same time, the forensic significance of a complainant's sexual history can be traced further back to the ambivalence of late medieval legal commentators as to whether virginity was a requirement for the commission of rape as well as to the preoccupation of early modern jurists with external signs and manifestations of non-consent. What seems clear is that as the concept of rape moved away from its early associations with *raptus* (understood as abduction/carrying off) and became more firmly grounded in sexual violation *against a woman's will*, the prior sexual behaviour and experience of the prosecutrix/complainant assumed greater evidentiary significance, initially as indicative of her moral character (and therefore credibility) and increasingly as relevant to the question of her (non)consent. These intellectual moves became crystallised in the 'twin myths' – in the legal acceptance of assumptions that unchaste women were more likely to consent to sex and were less worthy of belief.

Historically (and to a yet to be determined extent, contemporaneously), the use of sexual history evidence in the rape trial served two important functions. First, it enabled the formal exposition of the modern offence of rape in terms of lack of consent. As far back as Hale, as we have seen, rape of a prostitute was held to be within the scope of legal contemplation. Non-consensual sexual intercourse thus emerged as the manifest conception of rape. And yet, what the law gives, the law just as easily takes away. Here, evidence of a complainant's prior sexual behaviour provided the means of taking, her lack of chastity mobilised to evidence her consent notwithstanding her assertions to the contrary. Ngaire Naffine (2019) has highlighted the ability of criminal law scholarship to advance and defend apparently contradictory positions when it comes to sexual offences law. Sexual history evidence is a case in point, as its use simultaneously supports and denies the capacity of gender-coded moral agents ('women')[79] to withhold consent to sex where they have on a prior occasion agreed to it.

---

[79]   This point is further developed in Chapter 7.

This takes us to the second important function of sexual history evidence which our trawl through history reveals. By mobilising a complainant's sexual past to subvert an assertion of non-consent, rape law – as operationalised – continued to set the terms of men's sexual access to women largely within the normative parameters of the prevailing gendered social order. Virginity and wifely chastity were to be respected; women who stepped outside these socially circumscribed boundaries of female sexual agency were, to all intents and purposes, outside the protection of the law. This is not to say that sexual history evidence worked perfectly or uniformly to maintain this socio-sexual order. As Clark (1987), among others, points out, other factors came into play to shape the outcomes of rape trials, including the social status of the complainant and defendant, the complainant's age and, to an undetermined extent, other factors such as race and ethnicity.[80] Nevertheless, the way in which sexual history evidence functioned to align the application of rape law with social norms prescribing the scope and limits of male sexual entitlement is not difficult to discern.

In the two chapters which follow, we will look more closely at how sexual history evidence features in the contemporary rape trial. In Chapter 4, we assess the state and effectiveness of current law governing the use of sexual history evidence, both in England and Wales and in other common law countries. In Chapter 5, we evaluate the empirical evidence marshalled both for and against further legal restriction of sexual history evidence and consider some of the challenges scholars confront when researching this field. These two chapters prepare the groundwork for the more theoretical/ philosophical analyses in Chapters 6 and 7.

---

[80] Clark finds some evidence of the invocation of anti-Irish stereotypes in her study but otherwise finds reference to race absent from the historical record (1987: 143) (though this is not to say it did not feature). By contrast, Jennifer Wriggins' (1983) pioneering study of the history of rape law in the United States showed that the defendant's and complainant's race were often pivotal to trial outcomes.

4

Legal Regulation: Limits and Potentialities

Introduction: what constitutes sexual history evidence?

Sexual history evidence is a slippery concept which is difficult to define outside the contexts in which it is invoked.[1] We saw in Chapter 3 that it took legal shape and form within broader consideration of the relevance of evidence relating to a rape complainant's character or reputation: an accused might seek to introduce evidence of a complainant's propensity to lie or thieve, for example, to challenge the reliability and credibility of her testimony. In practice, the easiest way to call a woman's character into question was to expose her lack of chastity. In some contexts, too, prior sexual history with the accused functioned formally to restrict the scope of criminal proscription, as, for example, where a husband had non-consensual sex with his wife or, in the opinion of at least some medieval and early modern legal commentators, a man had non-consensual sex with his mistress or concubine.

Modern legislative frameworks are surprisingly shy about defining sexual history evidence with any precision. In England and Wales, section 41 of the YJCEA 1999 applies to evidence concerning 'any sexual behaviour of the complainant'. Section 42(1)(c) clarifies that 'sexual behaviour' encompasses 'any sexual behaviour or other sexual experience, whether or not involving the accused or another person, but excluding anything alleged to have taken place as part of the event which is the subject matter of the charge against the accused'. This latter clause introduces an important temporal element, which explains why this evidence is often referred to as 'history'. Technically

---

[1] An abridged version of this chapter was previously published as Conaghan, J. and Russell, Y. (2023) 'Sexual history evidence in review: Stasis in constant change', in Gleeson, K. and Russell, Y. (eds) *New Directions in Sexual Violence Scholarship: Law, Power and Change*, London: Routledge, 127–48. Reproduced by permission of the Taylor & Francis Group.

though, and depending on the scope of what is legally permitted, sexual history evidence may also encompass sexual behaviour taking place *after* the alleged offence.[2]

The 1999 Act does not define what is 'sexual'. However, section 78 of the SOA 2003 – which governs the definition, scope and content of a variety of sexual offences – states that

> penetration, touching or any other activity is sexual if a reasonable person would consider that –
> (a) whatever its circumstances or any person's purpose in relation to it, it is because of its nature sexual, or
> (b) because of its nature it may be sexual and because of its circumstances or the purpose of any person in relation to it (or both) it is sexual.

In other words, an activity may be sexual 'because of its nature' or because the circumstances or purposes of the activity make it sexual in nature. One might expect such a convoluted definition to invite judicial clarification of what falls within and without its scope. Again, surprisingly little in the way of clarity has been forthcoming, the Court of Appeal in *R v Mukadi*,[3] for example, merely observing that what constitutes sexual behaviour is 'a matter of impression and common sense'.[4]

In the Canadian Criminal Code, sexual history evidence covers 'evidence that a complainant has engaged in sexual activity whether with the accused or any other person' (section 276). As in England and Wales, this definition excludes sexual activity forming 'part of the subject matter of the charge', and while there is no definition of 'sexual', section 276(4) clarifies that sexual activity 'includes any communication made for a sexual purpose or whose content is of a sexual nature'. This clause is helpful in clarifying that, for example, digital messaging with a sexual purpose or content falls within the scope of legal protection; not all jurisdictions offer such clarity on this point.

The Scottish approach to sexual history evidence diverges from some other jurisdictions in schematically aligning sexual history evidence with evidence of a complainant's 'bad character'. Section 274(1)(a) of the Criminal Procedure (Scotland) Act 1995 prohibits evidence to show that the complainant 'is not of good character (whether in relation to sexual

---

2   In *R v Evans* (2016) EWCA Crim 452, part of the evidence allowed by the court related to the complainant's sexual behaviour two weeks after the disputed event.
3   [2003] EWCA Crim 3765.
4   *Mukadi*, [14].

matters or otherwise)', while section 274(1)(b) proscribes evidence that the complainant (in Scots law terms, 'the complainer') has at any time 'engaged in sexual behaviour not forming part of the subject matter of the charge'.

In sum then, and as this swift sampling of legislative provisions reflects, 'sexual history' appears to encompass a complainant's sexual activity, behaviour, experience, and in some contexts, depending on the legislative wording, reputation, whether with the accused or a third party, outside the immediate time frame of the event forming the subject matter of the charge. 'Sexual history *evidence*' refers to evidence of such activity, behaviour, experience and so on posited as relevant to the guilt or innocence of the accused.

'Sexual' most obviously includes sexual intercourse (sometimes euphemistically referred to as 'sexual relations'). In *R v A (No 2)*,[5] for example, evidence that the accused had been in a sexual relationship with the complainant for three weeks prior to the alleged rape fell within the scope of section 41 regulation. Similarly, evidence in *Evans*[6] that the complainant had sexual intercourse with persons other than the defendant plainly triggered section 41 scrutiny. In both cases, applications to introduce the evidence were eventually approved. By contrast, in *R v Harris*,[7] an application to adduce evidence gleaned from the complainant's private medical and psychiatric records, including an admission that some years previously she had engaged in risk-taking sexual activity (specifically sexual intercourse with a taxi driver), was denied on the grounds that it did not meet the admissibility requirements of the 1999 Act. In *R v CB and Sultan Mohammed*,[8] the Court of Appeal upheld a decision to reject an application to introduce evidence from a complainant's mobile phone of sexual activity with another person two years prior to the alleged rape. The accused in this case sought to argue that text messages sent by the complainant showed a past propensity to have casual sex while intoxicated which she failed to recall the following morning. In this case, as in *Harris*, the defence sought to rely on the same gateway (section 41(3)(c) YJCEA), although, unlike *Evans*, unsuccessfully.

What one gleans from these cases is an effort by the courts in England and Wales to distinguish between applications which rely on the mere fact of a complainant's previous sexual activity from applications which can successfully map that prior activity on to the gateway requirements laid out in the 1999 Act.[9] In this sense, the scope of admissible sexual history evidence is very much dependent on the legal regime regulating its use.

[5]   [2001] UKHL 25.
[6]   [2016] EWCA Crim 452.
[7]   [2009] EWCA Crim 434.
[8]   [2020] EWCA Crim 790.
[9]   The details and operation of s 41 YJCEA 1999 are considered later in this chapter.

Across regulatory frameworks, the law on sexual history evidence has yielded a range of distinctions imbued with legal consequence, for example between sexual activity with the defendant versus third parties, or between general accounts and specific instances of a complainant's sexual activity.[10] In other words, what passes for sexual history evidence in a particular jurisdiction will be significantly shaped by the history and development of the relevant law, crafting the doctrinal tools and concepts which support the legislative framework. In this context, the fact that the framework which emerged in England has come to underpin so many other common law jurisdictions is not insignificant.

Sexual history evidence is usually introduced to support or counter a factual assertion relevant to the guilt or innocence of the accused. Taking the form of testimony – whether of the defendant, complainant or trial witness – it is subject to the general rules governing the admissibility of evidence in a criminal trial (including those relating to cross-examination)[11] as well as any specific rules governing the introduction of this type of evidence. In addition, the precise details of the regulatory regime operate within the broader context of trial practice, comprising the conventions, techniques and values that have gained acceptance in a particular legal practitioner community. Over time and place too, accepted practices may change, with contestation arising as to what kind of evidentiary approach is most likely to ensure the fairness of the trial process. Lately, for example, evidence law scholars have begun to question the traditional approach to cross-examination that flourished in an adversarial context – what is sometimes described as the 'advocacy' model. Instead, scholars are propounding the benefits of a 'best evidence' model whereby cross-examination is approached as an investigative opportunity to test the veracity and completeness of witness testimony (Henderson, 2016; Williams, 2020). 'Fairness' too may be variously conceived and weighted, whether viewed solely (or primarily) in terms of fairness to the defendant or as encompassing and/or according some weight to the justice interests of the complainant (Gotell, 2006). It follows that in understanding the scope, nature and operation of sexual history evidence in rape trials, we must be attentive not just to the prevailing regulatory regime but also to the wider institutional and cultural features of a jurisdiction.

Scanning the juridic and policy landscape

The analysis which follows takes a closer look at the legislative and policy landscapes of a range of countries with jurisdictions comparable to England

---

[10] See, for example, YJCEA 1999, s 41(6).

[11] See further, Chapter 6.

and Wales. These include Ireland (both Northern Ireland and the Republic of Ireland), Scotland, New Zealand, Canada, Australia and the United States. All, with the partial exception of Scotland, are common law based, and all, albeit in different ways and to varying extents, bear the imprimatur of Hale's legacy. The colonial context too has played a role in shaping the way in which English common law principles have been received and applied in each jurisdiction. The many complexities and contradictions of the colonial legal inheritance are beyond the scope of this book, and for this reason we do not offer a detailed history of the emergence and development of legal regulation in each jurisdictional context. Rather our aim is to sketch out the operating regime governing the uses of sexual history evidence in each of the countries we consider in order to present a 'snap-shot' of the fast-moving currents which characterise the present moment, highlighting new directions and initiatives, and distilling key themes and challenges. As we shall see, virtually every country is in the process of reviewing their existing regulatory framework and/or trialling new approaches. Moreover, while the doctrinal and procedural structures may differ, reflecting the unique political, social and historical realities in which they were created, many of the problems, conceptual and practical, associated with the use of sexual history evidence recur regardless of regulatory configuration. In the final section of the chapter, we draw together some common themes to reflect critically on the cycle of policy making and law reform driving so much legislative and policy movement in this area. We conclude with a call to resist the artificially imposed strictures of the policy/reform cycle and return to the important and difficult work of reckoning with the underlying logic that continues to support the use and relevance of sexual history evidence in the rape trial. This task becomes the focus of Chapter 6.

England, Wales and Northern Ireland

In England and Wales, section 41 YJCEA 1999 governs the introduction of evidence 'about any sexual behaviour of the complainant'. These provisions are exactly mirrored in the law of Northern Ireland in articles 28 and 29 of the Criminal Evidence (Northern Ireland) Order 1999.[12]

Section 41 establishes a general rule of exclusion of sexual history evidence, whether relating to sexual behaviour with the defendant or with third parties, subject to four exceptions. Moreover, even where the requirements for these exceptions (or 'gateways') are met, leave to admit sexual history evidence

---

[12] For expediency, we refer in the subsequent discussion only to the precise sections of the English and Welsh provisions.

cannot be given unless the court is satisfied that 'a refusal … might have the result of rendering unsafe a conclusion of the jury or … the court on any relevant issue in the case' (section 41(2)(b)). At the time of enactment, the scheme created by section 41 was regarded by many to be strict, if not 'draconian' (Birch, 2002: 352). In fact, as Temkin pointed out soon after the 1999 Act became law, the new regime is far less restrictive than many made out and considerably more generous to defence interests than comparable jurisdictions (2003: 223–5).

Turning to the exceptions to the general rule of prohibition, the first is found in section 41(3)(a) and permits evidence of sexual behaviour that relates to a relevant issue in the case which is 'not an issue of consent'. Under section 42(1)(a), 'relevant issue in the case' means 'any issue falling to be proved by the prosecution or defence in the trial of the accused'. Therefore, section 41(3)(a) provides wide scope to admit sexual history evidence not relating to consent, but which otherwise satisfies the test of relevance. This might include evidence showing a complainant had a motive to lie[13] or supporting a defendant's claim of belief in the complainant's consent.[14] The second exception, section 41(3)(b), applies where the matter for which the evidence is sought *is* one of consent. In that circumstance, sexual history evidence may be adduced if it occurred *at or about the same time* as the sexual activity which is the subject matter of the charge. The vagueness of the temporal requirement in section 41(3)(b) invites interpretation. In *R v A (No 2)*,[15] which involved a legal challenge to section 41 on grounds of its alleged incompatibility with the defendant's right to a fair trial under Article 6 of the European Convention of Human Rights (ECHR), their Lordships agreed that sexual behaviour taking place one week prior to the disputed event fell outside the scope of 'at or the same time' but otherwise diverged as to the precise scope of contemporaneity required.[16]

The third exception in section 41(3)(c), what is sometimes called the 'similar fact' gateway, applies, as with the second exception, where the matter for which the evidence is sought is one of consent, but 'the sexual

---

[13] Although see YJCEA 1999, s 41(4), stating that

> no evidence or question shall be regarded as relating to a relevant issue in the case if it appears to the court to be reasonable to assume that the purpose (or main purpose) for which it would be adduced or asked is to establish or elicit material for impugning the credibility of the complainant as a witness.

[14] S 42(1)(b) explicitly clarifies that the defendant's belief in consent is not 'an issue of consent' for purposes of s 41.
[15] [2001] UKHL 25.
[16] L Steyn observed, not without a hint of disapproval, that s 41 imposed 'an extraordinarily narrow temporal restriction' [40]. However, L Slynn speculated that 'at or about the same

behaviour of the complainant to which the evidence or question relates is alleged to have been, in any respect, so similar' either to: any sexual behaviour of the complainant which took place *as part of the event* which is the subject matter of the charge; or, any other sexual behaviour of the complainant that took place *at or about the same time* as that event. Note again the reliance on vaguely worded temporal norms to set the limits of protection, including the notion of 'sexual behaviour … which took place as part of the event'. There is also the additional question of the degree of similarity required to trigger this gateway. According to section 41(3)(c), the previous behaviour of the complainant must be 'so similar … that the similarity cannot reasonably be explained as a coincidence'. In *Evans*, the Court of Appeal considered the operation of section 41(3)(c) in some detail, noting that its requirements were strict, and compelled the defendant to 'overcome [a] high hurdle of relevance and similarity'.[17] At the same time, the Court cited with approval the comments of Lord Clyde in *R v A (No 2)*[18] on the scope and meaning of section 41(3)(c), namely that '[i]t is only a similarity that is required, not an identity'.[19] Lord Clyde went on to observe that there was no need for the defendant to show that the similar conduct invoked was 'rare or bizarre … so long as the particular conduct goes beyond the realm of what could reasonably be explained as a coincidence, it should suffice'.[20] Indeed, his Lordship urged a flexible approach to interpretation,[21] particularly in relation to section 41(3)(c), to enable it to be read in a manner compatible with the defendant's fair trial rights. This 'interpretative gloss' allowed the House of Lords in *R v A (No 2)* to avoid making a Declaration of Incompatibility under the provisions of the Human Rights Act 1998 but adds to the vagueness and confusion surrounding the legislation's practical application.

Finally, section 41(5) contains an exception to the rule of exclusion which permits the defence to challenge any prosecution evidence about the complainant's sexual behaviour. Under sections 41(5) and (6) of the YJCEA, questioning by the defence must 'go no further than is necessary to enable

---

time' could extend to 'a few hours, perhaps a few days when a couple were continuously together' [12]. Lord Hope relied on the Explanatory Note accompanying the legislation which suggested no more than 24 hours before or after the offence [82]. Finally, L Clyde noted 'a degree of elasticity in the provision' and concluded that its precise application should be left to the judge [132].

[17] *Evans*, [48].

[18] [2001] UKHL 25.

[19] *R v A (No 2)*, [135].

[20] *R v A (No 2)*, [135].

[21] 'In my view section 3 requires the court to subordinate the niceties of the language of section 41(3)(c), and in particular the touchstone of coincidence, to broader considerations of relevance judged by logical and common sense criteria of time and circumstances' [45].

the evidence adduced by the prosecution to be rebutted or explained'. It must also 'relate to a specific instance or instances of alleged sexual behaviour on the part of the complainant'.

In 2019, the British Home Secretary, Lord Chancellor and Attorney General, spurred on by the freefall in prosecution and conviction rates for sexual offences across England and Wales, made a public commitment to 'understand[ing] why we are letting down rape victims and ... to build the confidence of victims to come forward and report these horrendous crimes' (Home Office, 2021: Ministers' Foreword). The publication of the 'End-to-end rape review report on findings and actions' in June 2021 was part of this process, announcing a long list of commitments to change at every point of the criminal justice response to sexual violence (Home Office, 2021). Linked to the 'End-to-end review', the Law Commission of England and Wales was tasked with 'examin[ing] law, guidance and practice relating to the use of evidence in prosecutions of serious sexual offences and consider the need for reform' (Home Office, 2021: para 114). This project was launched at the end of 2021 and is scheduled to produce a final report in 2024.[22] At the time of writing, the project is still at an early stage but includes a commitment to reviewing the provisions restricting the use of sexual history evidence, alongside review of the rules governing the use of a complainant's medical and counselling records at trial, special measures for vulnerable witnesses, and strategies to counter the effect of rape myths in courtroom proceedings.[23]

Meanwhile, Northern Irish law and procedure on sexual offences has also been subject to a substantial review in the aftermath of the 'Rugby Rape Trial' in 2018.[24] The 'Gillen Report into the law and procedures in serious sexual offences in Northern Ireland' was published in 2019, generating a range of recommendations including limiting public access to rape trials (Recommendation 2), introducing pre-recorded cross-examination (Recommendation 3), 'a measure' of publicly funded legal representation for rape victims (Recommendation 4), and the promotion of a 'more robust judicial attitude and case management approach to prevent improper cross-examination about previous sexual history' (Recommendation 7).

During the review, Gillen and his team considered the myriad problems with the operation and implementation of the provisions governing sexual

---

[22] 'Law Commission to review the trial process for sexual offences'. Available from: https://www.lawcom.gov.uk/law-commission-to-review-the-trial-process-for-sexual-offences/ [Accessed 24 August 2022].

[23] A pilot of taking pre-recorded evidence from rape victims began in Wales on 11 July 2022: https://www.gov.uk/government/news/pre-recorded-evidence-for-rape-victims-rolled-out-across-wales [Accessed 24 August 2022].

[24] See generally, Killean et al (2021).

history evidence in articles 28–30 of the Criminal Evidence (Northern Ireland) Order 1999 (Gillen, 2019: chapter 8). They noted that 'across the globe, research indicates that the problem is not so much the statutory regime adopted but the failure of the judiciary to apply the provisions correctly' (Gillen, 2019: para 8.22). Having considered the relevant law and secondary literature in England, Wales and Northern Ireland, Gillen concluded that while tightening legal tests of relevance and giving greater weight to a complainant's privacy rights were important, the law in practice was where change was most required. The Review emphasised the need to prioritise the enforcement of procedural rules along with rigorous and continual training of judges and counsel. Gillen also recommended the introduction of independent legal representation (ILR),[25] inter alia, to support complainants when applications to introduce sexual history evidence were heard (Gillen, 2019: chapter 8).

The use of ILR in sexual offence trials in adversarial systems is often held up as a way in which many of the ills associated with the prosecution of sexual offences may be cured (Smith and Daly, 2020). As we shall see, limited access to ILR is available to complainants in the Republic of Ireland, and there are examples of similar arrangements in other common law countries including Canada, Australia and the United States (Killean, 2021). At the same time, as Killean, among others, points out, the formal logic of the adversarial trial as a two-sided contest between the state and the accused presents structural and ideological obstacles to the introduction of ILR for rape complainants whose standing in criminal trials is merely that of a witness. In inquisitorial systems, by contrast, the idea that victims have an independent interest, or right to participate, in criminal proceedings, is more easily accommodated (Killean, 2021: 179–81).

In the aftermath of Gillen, Mary Iliadis and colleagues have revisited the arguments for using ILRs in sexual offence trials, arguing that the Gillen proposals do not go far enough (Iliadis et al, 2021: 255–7). Challenging the prevailing notion that providing ILR to complainants poses an inherent threat to defendants' right to a fair trial (a view which appears to unite the Criminal Bar), the authors propose a 'Gillen-plus framework' which would extend ILR beyond the parameters recommended by Gillen but without according formal party status to complainants (Iliadis et al, 2021: 267). Central to this argument is an insistence that complainants'

---

[25] Gillen (2019: chapter 5) accepts the case for publicly funded legal representation for complainants in serious sexual offences cases in the following circumstances: (1) to oppose cross-examination in relation to previous sexual history, (2) to oppose disclosure of a claimant's personal medical records and (3) from first report up to the commencement of (but not during) the trial, to explain the complexities of, and the legal developments occurring in, the legal process.

rights and interests do not neatly align with the prosecution stance, particularly in relation to matters of privacy and, to some extent, the risk of secondary victimisation also. These concerns arguably make the case for ILR throughout the trial process albeit 'confined to specific matters of evidence and procedure that touch on the interests and rights of complainants' (267): 'Representatives should be able to protect complainants' rights and interests by objecting to specific questions, especially in light of research evidence indicating that advocacy practice often departs from formal evidential and procedural rules, as well as from specific judicial instructions/guidance issued in the pre-trial phase' (Iliadis et al, 2021: 268). In response to the Gillen Report, the Northern Irish Department of Justice released an Implementation Plan in June 2020 (NIDJ, 2020). Although identifying (pre-trial) ILR as a 'strategic priority', the plan did not follow through with concrete proposals other than to recommend a limited pilot study.[26]

Republic of Ireland

The Irish Republic is of particular interest as an early pioneer of ILR for complainants in relation to applications by defence counsel to introduce sexual history evidence. The relevant law governing sexual history evidence in Ireland is found in section 3 of the Criminal Law (Rape) Act 1981. Prior to the 1981 Act, the complainant's sexual past was freely admissible. The defence had unlimited powers to question complainants about their past sexual experience, whether with the defendant and/or third parties[27] (Leahy and Fitzgerald O'Reilly, 2018: 137–8). Under section 3(1), evidence about the 'sexual experience' of the rape[28] complainant with any person (other than the encounter to which the charge relates) is not to be admitted except with leave of the trial judge. Notice of an intention to make an application must be given to the prosecution by or on behalf of the accused at the earliest available opportunity, namely 'before, or as soon as practicable after,

---

[26] In the meantime, Victim Support in Northern Ireland have launched an independent legal advice system for victims of sexual offences providing advice and support up to the start of the trial: https://www.victimsupportni.com/help-for-victims/solas/ [Accessed 23 March 2023].

[27] The 1981 statute, as originally enacted, was modelled on the provisions in s 2 of the English SO(A)A 1976 and, as with that Act, only covered sexual experience with persons other than the accused. The scope of protection was later expanded in the Criminal Law (Rape) Amendment Act 1990 to cover sexual experience with the defendant.

[28] S 3 applies to a range of sexual offences including rape, aggravated sexual assault, sexual assault and associated offences such as attempts to commit these offences. See generally Leahy and Fitzgerald O'Reilly (2018: 139).

the commencement of the trial'.[29] The courts have indicated a willingness to consider late applications, that is, after the commencement of the trial, where it is in the interests of justice to do so.[30]

Section 3(2)(a) prescribes that the judge cannot give leave unless the defence makes an application to the judge in the absence of the jury. Moreover, leave shall only be given if the court is satisfied that the exclusion of the evidence would be unfair to the defendant (section 3(2)(b)). The test of unfairness is a typical example of statutory linguistic contortion: leave shall be given

> if the judge is satisfied, on the assumption that if the evidence or question was not allowed the jury might reasonably be satisfied beyond reasonable doubt that the accused person is guilty, the effect of allowing the evidence or question might reasonably be that they would not be so satisfied. (Section 3(2)(b))

Case law suggests that the threshold applied in section 3(2)(b) is a 'high one, though … not an impossible or unattainable one'.[31]

The granting of leave does not give defence lawyers *carte blanche* to ask any questions they like about the victim's sexual experience. Section 3(3) empowers the judge to disallow a question if it is not thought to be in accordance with the leave given. In *People (DPP) v GK*, the Court was clear that section 3 should be interpreted restrictively and that, in general, sexual history evidence should be more likely excluded than admitted.[32] The Court also stated that where questioning is allowed, it must be confined to what is strictly necessary and should never be used as a form of character assassination.[33]

According to section 4A of the Criminal Law (Rape) Act 1981 (amended in 2001), victims in certain sexual offence trials are entitled to ILR in respect

---

[29]   CL(R)A 1981 (IRE) s 4A2.
[30]   *People (DPP) v Walsh*, extempore, Court of Criminal Appeal, 18 July 2008.
[31]   *People (DPP) v EH* [2019] IECA 30, [28].
[32]   [2007] 2 IR 92, 103–4.
[33]   *GK*, 103–4. Independent of s 3, s 21 of the Criminal Justice (Victims of Crimes) Act 2017 (IRE) provides further protection for crime victims questioned in criminal proceedings. S 21 provides that where the court is satisfied (a) there is a need to protect the victim from secondary/repeat victimisation and (b) it would not be contrary to the interests of justice to do so, the court may give directions as to the questions asked in cross-examination where it relates specifically to the private life of the victim. These provisions are notable in applying to all criminal proceedings (not just sexual offences) and in enshrining the concept of secondary victimisation in legislation. The onus lies with the judge to give the protection effect and much depends on their willingness to intervene on the victim's behalf.

of any application made to question them about past sexual experience. Section 28(5A) of the Civil Legal Aid Act 1995 (amended in 2001) requires legal aid to be provided to complainants to fund this legal representation free of charge.

The Irish legislation differs from the law in England, Wales and Northern Ireland in adopting a discretion-based approach rather than prescribing formal gateways through which the evidence in question must be judged to pass. Subject to the test of unfairness in section 3(3), the discretion is unrestricted, and several feminist commentators have criticised its breadth, arguing that it has led to an alarmingly high rate of admission of sexual history evidence in sexual offence trials (Rape Crisis Network of Ireland, 2009; Leahy, 2014). As Leahy and Fitzgerald O'Reilly point out, the only clear requirements are that the application for leave must take place in the absence of a jury and that the complainant is entitled to be present and have ILR for purposes of the application (2018: 145).[34]

While judicial guidance suggests that section 3 should be restrictively applied,[35] research suggests that, in practice, a broad approach to the admission of evidence is the more frequent interpretation (Rape Crisis Network of Ireland, 2009: 8; Leahy and Fitzgerald O'Reilly, 2018: 146–7). Further, the failure to define 'sexual experience' for purpose of the Act ensures that the boundaries of what falls within the scope of statutory protection remain unclear. Specifically, the statute provides no guidance as to the admissibility of 'secondary' evidence of sexual experience, for example evidence that a complainant has undergone an abortion or taken oral contraceptives in the past (Leahy and Fitzgerald O'Reilly, 2018: 144). In her recent report, *Realities of rape trials in Ireland*, Leahy (2021: 28–9) recommends that the definition of 'sexual experience' be statutorily clarified.

In 2020, prompted by widespread public concern about the treatment of victims of sexual offending, the Irish Minister for Justice and Equality constituted a working group tasked with 'examin[ing] certain key aspects of the criminal justice process in so far as it relates to vulnerable witnesses, and to identify ways in which the treatment of such witnesses might be improved' (O'Malley, 2020: 8). The group considered the law governing the introduction of sexual history evidence, concluding that the statutory scheme in section 3 struck 'a fair balance between protecting the rights of

---

[34] A further limitation (which applies to England and Wales also) is that the provisions apply only to evidence sought to be introduced by the defence. As Leahy and Fitzgerald O'Reilly (2018: 143–4) argue, the complainant can equally be distressed by the (often inadvertent) references to her sexual experience by prosecuting counsel, at the same time inviting the introduction of rebuttal by the defence (where the prosecution claims that the complainant is a virgin, for example).

[35] *GK*.

accused persons and those of victims in sexual offence trials' (O'Malley, 2020: 66). For this reason, they did not recommend any legislative changes to the core provisions. They did make an independent recommendation for the introduction of preliminary hearings to reduce delays and allow matters such as section 3 applications to be considered at a much earlier stage (O'Malley, 2020: chapter 5).

In respect of ILR specifically, the working group recommended the extension of ILR to encompass a broader range of sexual offences, and the enhancement of the ILR's role in monitoring the cross-examination of sexual offence complainants. They proposed that ILRs should be allowed to object to a question, or at least submit to the trial judge that a particular question did not come within the terms of the leave granted (O'Malley, 2020: 69). As things stand, the complainant is only entitled to legal representation in the section 3 hearing and not in relation to other aspects of the trial process such as cross-examination, where, as has been noted, much depends on the willingness of the judge to enforce the terms of leave granted.

Feminists remain unconvinced that ILR has fulfilled its undertaking to improve rape victims' experience of the legal process. Iliadis (2020) highlights several issues including the submission of late applications for admission of sexual history evidence and the unduly circumscribed role of the ILR. Other studies, in particular Leahy (2021), also highlight a tendency to appoint inexperienced junior counsel as ILRs, a problem exacerbated by late notice to the Legal Aid Board of applications (prompting the need to appoint a representative). As Iliadis concludes, ILR is only as effective as the regulatory system in which it operates allows, meaning that in practice, victims often remain 'equally as vulnerable as they would be if legislation did not exist' (Iliadis, 2020: 428). Indeed, she goes on to speculate that 'the implementation of ILR has had a counter effect of retaining sexual history evidence in trials' (429).

Scotland

Sections 274 and 275 of the Criminal Procedure (Scotland) Act 1995 (CP(S)A) govern the law of sexual history evidence in Scotland, which was radically amended by the Sexual Offences (Procedure and Evidence) (Scotland) Act 2002.[36] The Scottish approach differs from that of England, Wales and Northern Ireland in combining regulation of evidence of a complainant's bad character and sexual history into the same regulatory

---

[36] S 274 CP(S)A 1995 specifies the kind of evidence prohibited, including sexual history evidence; S 275 prescribes the circumstances in which s 274 prohibitions can be circumvented, essentially establishing a staged approach requiring that (i) the evidence is specific and relevant, and (ii) its probative value significantly outweighs any risk of prejudice to the administration of justice. See Campbell and Cowan (2017).

framework.[37] Historically, this makes some sense because the emergence of evidentiary rules around the use of a complainant's sexual history was partly driven by judicial concerns to protect complainants from unwarranted attacks on their character (and therefore credibility as witnesses). However, concerns about the use of bad character evidence – whether relating to witnesses or the accused – extend well beyond the sphere of sexual offences, and, in England and Wales, the interest in ensuring a defendant's right to a fair trial has led to a predominant doctrinal preoccupation with regulating evidence of a *defendant's* bad character, first through common law, and, since 2003, through a distinct statutory framework.[38] Although the English legislation places some restrictions on the introduction of evidence of non-defendants' bad character,[39] where evidence of a complainant's sexual history is at issue, section 41 of the YJCEA 1999 superimposes additional restrictions on the legal framework.[40]

Feminist analyses of the Scottish provisions draw attention to a dissonance between law in the books and law in action (Campbell and Cowan, 2017; Cowan, 2020). Early analysis of the current Scots law provisions found that paradoxically, the 2002 amendments had led to an increase in applications for sexual history evidence to be admitted and a subsequent increase in the admission of this kind of evidence (Burman et al, 2007: 7; Burman, 2009: 388). The requirement for detailed written applications to be submitted to the Court in section 275 appear to have stoked this phenomenon because the fulsome 'scatter-gun approach' often employed by defence counsel has increased the likelihood that at least some of the questioning contemplated will be allowed (Burman, 2009: 389). Burman's research is borne out by a more recent small-scale case study of section 275 applications in Scotland made between January and April 2016

---

[37] For proposals to combine sexual history evidence and evidence of bad character in sexual offences cases in the same regulatory framework in England and Wales, see Brewis and Jackson (2020).

[38] Criminal Justice Act 2003 (CJA), ss 98–113.

[39] See especially CJA s 100 which states that

> evidence of the bad character of a person other than the accused is admissible if ...
> a) It is important explanatory evidence,
> b) It has substantial probative value in relation to a matter which –
>   (i) Is a matter in issue in the proceedings, and
>   (ii) Is of substantial importance in the context of the case ... or
> c) All parties ... agree to the evidence being admissible.

[40] In a study of the operation of YJCEA 1999, s 41 in the courts of England and Wales, Hoyano (2018) highlights concerns within the Criminal Bar about the 'troublesome overlap' between s 41 and CJA s 100. For further discussion, see Chapter 5.

showing an approval rate of up to 84 per cent (Cowan, 2020: 16). Another recurring criticism of the Scottish law relates to the balancing that courts must effectively undertake to assess the probative value of sexual history evidence. According to section 275(1)(c), the probative value of the evidence must be 'significant' and 'likely to outweigh any risk of prejudice to the proper administration of justice'. Section 275(2)(b) goes on to clarify that 'the proper administration of justice' includes 'appropriate protection of a complainer's dignity and privacy'. Thus, the rights/interests of the victim are expressly enshrined in the legislation. Nevertheless, Burman et al (2007: 393) found that the balancing of these rights in section 275 applications remained weighed heavily in favour of a defendant's right to a fair trial. Moreover, in a recent review of the use of sexual history and bad character evidence, commissioned by the Scottish Equality and Human Rights Commission, Cowan identified a growing strain of case law[41] exposing judicial failures at trial court level adequately to protect the dignity and privacy of complainers (2020: 12–14). Similarly, a review of the management of sexual offence cases by the Lord Justice Clerk's Review Group in 2021 problematised the interpretation and application of the rape-shield provisions contained in sections 274 and 275, criticising their effectiveness and implementation in practice (LJCRG, 2021: 44–6). The report argues in favour of specialised sexual offences courts where all judges, lawyers, clerks and other staff are appropriately, uniformly and specifically trained (LJCRG, 2021: 46–7).[42] The case for introducing ILR for complainers is also growing, particularly given Cowan's findings that prosecutors rarely challenged the introduction of sexual history and bad character evidence.[43] Finally, a Scottish government-funded empirical project is currently being undertaken (somewhat delayed by the COVID pandemic) which will observe rape and attempted rape trials, and scrutinise the content of section 275 applications, to investigate how the rape-shield legislation and associated procedures are understood and applied during court proceedings. 'The use of sexual history, bad character and private data evidence in Scottish sexual offences trials', conducted by Cowan, Keane and Munro, is due to report in 2023.

---

[41] See in particular *MacDonald v HMA* [2020] HCJAC 21 and Cowan's discussion thereof (2020: 13).

[42] The introduction of specialist rape courts has also been mooted in England and Wales as a way of 'clearing the backlog' of rape cases (HMICFRS/HMCPSI, 2022: Rec 4).

[43] See also Raitt (2013); Chalmers (2014); Keane and Convery (2020).

New Zealand

New Zealand's law on sexual history evidence was wholly governed by common law until the Evidence (Amendment) Act 1977 provided the original 'rape shield' to limit the admission of private sexual evidence about rape complainants in proceedings concerning sexual offences. Section 44 of the Evidence Act 2006 currently governs sexual history evidence in New Zealand. Section 44A specifies the procedure that must be followed, including form and notice requirements, but which can be dispensed with by the judge in certain broadly drafted circumstances (section 44A(6)). These sections were replaced by new provisions on 21 December 2021.[44]

In its prior iteration, section 44 provided that evidence of a complainant's 'sexual experience' with any person other than the defendant would be inadmissible, except by leave of the court. The court would not grant permission for such evidence to be admitted unless it reached a 'heightened relevance threshold' (NZLC, 2019: para 3.2) which required a judge to find that 'the evidence or question is of such direct relevance to facts in issue in the proceeding, or the issue of the appropriate sentence, that it would be contrary to the interests of justice to exclude it' (section 44(3)). No evidence relating to the complainant's reputation in sexual matters was admissible (section 44(2)). Evidence of the complainant's sexual experience with the defendant was not governed by section 44 and was admissible subject to the general rules governing the admissibility of relevant evidence.[45]

As in other jurisdictions, case law governs the boundaries of what counts as 'sexual experience' for purposes of section 44(1). In some circumstances, the courts have held that evidence of a prior allegation of sexual offending by the complainant (against someone other than the defendant) is 'sexual experience' within the meaning of section 44(1).[46] However, sexual experience will not include general sexual knowledge,[47] nor will it include sexual activity with another person just prior to the alleged offending.[48] Sexual experience is likely to include, for example, evidence as to a complainant's virginity (NZLC, 2018: para 3.25) as well as sexually explicit text messages, even where no physical contact takes place.[49] New Zealand's Supreme Court have

---

[44] Sexual Violence Legislation Act 2021 (NZ).
[45] See in particular Evidence Act 2006 (NZ) ss 7 and 8.
[46] See *R v Morrice* [2008] NZCA 261; *Best v R* [2016] NZSC 122.
[47] *R v M* (2000) 18 CRNZ 368 (CA); *M v R* [2010] NZCA 620.
[48] *Jones v R* [2018] NZCA 288. This is another example of the regulatory significance of temporality in sexual history evidence: an event which has just occurred is too immediate to constitute a separate 'experience'.
[49] *R v Singh* [2015] NZCA 435.

commented in judicial dicta that the section may need further legislative clarification, particularly as to whether what has been termed 'sexual disposition' evidence – essentially evidence that goes to the complainant's sexual preferences or propensities rather than her actual experience or behaviour – comes within the scope of section 44.[50] The concern here, which feminist commentators have repeatedly raised, is that the narrow drafting and interpretation of 'sexual experience' in section 44 has allowed a lot of evidence relating to the complainant's sexual disposition to sneak into the courtroom 'through the back door' without defence counsel having to apply for leave.

Elisabeth McDonald's extensive study of the use of sexual history evidence in sexual offences trials in New Zealand found examples of cases in which evidence of sexual orientation, use or possession of contraceptives, possession of sex toys, and prior pregnancies were admitted in evidence without reference to section 44, but in a way that clearly implicated the sexual history of a complainant (2020a: 131–60). McDonald argues that a lot of 'sexualised behaviour' should be included within the regulatory ambit of section 44 (for example, evidence of a complainant kissing, flirting or cuddling) because it can have the same prejudicial impact on a jury as evidence of sexual intercourse (McDonald, 2020a: 149). McDonald also argues that the 'heightened relevance' requirement in section 44(3) – designed to ensure an 'extra check' on sexual history evidence before it is admitted – is applied by the courts in an inconsistent manner and cannot, therefore, be relied upon as a panacea to cure all problems (2020a: 160–86). The inconsistency in judicial application of the 'heightened relevance' requirement was particularly notable in cases where the complainant was in an intimate relationship with another person at the time of the alleged rape (McDonald, 2020a: 150).

The New Zealand Law Commission reviewed the Evidence Act 2006 in 2019 and considered the operation and implementation of section 44 in some detail, making several wide-ranging recommendations for reform (NZLC, 2019). These included clarifying section 44 to ensure that sexual disposition evidence came within the scope of protection. New Zealand's Labour government responded to the Commission's report in September 2019, accepting many of its findings and undertaking to initiate reform of the law around sexual history evidence.[51] The Sexual Violence Legislation Act 2021 passed into law on 21 December 2021.

Among other root and branch legislative reforms to the laws governing sexual violence in New Zealand, the Sexual Violence Legislation Act 2021

---

[50] *B (SC12/2013) v R* [2014] 1 NZLR 261, [56].
[51] See further: 'Sexual Violence Legislation Bill'. Available from: https://www.parliam ent.nz/en/pb/bills-and-laws/bills-proposed-laws/document/BILL_93010/sexual-viole nce-legislation-bill [Accessed 24 August 2022].

extends the protection conferred by section 44 to sexual experience with the defendant and clarifies that sexual disposition evidence falls within the scope of section 44 protection.[52] Interestingly, following a Law Commission recommendation, evidence seeking to establish 'the mere fact' that the complainant and defendant had prior sexual experience (as opposed to the nature or details of that experience) is explicitly excluded from the scope of section 44. The Law Commission concluded that this was evidence of a 'background or factual nature' which did not need to meet the heightened test of relevance prescribed by section 44 (NZLC, 2019: para 3.52).

Some commentators remain concerned that the Bill does not fully address the problems to which sexual history evidence give rise, and, moreover, that the gateways for the admission of such evidence will continue to be exploited (see further: McDonald, 2020b). Such objections notwithstanding, these newly enacted provisions represent some of the most restrictive rape-shield laws in the jurisdictions we are considering.

Canada

Canada's first rape-shield statute was passed in 1976, prior to which the use of sexual history evidence was governed by common law. The current law is found in sections 276 and 277 of the Canadian Criminal Code (RSC 1985). Those provisions have undergone several rounds of reform since they became law in 1983. Under section 276, as it was passed, admission of evidence of 'sexual activity' (with anyone other than the defendant) was prohibited unless it fell within one of three exceptions: (a) rebuttal evidence, (b) evidence going to a question of identity or (c) evidence relating to consent to sexual activity on the same occasion as the trial incident. Section 277 excluded evidence of sexual reputation for the purpose of challenging or supporting the complainant's credibility.

In 1992, in the *Seaboyer*[53] case, the Canadian Supreme Court struck down section 276[54] as an unconstitutional infringement on defendants' liberty and fair trial rights because it failed to provide sufficient scope for judicial determination of the relevance and probity of the evidence sought to be submitted. In response to the decision, Bill C-49 was passed, re-enacting section 276, albeit in a 'weakened form' (Gotell, 2006: 753). The new section 276 has been expanded to regulate the admissibility of all sexual activity, including between the complainant and the accused. Moreover, section

---

[52] See sections 4(a) and 4(b) Evidence Act 2006.

[53] [1993] 1 LRC 465.

[54] S 277 (excluding evidence of the complainant's sexual reputation) was held to be compatible with the defendant's constitutional rights.

276(1), drawing on judicial guidelines articulated in *Seaboyer*, categorically excludes evidence of prior sexual history where its relevance is premised on one or both of the 'twin myths', that is, to support an inference that the complainant, by virtue of her prior sexual history, is more likely to have consented to the sexual activity which forms the subject matter of the charge, and/or is less worthy of belief. Section 276(2) creates a presumption of inadmissibility unless the evidence relates to a specific instance of sexual activity, is relevant to the issue at trial and is of 'significant probative value' not outweighed by its prejudicial effect. Section 276(3) then requires the judge to perform a complex balancing act taking account of a prescribed list of factors including the defendant's right to make a full defence (s 276(3) (a)) and the potential prejudice to the complainant's personal dignity and right of privacy (s 276(3)(f)) to determine the admissibility of sexual history evidence.[55] Applications for the admission of sexual history evidence must also be heard *in camera*.

In this revised incarnation, section 276 adopts a two-stage approach to the admission of sexual history evidence, first positing a presumption of inadmissibility, followed by the structured exercise of judicial discretion prescribed by section 276(3). It is an approach that has met with wide approval across the common law world: in her evaluation of the Irish rape-shield framework, Leahy (2014) identifies it as best practice, while Gillen (2019) commends the Canadian model in his discussion of the operation of the legislative provisions governing the admissibility of sexual history evidence in Northern Ireland. A perceived strength of the Canadian approach is that it avoids the rigidity of the gateways approach adopted in England and Wales, retaining but structuring judicial discretion to direct and limit the application of the regulatory framework. An additional strength is the range of factors judges are directed to take into account, some of which extend beyond the direct interests of either the complainant or defendant. As Gotell (2006) observes: 'These provisions were clearly intended to compel judges to engage in a complex balancing exercise that extends beyond a narrow contest between the "privacy" of the individual complainant and the legal rights claims of individual defendants ... in effect, contemplat[ing] a contextual analysis of sexual history ... applications at trial' (755). And yet, in their operationalisation, this 'ideal framework' has disappointed, with feminist critics arguing that the rape shield has effectively been 'rendered permeable through judicial interpretation' (Gotell, 2006: 746). This is partly a failure of proper implementation – Gotell points to the continued high rates of admissibility of sexual history evidence after the 1990s reforms

---

[55] There are eight factors listed in total, including s 276(3)(h) – 'any other factor that the judge ... considers relevant'.

(2006: 757). More recently, Elaine Craig (2016), in her critical study of the role of the Canadian legal profession in sexual offences trials, argues that a general lack of understanding among trial judges of how section 276 is supposed to work, accompanied by a continued reliance on rape myths in decision-making, has meant that evidence that should rightfully be excluded is often admitted in practice. However, as Gotell in particular stresses, this is not just a problem of implementation. A stance of judicial resistance to 'feminist-inspired reforms' (2006: 758) has provoked judges to carve out a series of narrow exceptions to the application of section 276, thereby avoiding the requirement to 'balance' as prescribed by section 276(3).[56]

In 2018, Bill C-51 reformed section 276 further, introducing several new clauses into the statutory schema governing sexual history evidence. For example, section 278.94(2) allows a complainant to appear and make submissions at rape-shield admissibility hearings. Section 278.94(3), for the first time, also allows any participating complainants to be represented by counsel in such proceedings. Complainants must be informed by a judge of this right as soon as possible.[57] Nevertheless, Danielle McNabb and Dennis Baker (2021) argue that, in amending the rape-shield law, the disproportionate focus of the Canadian legislature on due process over problems of judicial interpretation mean that the reforms introduced by Bill C-51 in 2018 are unlikely to improve the experience of the trial for a complainant.

Australia

Every jurisdiction in Australia has a legislative framework that limits and governs the admission of complainant sexual history evidence.[58] All jurisdictions, apart from the Northern Territory where leave can be applied for its admission, prohibit the admission of evidence relating to 'sexual reputation'. Distinguishing between sexual history and sexual experience (which are sometimes admissible) and sexual reputation (which is never admissible, save in the Northern Territory) has presented problems for the

---

[56] Craig (2016) similarly critiques judicial interpretations of section 276, calling for a more 'rigorous' approach.

[57] See further McCallum and Ng (2020).

[58] Evidence (Miscellaneous Provisions) Act 1991, ss 75–8 (ACT); Criminal Procedure Act 1986, formerly s 293, since 2022 renumbered S 294CB (NSW); Criminal Procedure Act 2009, part 8.2 division 2, ss 341–52 (VIC); Criminal Law (Sexual Offences) Act 1978, s 4 (QLD); Evidence Act 2001, s 194M (TAS); Sexual Offences (Evidence and Procedure) Act 1983, s 4 (NT); Evidence Act 1929, s 34L (SA); Evidence Act 1906, ss 36B, 36BA and 36BC (WA).

courts, given the lack of legislative guidance on the boundaries between these categories (Heath, 2005: 7).

The scope and extent of judicial discretion in respect of the admission of sexual history evidence has been a key point of contention in the legislative debate in Australia. Because of the large discretion afforded judges in most Australian states and territories, critics argue that protections against intrusive questioning are limited in practice (Easteal, 2011: 22). Evaluation of the operation of various rape-shield provisions in different Australian jurisdictions has shown that intrusive questioning continues without reference to the relevant legislation, and contrary to their stated aims (Henning and Bronitt, 1998: 76, 84; Heath, 2005: 13). Sections 51 and 53 of the Evidence (Miscellaneous Provisions) Act 1991 (the relevant law in the Australian Capital Territory), for example, allow evidence of sexual activities of the complainant deemed to 'have substantial relevance to the facts in issue' or 'be a proper matter for cross-examination about credit'. 'Substantial relevance', Patricia Easteal points out, is always open to interpretation with reference to 'social myths about "real" rape, female sexuality, male sexuality, and intimate relationships' (Easteal, 2011: 22).

In New South Wales (NSW), the law takes the form of an absolute prohibition on the admissibility of evidence of a complainant's sexual reputation and a general prohibition on the admission of evidence of sexual experience or activity evidence unless it fits within a series of evidentiary gateways.[59] These include where the evidence relates to sexual experience or activity at or about the time of the offence alleged or forming 'part of a connected set of circumstances' of the alleged offence (section 294CB(4)(a)), or the evidence 'relates to a relationship' with the accused (section 294CB(4)(b)). In the case of each of the section 294CB(4) gateways, the evidence can only be admitted if the court finds that its probative value 'outweighs any distress, humiliation or embarrassment that the complainant might suffer as a result of its admission'. The NSW law is described as a mandatory model in that the court has no residual discretion to admit evidence if it is deemed not to come within the scope of the legislative exceptions.

Unsurprisingly, given that it is probably the most restrictive legislative regime of the many and varied jurisdictions we consider here, the effectiveness of the NSW model has been the subject of some contention in the literature. In the early operation of what was then section 293, several courts issued stay proceedings asserting that an accused was simply prevented from access to a fair trial by the restrictions imposed.[60] However, the Australian High Court put a stop to this type of reasoning by endorsing

---

[59] Criminal Procedure Act 1986, s 294CB(4)(a)–(f)(NSW).
[60] See, for example, *R v Morgan* (1993) 30 NSWLR 543; *R v Bernthaler* (NSW, Court of Criminal Appeal, No 60394/93, 17 December 1993, unreported).

the holding of NSW Court of Criminal Appeal that the right to a fair trial may be curtailed by statute, to the extent that the courts have no power to stay criminal proceedings on the basis that legislation operates in those proceedings to cause injustice to the accused.[61] Nevertheless, the courts in NSW appear to have 'got around' the restrictions ostensibly imposed by interpreting the legislative exceptions in the widest possible terms.[62]

Critics of the NSW approach emphasise that the same problems in the case law arise under the 'mandatory approach' as they did under the common law before the advent of the rape shield, with 'rape myths' continuing to hold sway in decision-making by the courts in sexual offence trials. In *Burton*, for example, the original trial judge admitted evidence that the complainant, in the company of the accused, had expressed sexual interest in a stranger on the grounds that it communicated her 'sexual availability'. The judge's reasoning was robustly rejected on appeal, but the case illustrates the extent to which myths about women's sexuality still find their way into legal proceedings.[63] The NSW Law Reform Commission has recommended that the rape-shield provisions be periodically reviewed so that their efficacy in relation to other developments in the law around sexual offences can be monitored.[64]

United States

The first state to enact a rape-shield law in the United States was Michigan in 1974. Many states followed, adopting 'rape-shield' provisions during the course of the 1970s and into the 1980s, with the combined goals of encouraging the increased reporting and prosecution of sexual offences, protecting the complainant's privacy in court, and trying to prevent jury decisions based on prejudice against women perceived to be of 'poor moral character' (Cavallaro, 2019: 302).[65] Rape-shield laws in the United States generally prohibit invoking either a complainant's sexual reputation or specific sexual experience, whether to evidence a propensity to consent, or to call her credibility into question. Moreover, most regulatory regimes

---

[61] *R v PJE* (NSW, Court of Criminal Appeal, No 60216/95, 9 October 1995, unreported); *PJE v The Queen* (High Court of Australia, No S8/1996; S154/1995, 9 September 1996, unreported).

[62] See discussions in *R v Taylor* [2009] NSWCCA 180 at 36; *GP v R* [2016] NSWCCA 150 at 40; although see recently *Jackmain v R* [2020] NSW 150.

[63] *R v Burton* [2013] NSWCCA 335, discussed in Brown et al (2020: para 8.5.2.4).

[64] New South Wales Law Commission (2020) 'Consent in Sexual Relationships', https://www.lawreform.justice.nsw.gov.au/Documents/Publications/Reports/Report%20148.pdf [Accessed 5 June 2023].

[65] See the discussion in *US v Dorsey*, 16 MJ 1 (CMA 1983) [7].

only apply to sexual history evidence with third parties. Beyond these broad commonalities, states differ on their legislative approaches to exceptions to the general rule, the extent of judicial discretion and the purpose for which the evidence is being admitted.

Most states fall into a group that broadly follows the Federal Rules of Evidence (rule 412), what Anderson describes as the 'legislated exceptions' category (Anderson, 2002: 59, 81–3).[66] States with these laws prohibit the admission of sexual history evidence and then provide several exceptions to the general rule, where the evidence may be considered relevant to the charge under consideration. Not all states list the same exceptions. However, under rule 412, exceptions to the general rule include: evidence of 'specific instances' of the complainant's sexual behaviour where the evidence proves that 'someone other than the defendant was the source of semen, injury or other physical evidence' (412 (b)(1)(A)); evidence of specific instances of sexual behaviour by the alleged victim with respect to the person accused of the sexual misconduct offered by the accused to prove consent or by the prosecution (412 (b)(1)(B)); and evidence the exclusion of which would violate the constitutional rights of the defendant (412 (b)(1)(C).

The 'constitutional catch-all' in rule 412(b)(1)(C) is not a feature of all 'legislated exception' states, but as Anderson points out, because the Constitution functions as a mandatory constraint on all Acts of Congress, the inclusion of the catch-all clause in state legislation is arguably superfluous, serving to 'simply [reemphasise] judicial authority to admit evidence of a complainant's prior sexual history when a judge concludes that the Constitution demands it' (Anderson, 2002: 84; see also Galvin, 1985: 886). Anderson also criticises rule 412(b)(1)(B) on the grounds that it 'cracks the [rape] shield because men with whom the complainant has been previously intimate commit 26% of all rapes' (2002: 56). States that follow the Federal Rules of Evidence will also have procedural notice requirements and specify that hearings regarding the admission of sexual history evidence must be held *in camera*.

---

[66] States that fall into this category include: ARIZ. REV. STAT. § 13–1421 (2021); COLO. REV. STAT. § 18-3-407 (2021); MD. CODE ANN. CRIM. LAW § 3-319(c) (2021); MASS GEN. LAWS ch. 233, § 21B (2021); MICH. COMP. LAWS ANN.§ 750.520j (2021); MINN. STAT. § 609.347 (2021); N.J. STAT. § 2C:14-7 (2021); N.Y. CRIM. PROC. LAW § 60.42 (2021); TEX. R. EVID. 412 (2021); WIS. STAT. § 972.11 (2021–22). Anderson's taxonomy of rape-shield legislation broadly follows that of Galvin (1985), who developed her categories from particular state models ('Michigan', 'Texas', 'Federal' and 'California'). For exposition purposes here, we have effectively merged the Michigan and Federal models.

The second group of states follow what Anderson labels the 'discretionary approach'.[67] These states specify the procedural requirements for notice and relevant hearings while requiring the trial judge undertake a balancing exercise to determine the probative value of the evidence in relation to its prejudicial effect (Cassidy, 2021: 156). In some instances, there is no legislative guidance or constraint on the operation of judicial discretion. In Rhode Island, for example, a defendant is simply required to follow notice procedures if they want to introduce sexual history evidence. The court is then required to follow the stipulated hearing procedure before it 'rule[s] upon the admissibility of the evidence offered'.[68]

The third group follow an 'evidentiary purpose' approach (Anderson, 2002: 85) in which the admissibility of sexual history evidence turns on the purpose for which admission is sought. Typically, such laws distinguish between evidence that is being deployed to impugn credibility, and that being used to prove consent. States tend to prohibit one and allow the other in certain circumstances. In California and Delaware, for example, sexual history evidence may be admitted for the purposes of challenging a complainant's credibility, but not as proof of her consent.[69] In Nevada and Washington, the exact opposite prevails: evidence of a complainant's sexual history cannot be used to attack her credibility but may be admitted to prove her consent to sexual intercourse with the defendant 'upon a showing of relevance and a determination that relevance is not substantially outweighed by prejudice' (Anderson, 2002: 85).[70]

At this point, the reader can probably predict the likely criticisms that have been levelled at the different approaches to sexual history evidence across the varied jurisdictions of the United States. As regards the discretionary approach, with no real limits on judicial discretion or any guidelines to determine relevance, critics point out that the legislation amounts to a 'rape shield' in name only (Robayo, 1994: 302; Wallach, 1997: 494). Galvin, however, has argued that the lack of flexibility in the 'legislated exceptions' approach had created the conditions under which the discretionary approach flourished in some states (1985: 829).

As to the 'evidentiary purpose' approach, critics point to the permeability between evidence of consent and as to credibility, which in all cases requires that the court be able readily to distinguish one from another to accurately

---

[67] States following this approach include: ALASKA STAT. ANN § 12.45.045 (2020); ARK. CODE ANN. § 16-42-101 (2021); KAN. STAT. ANN. § 21-5502 (2021); N.M. STAT. ANN. § 30-9-16 (2021); WYO. STAT. ANN. § 6-2-312 (2021).

[68] R.I. R. EVID. § 412 (2021); R.I. GEN. LAWS § 11-37-13 (2021).

[69] CAL. EVID. CODE §§ 782, 1103 (2021); DEL. CODE ANN. tit. 11, §§ 3508, 3509 (2021).

[70] NEV. REV. STAT. §§ 48.069, 50.090 (2021); WASH. REV. CODE § 9A.44.020 (2021).

apply the law. Discussing the law in California, which allows the admission of sexual history evidence for purposes of challenging a complainant's credibility but not as proof of her consent, Wallach points out that the lack of guidance between what amounts to evidence proving consent and evidence impeaching credibility introduces ambiguity in the operation of the discretion given to judges, presenting a risk both to the rights of the defendant and the victim (Wallach, 1997: 514). The functional equivalency between evidence proving consent and evidence impeaching credibility (Galvin, 1985: 775) means that all that a defendant has to do is simply change the purpose for which he is using the evidence to make it admissible under the credibility section, in the case of California, despite it not being admissible had it been used to show consent (Robayo, 1994: 301–2). In a fairly comprehensive review of rape-shield legislation in the United States, Anderson (2002) has argued that, because of the holes in statutory protection, US laws are more akin to a 'sieve' than a shield. Evidence of prior sexual intimacy between the defendant and the complainant, which might help to support an argument of reasonable belief in consent, or which shows a pattern of sexual misconduct/promiscuity on the part of the complainant, are among the gaps which, Anderson argues, prevent the realisation of rape-shield legislative goals.

Recurring themes and patterns

Several themes and patterns emerge from our pan of regulatory trends and directions in a selection of jurisdictions. First, as we have noted, the law, in almost every jurisdiction we looked at, has undergone several rounds of review and revision, many in the last five years. McNabb and Baker analyse this process using a 'policy cycle' framework drawn from public policy literature to highlight a distinct cyclical pattern: a problem is identified and an agenda for investigation set; a policy approach is formulated and buy-in from relevant actors sought; decisions are made, legislation drafted and policy and guidance issued; implementation is executed; and finally, the changes are evaluated against identified criteria (2021: 26). In theory, as the policy cycle repeats, the 'best model' should reveal itself through a natural dialectic. In the case of sexual offences reform, this process of repetition seems to be occurring with increased regularity – often sparked by public outrage triggered by media reports of watershed cases. In their analysis of the policy cycle as it has manifest in Canadian sexual history evidence law and policy, McNabb and Baker identify a trend towards the 'judicialization of politics' in which policy problems with questions of social and political justice at their heart are stripped of their complexity and transformed into matters of legal doctrine that privilege due process concerns, particularly as they relate to the accused (McNabb and Baker, 2021: 25). Not that due process concerns are unimportant. The problem that McNabb and

Baker identify is that they attract undue legislative and policy attention (2021: 40) and side-line, inter alia, problems of judicial implementation. In general terms, the policy focus is becoming increasingly directed towards procedural rather than substantive interventions. We observed this shift towards procedural norms in several jurisdictions we reviewed, for example in New Zealand, in the legislatively enhanced elaboration of steps to be followed when leave to admit sexual history evidence is sought, or in the island of Ireland where ILR has been embraced as a key technique to countervail instances of evidentiary abuse. Yet problems of judicial implementation and courtroom culture continue to surface in virtually every jurisdiction we surveyed.

The review and revision of protective legislative frameworks is often the first port of call for critical attention whenever an injustice is perceived. Legislatures and policy makers interpret the need to be 'seen' to be addressing the issues raised with tangible change, measured in terms of updated directives or new procedures and enactments. Such measures often require little financial commitment, making them a palatable compromise for legislatures, particularly where services have been ravaged by decades of austerity and virtually all aspects of the criminal justice apparatus cut back.[71] At the same time, the successive introduction of new measures to improve criminal justice responses to sexual violence sits uneasily alongside continued accounts of rising rates of reporting and decreasing rates of prosecution or conviction rates for sexual offences.[72] Indeed, across many of the jurisdictions we reviewed, there is a paradoxical sense of stasis in constant change, which the frequency and strictures of the policy cycle promotes.

A striking feature of the regulatory landscape governing sexual history evidence is its increased opacity and technical complexity.[73] The need to capture and contain an approved sexual imaginary in legislative form has produced a doctrinal edifice which is constantly called upon to respond to the fluidity and contentiousness of (hetero)sexual norms. The result is a plethora of legal regimes which rely simultaneously upon sharp binaries

---

[71] In England and Wales, for example, a report in 2019 found that government cuts to service provision were directly related to the fall in rape prosecutions, having left the criminal justice system 'close to breaking point': https://www.justiceinspectorates.gov.uk/hmc psi/wp-content/uploads/sites/3/2019/12/Rape-inspection-2019-1.pdf [Accessed 20 March 2023].

[72] A Home Office inquiry was launched in 2021 after successive reports found rape prosecutions in England and Wales to be at their lowest since records began, while the number of police-recorded rapes were at their highest level (House of Commons Home Affairs Committee, 2022).

[73] See, for example the findings of Hoyano (2018) showing that a significant proportion of the English Criminal Bar viewed the provisions of section 41 YJCEA as 'overly complex' and 'restrictive'.

and loose, underdetermined norms to structure decision-making. In early legislative incarnations, for example, considerable weight was placed, for purposes of setting the limits of legal protection, on distinguishing between a complainant's sexual behaviour with third parties (usually within the scope of rape-shield regulation) and her sexual behaviour with the defendant (often without). This distinction has assumed less formal significance in more recent rounds of reforms but continues to reappear in judicial reasoning[74] as well as academic commentary (Kibble, 2001, 2008; Thomason, 2018), indicating that it remains well embedded in the legal conceptual infrastructure. Other distinctions or binaries which do similar mapping and boundary work (with varying degrees of success) include evidence pertaining to consent versus credibility (see, for example, the swings and roundabouts of US legislative models) and, of course, the sharp demarcation of defendant 'rights' and complainant 'interests', described by Lord Slynn in *R v A (No 2)* as positing an 'obvious conflict',[75] and reinscribing an analytical framework in which the evidentiary stakes are placed in a relation of inescapable competition.

Terms such as 'sexual behaviour' or 'experience' also set the limits of legislative reach. As we have seen, legal approaches vary across and even within jurisdictions, with confusion surrounding the extent to which evidence with a sexual element, but which arguably extends beyond accepted legal understandings of behaviour or experience, can bypass the constraints of statutory rape shields. Concerns have been expressed in this regard by McDonald (2020a, 2023) in relation to New Zealand law and Leahy (2021) in her critique of the Irish provisions. Similarly, temporal norms, while functioning in most legislative schema to contain the operation of exceptions to rules of evidentiary exclusion, are troublingly ill-defined, causing frequent problems of interpretation and application. Behind this statutory nebulosity is a detectable unwillingness in legal discourse to draw bright lines between the end of one sexual encounter and the beginning of another, a historical hangover perhaps of the very different temporal norms which used to govern sexual relations, particularly, though not exclusively, in marriage. Yet, this residue of the patriarchal past goes to the heart of concerns about why sexual history evidence is so often deeply problematic: once we accept, as most legislatures and legal actors now purport to do, that the purpose of sexual offences law is to protect the sexual autonomy of individuals, that is, to give meaningful effect to the right to choose when, where and

---

[74] For example in *R v A (No 2)*, Lord Steyn asserted that while evidence of a complainant's sexual experience with other men was 'almost always irrelevant' to the question of consent, 'as a matter of common sense' evidence of prior sexual behaviour with the defendant may well be relevant to consent ([40–1]).

[75] *R v A (No 2)*, [5].

with whom we have sexual relations, the temporal specificity of each and every sexual encounter assumes an importance that appeals to past sexual behaviour appear to deny.

The fact is that notwithstanding an apparent consensus about the normative foundations of modern sexual offences law, rehearsed in judicial opinions as well as in legislative and policy texts, the use of sexual history evidence in rape trials remains mired in deep contestation. Controversy was a feature of virtually every jurisdiction we explored. While academics and victims' rights advocates are largely united in the view that law and policy is failing in the area, judges and legal practitioners continue to be less convinced, considering the 'problem' of the (mis)use of sexual history evidence to be largely resolved (O'Malley, 2020), only rarely problematic (Hoyano, 2018), or subject to legislative overkill to the detriment of the interests of justice (Birch, 2002; Marsh and Dein, 2021). This disagreement over the effectiveness of the relevant law mirrors a deeper clash of worldviews as to the evidentiary significance of a complainant's sexual history in which 'common sense' assumptions about (women's) sexual behaviour increasingly struggle to command the necessary consensus to found claims of relevance. Rape-shield laws act here to trouble courtroom assumptions which have operated unchecked for centuries, exposing to critical scrutiny figurations of feminine sexuality which, while rooted in the patriarchal past, continue to reside in legal reasoning and decision-making.[76] Landmark cases such as *Seaboyer*[77] and *R v A (No 2)*[78] provide judicial opportunities for working through the clash of social and legal imaginaries to which the use of sexual history evidence gives rise. This has yielded undoubted gains, including the official rejection by most legal models of the 'twin myths'. Yet the 'impermissibility' of reasoning based on the twin myths has not met with universal approval. Mike Redmayne, for example, questions the mythical status of the belief that unchaste women are more likely to consent to sex, drawing on data from a 1994 survey of sexual attitudes to support the proposition that women who have 'multiple sexual partners' are more likely to consent to sex (2003: 76–7). Similarly, Thomason argues that the propensity argument – the assertion that people who have consented to sex before are more likely to do so again – is 'no more than an analytic truth'

---

[76] Thomason's (2018) analysis of the relevance of sexual history evidence is particularly reliant on problematic tropes of female sexuality. His contemplations conjure conspiracies by secret lovers, acts of revenge triggered by sexual rejection, and the anachronistic proposition that 'relatively young' complainants can only have obtained knowledge of sexual matters through direct sexual experience. Such figurations of femininity would not look out of place in the court of Matthew Hale.

[77] [1993] 1 LRC 465.

[78] [2001] UKHL 25.

(2018: 347–8). The effect of such arguments is to affirm the holy grail status of 'relevant' evidence, placing logic at apparent odds with legislative enactments that exclude the twin myths from the repertoire of potential defence strategies. New Zealand's approach is interesting in this context as section 44 Evidence Act 2006 prescribes a heightened test of relevance for the admission of sexual history evidence: the judge must not admit such evidence 'unless satisfied that the evidence or question is *of such direct relevance* … that it would be contrary to the interests of justice to exclude it' (section 44(2) EA 2006, our emphasis). By deploying a scalar rather than binary concept of relevance, the New Zealand legislation tightens the net around the 'logic' which supports, inter alia, the twin myths.[79]

For judges and criminal law practitioners, such regulatory intensification merely heightens the appeal of discretionary approaches to regulation and the deep legal suspicion of 'gateways' regimes. By placing matters in the 'safe' hands of the judiciary, the argument goes, complexity gives way to simplicity, and the conceptual structure of Evidence Law remains intact. A key feature of this structure is the weight traditionally given to the defendant's right to a fair trial. Indeed, in an adversarial culture, this is the predominant measure of justice. The parameters of deliberation are set within a frame in which the rights of the defendant and the interests of the complainant are conceived as 'diametrically opposed', encouraging a 'winner takes all' approach to these critical evidentiary matters rather than striving for middle ground (Ozkin, 2011). The differential weighting of these apparently conflictual concerns poses real problems for 'balancing' regulatory techniques, which are often at the forefront of discussions around how to improve the law governing sexual history evidence.

At the same time, the rise of victims' rights discourses and the development of human rights thinking has undoubtedly encouraged the articulation of rights-based groundings for rape-shield laws. In Scots and Canadian law, for example, a complainant's right/interest/entitlement to the protection of her privacy and dignity is explicitly (if ambiguously) enshrined in the legislative provisions.[80] Gotell has characterised the relationship between the rights of the complainant and the rights of the accused as a 'zero-sum' game (2006: 767). The play of rights is zero-sum because howsoever the complainant's rights or interests are characterised,[81] they too easily yield to

---

[79]   Discourses of relevance are explored in detail in Chapter 6.

[80]   Criminal Procedure (Scotland) Act 1995, Section 275(2)(b)(i); Canadian Criminal Code (RSC 1985), Section 276(3)(f). CP(S)A 1995, s 275 (2)(b)(i) refers to 'appropriate protection of the complainer's dignity and privacy', while CCC s 276 (3)(f) lists 'potential prejudice to a complainant's personal dignity and right of privacy' as a factor a judge must consider when assessing the probative value of the evidence at issue.

[81]   Gotell's primary focus of analysis is on the complainant's 'fragile and illusive' right to privacy (2006: 747).

the accused's right to call any and all evidence relevant to their defence, framed in terms of fair trial rights and fundamental justice principles. While legislatures may prescribe that these concerns be balanced, in practice, they are put into competition with each other with a hierarchical approach prevailing in which defendants' rights are always seen as tangible, weightier and more urgent (Gotell, 2006: 766). While an attempt to give substance to complainant rights through limited entitlement to ILR, for example, certainly challenges the inevitability of the normative schema in operation where sexual history evidence is at issue during the trial, such initiatives appear piecemeal when set against the full force of a legal and policy framework that remains otherwise unmoved.

If we look at prosecution and conviction statistics or studies of victims' experiences of the criminal justice process (see, for example, Gillen 2019), we might well wonder whether rape-shield regulation has in any way contributed to improving the criminal justice response to sexual violence. Some feminist commentators speculate that it has not – indeed, some are concerned that it may have further entrenched the use of sexual history evidence in the trial process (see, for example, Burman, 2007, 2009; Leahy and Fitzgerald O'Reilly, 2018). This prompts a further question about how the success or otherwise of such legislative interventions should be measured, a question which is intimately connected to efforts to distil 'best practice', a common goal of comparative or jurisdictional reviews. One interesting by-product of rape-shield regimes, and the discussions they have engendered, is that a space has been opened for the articulation of counternarratives of criminal justice. We have seen in Chapter 3 how the historical conditions in which the adversarial model assumed foundational significance were such as to tilt the normative balance towards the institutional embedding of the accused's right to a fair trial (Beattie, 1991; Cairns, 1998), yielding a discourse in which defendants' rights became synonymous with criminal justice. Within this frame of reference, advancing the interests of the complainant appears to be in competition with justice itself. The development of rape-shield regimes, however, has compelled the articulation of additional justice concerns, such as the interest in ensuring that crimes are reported and citizens properly protected from harms which the state is committed to guard against. These and other concerns are expressly enshrined in section 276 of the Canadian Criminal Charter, albeit, according to Gotell (2006), unduly restricted by judicial interpretation. Similarly, in *R v A (No 2)*, Lord Slynn acknowledges that the unfair harassment of rape victims in court is 'bad for society in that women will be afraid to complain and as a result men who ought to be prosecuted will escape'.[82]

---

[82] *R v A (No 2)*, [1].

While it may be that rape-shield laws do not yet conform to conventional measures of success, whether understood in terms of prosecution and conviction rates or victims' experience of the trial process, that does not mean that there is not something interesting – and tentatively progressive – going on. Slowly and provisionally, often in the face of considerable resistance, rape-shield legislation is creating a space for the articulation of a more expansive conception of criminal 'justice', one which does not compete with the defendant's fair trial rights but locates those rights within a more capacious justice imaginary. Our jurisdictional survey has revealed incremental signs of such hopeful developments in the legislative articulation of a range of justice concerns and rights engagements. Legislative processes and initiatives are helping to forge a new language of rights centred on the harmful and exclusionary effects of the trial process on vulnerable witnesses. A range of potential rights infringements are now implicated in the misuse of sexual history evidence, including the complainant's right to have her dignity and privacy protected, her physical autonomy and security upheld and her equality fully realised.[83] Even the promotion of ILR, while delivering mixed results in terms of experience on the ground, is prompting a discourse of participation rights which problematises the traditional marginalisation of witnesses in the adversarial criminal trial.[84] Again, while the current tendency is still to view such initiatives in terms of a clash of rights which, in the interests of justice, courts and legislatures are required to 'balance', the idea of rights in inevitable conflict holds far less water once fairness is recalibrated to align with a continually evolving criminal justice imaginary.

Of marked importance in this context is the growing policy attention accorded to the notion of secondary victimisation, often referred to as a 'second rape' (Russell, 2023). This theme was present throughout the jurisdictions we reviewed, with reformatory energies increasingly attached to efforts to mitigate or cure the harms to the complainant occasioned by the trial process. We particularly noted the legislative enshrinement of the concept of 'repeat or secondary victimisation' in Irish law. Strikingly too, this provision applies beyond the context of sexual offences, serving as an example of the wider discursive impact of rape-shield legislation on criminal justice norms. At the heart of the concern to avoid repeat or secondary victimisation is the disturbing idea that the justice process is itself actively implicated in the perpetration of sexual violence (Russell, 2016). This is an extraordinarily strong indictment of the legal process, and yet the impetus to improve the experience of the trial for the complainant where sexual history

---

[83] For an excellent articulation of these concerns, see Heureux-Dubé's partial dissent in *Seaboyer*, 529.

[84] See Chapter 8 for further discussion of this point.

evidence is concerned continues to rub up against the seemingly intractable wall of evidentiary 'relevance' as the cornerstone of the accused's right to a fair trial. As we have seen, rather than confront the changing landscape of justice to which a concern with sexual history evidence has undoubtedly contributed, the trend in many jurisdictions is to channel legal anxieties into bolstering procedural rights, for example by introducing or extending victims' access to ILR or by directing courts explicitly to consider a wider range of factors in the conduct of modified balancing exercises (as, for example, in section 276(3) of the Canadian Criminal Code).

While we have highlighted the scepticism of some commentators observing this trend towards proceduralism (Illias, 2020; Illias et al, 2021; McNabb and Baker, 2021), this too is indicative of efforts to reframe the schema of norms that govern discourse around sexual history evidence. Embedding norms for victim inclusion or participation through ILR, for example, is posited as a way of pushing back against the inevitability of the secondary victimisation of the complainant during the trial and to articulate better what is at stake when a court is called to consider the admission of sexual history evidence. These initiatives can be read as attempts to intervene in and displace the assumption that the idea of a fair trial aligns perfectly and exclusively with defendant rights.

Conclusion

This chapter has conducted a 'state of the field' analysis of several similar common law jurisdictions. We have found that the laws and policy around sexual history evidence are subject to constant review and revision, and that discussion of the best way forward remains highly contested. We have highlighted some of the recurring themes which emerged from our panoramic overview, including the shared sense of stasis in change brought on by frequent calls for review and revision of a legislative framework that continues to be highly resistant to meaningful change. We also observed the persistent and deep disagreement between scholars, activists, criminal justice actors, policy makers and others about what to 'do' about or with sexual history evidence, adding to the difficulties around enacting meaningful change in the area or even how to measure that change. We noted the attempts in many jurisdictions to give substance to the notion of 'victims' rights' through ILR. These types of measures endeavour to change the normative schema governing sexual history evidence, which has historically been dominated by defendant-centred notions of a 'fair trial', invariably the principled founding for efforts to circumvent rape-shield regimes.

What is more difficult to assess in the context of mainstream debates taking place in the jurisdictions we reviewed is the extent to which efforts to date have upset the frame and/or underlying logic which supports the use of sexual history evidence. There is a constant reassertion, consciously or unconsciously, of the integrity and coherence of the common law evidentiary framework, continued appeals to 'common sense', and a legal practitioner preference for a flexible framework to manage the exclusion – and by implication, the admission – of sexual history evidence. There is little in the way of a direct reckoning with the normative structure which supports the admission of such evidence. Yet, a closer look reveals that the foundations are nevertheless under stress: the logic supporting claims of relevance is becoming increasingly strained, and criminal justice discourse is slowly moving towards the contemplation of new justice imaginaries. At the same time, the strictures and timescales of the policy cycle inhibit our ability to recognise and assess these developments, diverting attention towards strategies with more immediate political appeal. We need to hone our ability to look carefully at and question the structure and logic that supports the use of sexual history evidence in the rape trial as well as to excavate and critique the barely articulated but nevertheless operative assumptions that continue to underpin claims to relevance. Perhaps, most importantly, we need to engage directly with ideas of criminal *justice* and contemporary critiques thereof, harnessing our concerns about sexual violence to new criminal justice imaginaries emerging from the wreckage of a system whose decline appears increasingly inevitable.

These issues are taken up directly in Chapters 6 to 8. First, however, in the chapter that follows, we look at empirical studies of the use of sexual history evidence to inform our assessment of the kind of problem that sexual history evidence presents for criminal justice processes and the extent of that problem, viewed from the perspective of a range of stakeholders.

5

Tracking the Use of Sexual History Evidence in the Courtroom

Introduction

This chapter considers the degree to which the use of sexual history evidence continues to pose a problem in contemporary rape trials. To this end, we collate and analyse empirical studies, evaluating the extent to which these support claims *either* that the problems associated with the use of sexual history evidence have been resolved *or* that it continues to present justice challenges in the courtroom. As always, England and Wales, and to a lesser extent Scotland and Northern Ireland, are our primary jurisdictional focus, although we also highlight evidence that has emerged elsewhere, most notably from the jurisdictions considered in Chapter 4. As we shall see and based on the evidence available, the picture remains patchy and incomplete. Moreover, contestation abounds not just as to what can be gleaned from existing studies but also as to whether their conception and design is sufficiently robust to allow credible conclusions to be drawn. Part of the problem here is that the issue itself – the issue of what inferences can properly be drawn from evidence of a complainant's prior sexual behaviour – garners little in the way of consensus among those who express a view: one person's 'use' of sexual history evidence is another person's 'misuse', with what passes for some as 'common sense' presenting as patriarchal ideology to others. In Chapter 6, we address this contestation head on, focusing directly on the nature and validity of relevance claims underpinning the use of complainant sexual history evidence in rape trials. For the moment, we draw attention to the fact that the underlying premises justifying the use of sexual history evidence are deeply disputed to highlight a particular problem associated with empirical efforts to chart its use and misuse.

A range of approaches have nevertheless been adopted to precisely this end. Studies of the use of sexual history evidence and/or of the operation of legal regulatory frameworks designed to prevent or minimise its misuse have taken a variety of forms, including trial observations, analyses of court transcripts, audio files and other kinds of criminal justice records (for example, police files), surveys of or interviews with judges, lawyers, victims and diverse criminal justice stakeholders, jury simulation studies and analyses of case law. New forms and sites of enquiry continue to emerge: for example, Canadian scholar Elaine Craig has conducted an analysis of the marketing content on the websites of prominent criminal law firms (2018: 20–1). Some approaches speak more directly to the issue than others. Obviously, reported cases concerning the admissibility of sexual history evidence give some indication of the groundings for and parameters of its use. However, relying on case law alone is limiting, particularly if the primary focus is appellate decisions, as these cannot provide any real sense of the extent to which sexual history evidence features uncontested in rape trials, including in circumstances where its admission may be technically impermissible. That said, in jurisdictions where criminal trials are commonly reported, much can be gleaned from a systematic analysis of trial court decisions.[1]

Trial observations, audio files and transcripts can provide a better sense of how, and to what extent, sexual history evidence is a trial feature. However, much depends on the scale, design and execution of the research study, as this kind of research is time and labour intensive. Interviews with criminal justice stakeholders may also yield some valuable qualitative data but present problems of partiality in so far as the views of criminal justice actors tend to reflect the angle of vision which their role in the criminal justice system provides. This is something which can and should be mitigated by research design. The merits of jury simulation continue to be debated, although the research on rape trials using this approach is increasingly sophisticated and compelling. Finally, empirical as opposed to doctrinal analysis of cases is developing apace with the help of software applications such as NVivo, although we have not encountered this approach with regard to sexual history evidence. More common is the discursive deconstruction of judicial texts, particularly higher court judgments, drawing out the underlying values, assumptions and epistemological premises which inform judgment.[2] The decision in *R v A (No 2)*,[3] in which the House of Lords held that the provisions in YJCEA 1999, sections 41–3 should be read to be compatible with the defendant's fair trial rights is a popular focus of this kind of analysis.[4]

---

[1] See, for example, Craig's (2016) analysis of recent Canadian cases in which s 276 CCC applications have been made.

[2] Single trial transcripts may also be subject to this kind of analysis. See Chapter 7 and Russell (2016).

[3] [2001] UKHL 25.

[4] Clare McGlynn's (2010b) 'feminist judgment' of *R v A (No 2)* is a striking example of innovative approaches to case law analysis.

Cases involving high-profile defendants also attract academic attention, partly because the level of publicity poses particular problems for protecting the dignity and privacy interests of complainants,[5] but also because such cases provide researchers with an entrée into public debate (see, for example, McGlynn, 2017a, 2017b).

It follows that in weighing the evidence mobilised to support or deny the misuse of sexual history evidence, we must be equally attentive to the method and stance adopted by the researcher(s). With these provisos in mind, we begin by exploring how early studies of the use of complainant sexual history evidence prompted and shaped a policy agenda around this issue.

Early studies

Sexual history evidence emerges as a legislative and policy concern

A good starting point to modern consideration of the use of sexual history evidence is the Heilbron Report in 1975, which, as we saw in Chapter 2, was convened to advise the Home Office after the public controversy sparked by *R v Morgan*.[6] The precise task conferred upon the Advisory Group was 'to give urgent consideration to the law of rape in the light of recent public concern and to advise the Home Secretary whether early changes in the law are desirable' (Heilbron, 1976: para 1). The brief, therefore, was wide, and the resulting report considered several issues that had emerged from public consultation. Among the most prominent of these was the poor treatment of complainants during the trial process, particularly during cross-examination. As Heilbron observed:

> We start from the position that all relevant and proper cross-examination, even though it distresses, must be permitted in order to ensure a fair trial. But we have come to the conclusion that, unless there are some restrictions, questioning can take place which does not advance the cause of justice but in effect puts the woman on trial. Such procedure often tends unjustly to stigmatise the woman. This may result in the jury feeling that she is the type of person who either should not be believed, or else deserves no protection from the law, or was likely to have consented anyway. In particular, we are concerned about the extent to which, in a rape trial, the personal history and character of a rape victim can be introduced. It is very dubious whether it is today

---

[5]   See, for example, Haddad's (2005) analysis of the trial for sexual assault of US NBA superstar Kobe Bryant in 2003.

[6]   [1976] AC 182.

of very much relevance and often it serves only to cloud the real issues. (Heilbron, 1976: paras 90–1)

The Advisory Group had no empirical research upon which to draw, the evidence for their conclusion about the misuse of sexual history evidence coming primarily from the consultation submissions.[7] Surveying the relevant law, Heilbron recommended statutory restrictions on the use of sexual history evidence. These were enacted in attenuated form in the SO(A)A 1976, section 2, prescribing leave from the presiding judge before evidence of a complainant's sexual history could be admitted into trial.[8]

Studies conducted after the introduction of the SO(A)A 1976

The introduction of a legislative framework provided a new focus for researchers. Susan Edwards, in her pioneering text *Female Sexuality and the Law* (1981), was among the first legal scholars to draw attention to the continued misuse of complainant sexual history evidence after the introduction of statutory measures. Her analysis drew on a sample of recent cases, including newspaper reports, to highlight the lack of guidelines informing the exercise of judicial discretion and the resultant inconsistencies in decision-making (Edwards, 1981: 163–5). A more systematic early study of the operation of section 2 was conducted by Zsuzsanna Adler (1982, 1987). Adler observed and analysed rape trials in the Central Criminal Court in 1978–79.[9] Her sample comprised 50 trials involving 80 defendants and covering 85 per cent of rape trials heard in the Old Bailey during that period. She noted that applications to introduce evidence relating to a complainant's sexual history were made on behalf of 40 per cent of rape defendants. Of these, 75 per cent were successful in that at least some of the evidence sought to be admitted was allowed. Strikingly, Adler found that in a number of cases, defence counsel ignored the requirement to ask for leave and introduced evidence unchallenged by the judge or prosecuting

---

[7] Parliamentary papers suggest that members of the Heilbron Group may have sat in on some trials (HC Standing Committee F, cols 80–2 [31 March 1976]). A full list of written and oral submissions, running to no more than one page, is included in appendix 1 of the report. For discussion of the content of submissions, see Edwards (1981: 158–60).

[8] See further Chapter 3.

[9] Adler tells us that 'notes were taken of all the trials included in the study. Applications by defence counsel to introduce evidence of the complainant's sexual experience and the ensuing legal argument and judicial decisions were, in particular, fully recorded' (1982: 665). The need to hand-record notes in trial observations is a consequence of a legal prohibition on the use of audio recording devices (Contempt of Court Act 1981, s 9).

counsel (1982: 673). She also encountered several cases where the judge himself interrogated the complainant in detail about her past sexual history without engaging in any formal process to consider whether such evidence should be admitted (1982: 673). Overall Adler concluded that sexual history evidence featured in some way in most of the cases she observed, in relation to which more than half (59 per cent) concerned sexual behaviour with third parties (see generally 1987: 75–100). Adler also noted that the vast majority of applications were argued on the basis of their relevance to consent (Adler, 1982: 669).[10]

Adler's study was important in highlighting inconsistencies in the exercise of judicial discretion as well as the level of non-compliance with the regulatory framework. A decade later, her findings were amplified by Sue Lees' (1996) catalytic study of rape and criminal justice. *Carnal Knowledge* constituted a comprehensive critique of the criminal justice response to rape, triggering public concern about the high rate of attrition in sexual offence cases, and foretokening its importance as a key focus of contemporary criminal justice policy. The study drew on various data sources, including victim surveys, media reports and discrete studies of police practices to paint a damning picture of the traumas and indignities experienced by rape victims pursuing justice. With co-researchers, Lees monitored a selection of rape trials (38 in total) at the Old Bailey, Nottingham Crown Court and a London crown court over a four-month period in 1993. The use of sexual history evidence in the courtroom was a significant focus of Lees' subsequent analysis. She presented graphic accounts drawn from trial transcripts of the tactics used by defence counsel to discredit rape victims, including questions about the complainant's style of dress, whether she had undergone an abortion, references to her single motherhood status, and her alleged sexual preference for 'ethnic' men (1996: chapter 5).[11] Lees' approach differed from Adler's. Lees engaged in no formal 'number-crunching' to gauge the proportion of cases in which complainant sexual history evidence featured but relied instead on the shock impact of extracts from trial transcripts and related material:

---

[10] A larger study carried out in Scotland in the late 1980s produced not dissimilar findings. Brown et al (1992) monitored, inter alia, 305 High Court trials in Scotland between January 1987 and May 1990. They found that applications to introduce sexual history evidence were made in around 32 per cent of cases (a lower proportion than Adler) but that, of those, 85 per cent were successful. In most instances, the prosecution did not oppose the application, and in an additional 15 per cent of cases (n=46) sexual history evidence was introduced without an application. Overall, Brown et al concluded that sexual history was an issue in almost half of all cases (n=144, 47 per cent).

[11] Thereby providing evidence of the mobilisation of racism by defence counsel to undermine the credibility of white rape complainants who had sexual relations with Black men (1996: 138–9).

Have you ever asked a woman who has been raped whether she enjoyed it? Have you ever asked her whether she asked for it by wearing a short skirt or false eyelashes, going out late at night or inviting someone in for coffee? Have you ever asked her whether her shoes are not 'real' leather but 'cheap' implying she may be too? (Lees, 1996: 129)

By exposing the troubling techniques of defence counsel in rape cases to public scrutiny, Lees' analysis influenced public policy thinking around the protection of vulnerable and intimidated witnesses. In conjunction with Adler's (1987) study, Lees' work appeared to confirm both that the practice of putting demeaning, irrelevant and impermissible questions to vulnerable complainants was a staple ingredient of rape trials, and that the 1976 Act was not working to screen out abusive practices.[12]

Studies conducted after the introduction of YJCEA 1999

New restrictions on the use of sexual history evidence in sexual offences in England and Wales were introduced in YJCEA 1999, sections 41–3. However, any hope that the problems identified by Adler, Lees and others had been satisfactorily addressed did not appear to be borne out by a detailed study commissioned by the Home Office on the operation of the legislation carried out in the early 2000s. Among the findings, Kelly et al (2006) determined that section 41 applications occurred in just under a third of jury trials and, of these, two thirds were successful.[13] They also found

---

[12] Other influential studies include Harris and Grace (1999), a Home Office study tracking 500 rape cases heard in 1996 from report to final outcome, highlighting, inter alia, the pressing need for better support for complainants at all stages; and Temkin (2000), a study of barristers' views on prosecuting and defending rape in the 1990s, demonstrating the continued importance of sexual history evidence as a weapon in the armoury of defence barristers. Temkin's study involved ten in-depth interviews with experienced barristers, and what it lacked in terms of sample size, it more than made up for in terms of sheer shock value. Consider the following jaw-dropper:

> I feel very strongly about this. I feel very strongly that it's a great waste of public money to prosecute the ex-husband rape or the ex-boyfriend of rape unless there is extreme violence involved or it's part of a sort of campaign of harassment. I have had to prosecute an awful lot of cases where people have still been sort of seeing each other after having a relationship, where he wants it and she doesn't and it happens. Well she says it was a rape and probably, yes, it really was. But frankly does it matter? (barrister's quote reproduced in Temkin [2000: 226])

[13] A study conducted in Ireland, including an analysis of 35 transcripts of rape trials taking place between 2002 and 2005, found that applications to introduce sexual history evidence

that procedures for introducing sexual history evidence were used in only a minority of cases: most applications were made verbally at trial rather than privately and in accordance with the Crown Court Rules.[14] Generally, the study found low awareness and understanding of the provisions among the judges and practitioners they interviewed. Moreover, in addition to specific references to section 41, references to complainant sexual history were found in over a third of the Crown Prosecution Service (CPS) files they examined. Overall, Kelly et al concluded that sexual history material featured in some way in more than three quarters of trials (2006: vi). Significantly, too, they concluded that the introduction of section 41 appeared to have no discernible impact on the rate of attrition in rape cases. This is notwithstanding that the poor treatment of complainants was identified as a key contributor to high rates of attrition in previous studies (Harris and Grace, 1999).[15]

Kelly et al (2006) was a large, multimethodological study, encompassing findings drawn from analysis of Home Office statistical data, prospective case tracking, examination of CPS files, trial observations, interviews with key stakeholders, a questionnaire survey of support services and analysis of reported legal cases. The geographical scope of the study included Greater Manchester, London, Sussex and Newcastle. A total of 236 Crown Court cases were tracked over a three-month period, 170 CPS files were analysed, 31 trials observed and over 100 people, including barristers, judges, complainants and police officers, interviewed. By any standards, this was a major study, the results of which merited serious consideration. Aside from the headline findings, the report offered a treasure trove of insights into the operation and impact of section 41, confirming, for example, the findings of other studies showing a strong association between the application to introduce sexual history evidence and chances of acquittal (2006: 28), multiple examples of evasion of prescribed procedures (2006: 28, 36, 47), and a perhaps surprising

---

under s 3 of the Criminal Law (Rape) Act 1981 were made in seven cases, of which six were granted (Rape Crisis Network Ireland, 2009: 342).

[14] The Irish study also revealed a lack of compliance with relevant procedural requirements: although applications to introduce sexual history evidence were made in only seven cases, complainants were asked questions about their prior sexual behaviour in 13 of the 35 cases analysed. Strikingly, too, all seven applications were made after the trial had started (Rape Crisis Network Ireland, 2009: 340–3). See also Heath (2005: 10) highlighting lack of compliance as an emerging issue in Australian jurisdictions in the 1990s.

[15] Another study commissioned by the Scottish Executive to evaluate the effects of new rape-shield legislation introduced in Scotland in 2002 yielded equally disappointing findings, including, strikingly, that the number of applications to introduce sexual history evidence appeared to have increased since the rape-shield provisions had been tightened (Burman et al, 2007).

degree of reliance on sexual history evidence in cases involving minors (2006: 28, 36). Interestingly, the study found 'few examples of the lengthy and humiliating questioning that has been documented in other studies [for example, Lees]', suggesting that some of the worst excesses had been curbed by legislative intervention: 'Defence counsel were more effective when a subtler approach was taken', Kelly et al observed (2006: 47). This did not halt reliance on problematic stereotypical notions of acceptable femininity in the courtroom but did, the authors speculated, compel courtroom actors to adopt less overtly sexist tones (2006: 47).

The views of legal professionals

Kelly et al (2006) found that while judges and barristers broadly accepted the need for restrictions on the use of sexual history evidence, they were in full agreement that such evidence remained relevant in at least some cases. Judges, unsurprisingly, expressed a preference for a discretionary approach to the admission of sexual history evidence, and barristers and judges shared the view that sexual history evidence featured only infrequently in trials, notwithstanding the broader findings of Kelly et al (2006: 58–9). A separate study of judicial attitudes to section 41 carried out by Neil Kibble (2005a, 2005b) around the same time confirmed a judicial preference for discretion over legislative prescriptions.[16] Indeed, this view was strongly held: "[I]t is fundamentally wrong for Parliament to rob judges of discretion as to the admissibility of evidence" (interviewee quote reproduced in Kibble [2005b: 264]).[17] Judges welcomed the decision in *R v A (No 2)*,[18] which they saw as necessary to mitigate the strictness of the section 41 regime. Interestingly, while other studies highlighted inconsistencies in the judicial application of section 41, Kibble found 'a substantial degree of consistency in judicial approaches to questions of relevance and admissibility' (2005b: 263). He reached this conclusion after analysing judicial approaches to four hypothetical scenarios, each of which posed a question about the admissibility of sexual history evidence. Subsequently, Kibble clarified that his research concern was less with the final decisions reached by his research subjects and more with exploring the reasoning and approaches adopted and the perceptions of relevance held (2008). However, the fact that the majority

---

[16] Kibble conducted individual and group interviews with 78 (mainly circuit court) judges in England and Wales, presenting his subjects with a range of hypothetical scenarios and soliciting their views on the structure and operation of section 41 (2005a: 192).

[17] The hostility of lawyers and judges towards laws restricting the use of sexual history evidence emerges as a strong theme in Canadian studies. See, for example, Gotell (2006: 756) and Craig (2016).

[18] [2001] UKHL 25.

of judges were willing to admit sexual history evidence in all four scenarios is not insignificant.

There is a dissonance between Kibble's approach to researching the use of sexual history evidence and that of other studies we have considered: Kibble is concerned with assessing the effectiveness of the legislative framework on its own terms, gauged according to judicial understanding and application of the statutory provisions, whereas the aims of Kelly, Burman and others encompass but extend beyond questions of legislative effectiveness and compliance to investigate the prevalence and significance of sexual history evidence in rape investigations and trials and its contribution to the broader problem of attrition. Simply put, while Kibble is concerned with the *misuse* of sexual history evidence (where the scope of legitimate usage is defined by the legislation), other studies address the *use* of such evidence within and beyond the bounds of legal permissibility. As we shall see, such differences in purpose and scope also feature in studies conducted post-*Evans*.

The experiences of victims and victim support organisations

Looking at the range of studies carried out in the wake of the enactment of legislative protections in UK jurisdictions, one detects a striking contrast between the attitudes of judges and legal practitioners, on the one hand, and those of rape complainants, and the organisations which support them, on the other. For the former group, sexual history evidence, properly used, plays an important role in securing justice, understood in terms of ensuring a fair trial for the defendant. For the latter, however, the legal preoccupation with sexual history evidence is not only experienced as harmful, indeed violative, but is also thought to deter rape victims from seeking justice – where justice is understood in terms of the operation of effective mechanisms to redress acts of sexual violence. The visibility of these very different mindsets and angles of vision is dependent upon the extent to which researchers seek to include them. Both Kelly et al (2006) and Burman et al (2007), the Scottish study, sought to elicit views on how the use of sexual history evidence was perceived and experienced by complainants and/or those supporting them through the trial process. Drawing on 19 in-depth interviews with rape victims,[19] Kelly et al found that concern about the way in which their prior sexual history might be used did feature in some women's decision not to report that they had been raped; the majority who did report said they were questioned about

---

[19] All the interviewees were white women contacted through the police or a Sexual Assault Referral Centre; 15 of the 19 women chose to make a formal report, and around half the sample proceeded to trial.

their sexual history and sexual lives during the police investigation; and, of those who went to court (about half the sample), four were subject to questions about their sexual history, in relation to which they were both unprepared and lacked understanding of the section 41 process or what kinds of questions were and were not permitted (2006: 62–3). Kelly et al also solicited the view of professionals, including police officers and victim support agencies. Most police officers agreed that concern about enquiries into their prior sexual history contributed to complainants' decisions to withdraw (2006: 63). In addition, a survey of victim support groups confirmed that rape complainants displayed anxiety about the possibility of unwarranted intrusion into their private and sexual lives during the investigative and trial process (Kelly et al, 2006: 63–5).[20]

Burman et al's (2007) study of the use of sexual history evidence in Scotland also sought the views of rape complainants ('complainers' in Scottish terminology). Like Kelly et al, this was a large-scale multimethodological study which included case tracking, in-court observations and interviews with a range of stakeholders including judges, advocates and complainers.[21] The scope and focus of this study did not map neatly on to that of Kelly et al (2006), mainly because of differences in legislative approach. As we noted in Chapter 4, Scots law combines sexual history and bad character evidence within the same regulatory framework, and although the research focus was on sexual offences trials, some of the section 275 applications[22] concerned evidence of bad character of a non-sexual nature.[23] On the other hand, both the Scottish and the English studies, while tasked with evaluating the operation of new legislation, conceived this mandate broadly to encompass

---

[20] In a survey of sexual assault referral centres in Canada in 2005, 85 per cent reported that rape victims were concerned about the possibility of their sexual history being raised at trial, with heightened concern expressed where the victim had been in a previous sexual relationship with the perpetrator, was a sex worker, an ethnic minority or a lesbian (cited in Gotell, 2006: 774).

[21] See generally Burman et al (2007: chapter 2).

[22] Sexual Offences (Criminal Procedure) (Scotland) Act 2002; see further Chapter 4.

[23] For this reason, any reading of the study's finding that the number of s 275 applications had substantially increased since the legislative reforms of 2002 must take account of the fact that a proportion of such applications (the researchers estimate around 24 per cent) related to character evidence (Burman et al, 2007: 6). Nevertheless, as Burman et al go on to observe, it can certainly be concluded that the 2002 reforms have not reduced the extent to which complainers are subject to questioning about their sexual history and character. Moreover, although the greater take up of procedural requirements has made the use of such evidence more visible, the low proportion of Crown challenges to, and judicial refusals of, such applications, leads the researchers to conclude that a substantial net increase in the use of sexual history evidence has been a direct result of the legislative intervention (Burman et al, 2007: 6–7 and 134–5).

not just the extent to which the new legislative provisions were properly applied, but also to gauge the wider impact of reforms on the prosecution of sexual offences and acquire a general sense of how and when sexual history evidence was being used. To this end, Burman et al sought to interview a sample of rape complainants who had given evidence in court since the introduction of the 2002 reforms. Finding willing subject participants proved to be a challenge, and the resulting sample – four interviewees – was disappointingly small (Burman et al, 2007: paras 2.26–2.298). Soliciting input from often traumatised research participants presents obvious difficulties which curtail the ability effectively to research this issue. In any event, the picture emerging from this small sample of in-depth interviews corresponds with the findings of Kelly et al. Complainers reported feeling inadequately prepared for the process of giving evidence, lacking understanding of the evidence-giving process, including what kinds of questions/evidence were permissible or impermissible. Not all of them were informed that a section 275 application had been made or what that would entail for them. Most notably, all four interviewees reported feeling very distressed during cross-examination, with attacks on their character proving particularly upsetting.[24]

Rape myths research and jury studies

Aside from research directly targeting the use of complainant sexual history evidence in the courtroom, much can be gleaned from wider studies of the effectiveness of legal responses to sexual violence. The phenomenon of attrition in rape cases has, as we have seen, spawned a veritable mountain of studies tracking the operation of rape claims through every stage of the criminal justice process. Much of this research is of value for our purposes, not least in demonstrating how attitudes towards, and concerns about, a complainant's sexual history shape and inform proceedings long before her complaint reaches the courtroom.[25]

Two types of research are particularly relevant to how sexual history evidence features in legal fora. The first is the burgeoning literature on the effect of rape myths on judgement and decision-making; the second is the growing body of research examining jury deliberations, primarily though not exclusively through the conduct of mock trials and jury simulations. As we shall see, these two bodies of literature interact to enrich our

---

[24] One complainant was asked about her single motherhood status and the fact that she had children by two different fathers; another about being homeless and having a history of self-harm (Burman et al, 2007: 127–9).

[25] See, for example, Smith and Daly (2020), who found that 77 per cent of victims/survivors stated that they agreed that people who report sexual violence to the police can expect to have their medical and sexual history discussed at court.

understanding of the forensic significance of sexual history evidence, albeit in problematic ways.

Rape myth studies

Rape myth studies explore the presence and effects of attitudes and beliefs which legitimise sexual violence and inhibit law's ability to redress it. The concept of rape myths derives from social psychology, the notion of 'myth' serving to capture the way certain beliefs and assumptions, for example about how women behave in sexual situations, assume the status of general facts, which are normatively deployed to evaluate behaviour and assign responsibility in sexual encounters, including those which form the subject of legal proceedings. A central concern of rape myth research is to expose the operation of victim-blaming and perpetrator-exonerating beliefs in cultural and legal discourse. Bohner et al describe rape myths as 'descriptive or prescriptive beliefs about rape ... that serve to deny, downplay or justify sexual violence that men commit against women' (2009: 19).[26] Examples include a range of beliefs about: how 'normal' rape victims behave, for example by resisting their assault, reporting the rape promptly and so on; how women 'provoke' rape through their appearance and behaviour; and what motivates rape, including beliefs about men's limited ability to control their sexual impulses and women's corresponding responsibility to act as sexual gatekeepers. Beliefs that false rape allegations are common or that sexual assault by a stranger is more serious or 'real' also fall into the category of rape myths.[27]

While most of these beliefs and attitudes recognisably circulate in social discourse, the extent to which individuals or groups subscribe to them is an empirical matter. Rape myths do not exist or operate in abstraction; they are spatially, temporally and culturally bound, so that questions about their prevalence, influence and effects can only be answered contextually. Indeed, as the body of literature engaging with rape myths has developed over time, researchers have begun to track and analyse changes in the way in which some rape myths are conceived, maintained and mobilised, adapting their methods to take such changes into account (Bohner et al, 2023).

A range of tools have been developed by rape myth researchers to measure the extent to which rape myths are held and explore the correlation between

---

[26] Rape myths thus have both explanatory and justificatory functions, that is, they are deployed to explain sexual behaviour (to make sense of what has happened) and to justify it (Hänel, 2018: 37).

[27] On the range and types of rape myths, see Bohner et al (2009); Leverick (2020); Cowan (2021).

subscribing to rape myths and making judgements about responsibility and blame in sexual scenarios. Among the most deployed tools of measurement is AMMSA (the 'acceptance of modern myths about sexual aggression' scale) developed by Gerger et al (2007). AMMSA takes the form of a psychometric test comprising 30 statements to which research participants are invited to respond using a seven-point scale, ranging from 'not at all agree' to 'very much agree' (Leverick, 2020: 257; Bohner et al, 2023: 160–1).[28] The results of AMMSA and similar psychometric tests can be used, for example, to identify the characteristics of groups more likely to hold rape myths or to track correlations between the degree to which rape myths are held (the level of 'Rape Myth Acceptance' or 'RMA') and assignments of responsibility in hypothetical sexual scenarios. Leverick (2020) has recently conducted a comprehensive review of these kind of studies, concluding that the evidence of a correlation between RMA scores and evaluations of responsibility is 'overwhelming' (2020: 256), with studies 'near unanimous in finding a significant relationship between scores on RMA scales and judgments about victim/perpetrator blame in a specific scenarios' (2020: 257).

How does this body of research speak to our concerns about complainant sexual history evidence? As we have seen, rape myths often lurk within arguments supporting the admission of sexual history evidence, frequently clothed in the guise of 'common sense'. Indeed, the 'twin myths' – the beliefs that unchaste women are more likely to consent and are less worthy of belief – constitute the historical foundation of legal appeals to sexual history evidence. Rape myth research aids the identification and interrogation of beliefs and attitudes that attribute particular significance to a complainant's sexual history when making judgements about sexual assault. Take, for example, the 'real rape' myth, captured in the popular stereotype of a violent rape perpetrated by a stranger in a park or alleyway (Estrich, 1987). This stereotype invokes an understanding of rape in which certain features – the presence of violence, the absence of a prior relationship between victim and perpetrator, the public nature of the location (park, alleyway) – are thought to be especially indicative of the offence. Many studies have shown that the real rape stereotype operates prescriptively to shape criminal justice processes at all stages, from initial report to final verdict (Jordan, 2004; Ellison and Munro, 2009a). Another myth which features in invocations of complainant sexual history evidence is the 'ideal victim'. Several studies have highlighted the way in which assumptions about women's behaviour inform judgements of rape scenarios: women

---

[28] Examples of statements in the AMMSA test include: 'Many women tend to interpret a well-meant gesture as a "sexual assault"'; 'Alcohol is often the culprit when a man rapes a woman' (Bohner et al, 2009: 22).

who dress 'provocatively', get drunk or have had multiple sexual partners are less likely to fit expectations of victimhood and are correspondingly perceived to be less credible or deserving (Lees, 1996; Finch and Munro, 2005). Studies have also highlighted how these victim-blaming attitudes are deployed in court by defence barristers to discredit complainants and undermine their testimony (Adler, 1987; Lees, 1996; Burman et al, 2007), although more recent research, taking the form of trial observations, suggests the adoption of subtler techniques by defence counsel, for example by highlighting the 'abnormality' of the complainant's behaviour as compared to what a normal or reasonable person would do in the same circumstances (Smith and Skinner, 2017; Daly, 2022).[29] This subtler use of rape myths also aligns with Kelly et al's findings (2006: 47). It may be that restrictions on the use of sexual history evidence and greater public awareness of the presence and operation of rape myths are compelling defence lawyers to pursue less overtly sexist strategies of cross-examination.

This observation does not necessarily apply cross-jurisdictionally (or even within a single jurisdiction). Its validity requires empirical determination, with the normative pull of rape-shield laws likely to be offset in some contexts by the robustness of the adversarial culture. Take, for example, the observations of Abbe Smith, a self-described 'feminist defense lawyer', in an article published in the *American Criminal Law Review* entitled 'Representing rapists' (Smith, 2016). In this honest and highly reflective piece, Smith explains how she reconciles her role as a lawyer representing rape defendants – many of whom she acknowledges are likely to be guilty – with the unflinching cross-examination of traumatised victims of sexual offences. Her assertion of a commitment to a ' "feminist defense ethos" – built on an abiding skepticism of the reflective use of state power and a deep commitment to individual human dignity' (2016: 257) is of less interest, for purposes here, than her comments about cross-examining rape victims (although in so far as she expresses doubt about the value of carceral responses to criminality, we are not without some sympathy).[30] It is nevertheless the culture of cross-examination which she represents, indeed extols, that is both fascinating and disturbing. Notwithstanding her distaste and distress when questioning rape victims, Smith is unwavering in her commitment robustly to defend adversarial criminal justice processes. Impugning the complainant's testimony, she argues, is unavoidably part of the job:

---

[29]   Although see Temkin et al (2018) highlighting the persistence of flagrant attacks by defence counsel on complainants' moral character, including putting questions about their sexual history without previously applying for leave to do so (213–14).

[30]   For consideration of anti-carceral arguments, see Chapter 8.

[L]et's be honest. Especially when the defense is fabrication or consent – as it often is in adult rape cases – you have to go at the witness. There is no way around this fact. Effective cross-examination means exploiting every uncertainty, inconsistency, and implausibility. More, it means attacking the witness's very character. (Smith, 2016: 290)

Smith regards the deployment of rape myths, what she describes as 'cultural understandings and misunderstandings about sex' (2016: 283), as the stock-in-trade of criminal defence lawyering: '[I]t is not unusual for defense lawyers to play into sexism, racism, or other biases when it might be advantageous to do so. Exploiting prejudice is part of advocacy. The ability to persuade sometimes relies on an underlying ability to recognize and play off biases and stereotypes' (2016: 284).[31] It is up to the prosecutor, Smith argues, to anticipate and rebut these kinds of strategies.[32] Thus, in so far as rape myths circulate and influence how people respond to sexual assault scenarios, they are, in the perception of at least some legal practitioners, fair game for defence lawyers.

Jury studies

In the previous section, we introduced the concept of rape myths and considered the body of literature exploring what they are, how widely and deeply they are held, and how they might operate to blame victims and/or exonerate perpetrators of rape. We also highlighted particular rape myths, prefiguring a paradigmatically real rape or ideal victim that aids the construction of a normative frame within which a complainant's sexual history emerges as relevant to judgements of responsibility and blame.

However, just because rape myths are shown to be culturally circulating and variously held by selected research subjects does not necessarily prove that they inform judgement and decision-making in legal fora. Indeed, in a recent study of juror attitudes, Cheryl Thomas (2020) strongly argues they do not.

---

[31] In a recent joint review of the criminal justice response to rape, a coalition of anti-violence NGOs recommended that the rape-shield law in England and Wales be amended 'to create an up-to-date, clear and meaningful ban on the use of "SHE" ... [which] should explicitly refer to attempts to relate sexual history invoking race/class/disability and sexual orientation prejudice as well as sex' (Centre for Women's Justice et al, 2020: 78).

[32] In placing her faith in prosecutors to mitigate the worst excesses of ruthless defence advocacy, Smith makes the common error of assuming that prosecutorial and complainant interests align. Multiple studies show that they do not (Cowan, 2020). Interestingly, it does not seem to cross Smith's mind that the complainant, whose traumatic experience is at the heart of the trial, has no independent voice in the proceedings.

Thomas's study is unique in that she was given unprecedented access by the Ministry of Justice (MoJ) to subjects who had recently served as jurors in criminal trials, including but not limited to sexual offences trials. Her study, the object of which was to gauge 'the extent [to which] real jurors who have served on juries believe rape myths and stereotypes' (2020: 1001), was conducted in 2018–19, eliciting the participation of 771 jurors over four court regions in England and Wales. Each of the jurors was invited to respond to a survey distributed after they had concluded jury service. The survey probed juror attitudes to rape, sexual offences, sexual behaviour and rape myths through their response to a series of statements, variously drawn from public opinion polls and RMA scales, specifically, the Illinois Rape Myth Acceptance scale.[33]

Thomas's findings are interesting. Based on the survey responses, she concluded that 'hardly any jurors believe what are often referred to as widespread myths and stereotypes about rape and sexual assault' (2020: 1001). On the contrary, jurors came across as reasonably well informed about the realities of sexual offences, including the fact that rape could occur between intimates, that testifying about being raped in court was very challenging, and that rape victims might have good reasons for their reluctance to report rape in a timely manner or indeed at all (2020: 1002). In other words, Thomas concluded, rape myths were not widely held among actual jurors. Moreover, claims – primarily derived from jury simulation studies – that rape myths did feature in jury decision-making were plainly wrong. Her study, Thomas declared, revealed that such research methods were 'fundamentally flawed' (2020: 987).

Thomas's research is illustrative of the deep contestation which continues to rage in criminal justice discourse as to the existence, operation and effects of rape myths. However, her research is important for another reason: it shows how important research design and method are to the production of sound research outcomes. Thomas's study has been strongly criticised by experienced researchers in the sexual violence field. Chalmers et al (2021) note that Thomas's findings 'are more limited in their reach and robustness than she suggests' (755). They go on to highlight 'missed opportunities in the way the research was framed from the outset, limitations in the methodology used ... and potential slippages and overreach from the conclusions drawn' (Chalmers et al, 2021: 755). Daly et al (2023) also criticise Thomas's research design and the conclusions she purports to draw, focusing, inter alia, on the narrow three-point response scale used in the survey, the limitations of survey studies generally, and the interpretation,

---

[33] Thomas makes no mention of the AMMSA scale.

both by Thomas and other sympathetic commentators, of the raw data generated by the study.

The critical question, of course, is how one should approach the lack of correspondence between Thomas's research and that of jury simulation studies. One might speculate perhaps that where a single limited study produces results which appear wholly out of line with a large body of extant research on the same topic, legitimate questions may be raised about the design and conduct of the dissonant study. Thomas places a lot of weight on the fact that she had access to 'real jurors', but as Daly et al (2023) suggest, this hardly explains what amounts to a huge divergence in research outcomes. Equally, as critics have noted, Thomas's study is quite limited, taking the form of a simple survey, albeit of hitherto untapped research participants. The literature she so quickly dismisses is far more sophisticated in design and execution. Much of it is triangulated, combining quantitative studies of attitudes via surveys and psychometric tests with qualitative explorations of how subject attitudes and beliefs are manifest and mobilised in deliberative fora (as, for example, when mock juror deliberations are observed and analysed). While the quality and soundness of jury simulation studies will vary depending on factors such as the size of the study, selection of research participants and extent to which the research design replicates 'real' trial processes (Leverick, 2020: 258–9), the best of this work achieves high levels of sophistication in terms of methodology and analytical rigour.

A particular merit of jury simulation studies is that they seek to chart and document precisely how rape myths are mobilised in deliberative fora. Although surveys and tests do give some indication of the extent to which prejudices and stereotypes feature in selected populations, the soundness of research outcomes must be offset against the level of awareness among research subjects of the social undesirability of professing certain views – and thereby, their reluctance to express them (Bohner et al, 2023: 160). In addition, rape myths, indeed biases and prejudices more broadly, may be held unconsciously as well as consciously, a product of learned associations and social conditioning of which we are not always fully aware but nevertheless draw upon, particularly when called upon to make decisions in pressurised circumstances (Greenwald and Banaji, 1995; Kahneman, 2011). Increasingly, research has shown that rape myths function less as consciously held views of cognitively deliberative subjects and more as culturally prevalent tropes and images upon which people, including those involved in criminal justice operations, draw – often unconsciously – when exercising judgement. Bohner et al (2009) argue that RMA is best conceived as a 'general cognitive schema [understood as a knowledge structure that aids the processing of information] ... which guides and organises an individual's interpretation of specific information about rape cases' (23). Temkin and Krahé's (2008) research also shows evidence of schematic processing in rape deliberations. In a series of studies involving the presentation of hypotheticals to law students, as well as to members of the general public, Temkin and Krahé explore how rape myths, particularly the 'real rape' myth, operate as heuristics, that is, 'mental shortcuts and rules of thumb, to engage in speedy and relatively effortless cognition processing of information' (2008: 49).

In a compelling analysis of rape culture, Nicola Gavey makes the case for linking rape myths to broader discourses of sex and sexuality, claiming that 'everyday taken-for-granted normative forms of heterosexuality work as a cultural scaffolding for rape' (2019: 2). Gavey criticises the dominant form of rape myths research (what she describes as 'attitude research') for seeking to locate the problem of sexual violence in the biases of individuals (2019: 44–5). Instead, Gavey draws on social constructivism to argue that discourses of heterosexuality 'legitimate particular forms and circumstances of sex ... and delegitimate others' (2019: 131). The resulting structure of norms and standards serves as the cultural scaffolding within which individual choices about and assessments of sexual behaviour are made.[34] Gavey's concept of scaffolding has been taken up by other rape researchers, for example Smith, who uses Gavey's framework to probe the persistence of rape myths and gender stereotypes in courtroom settings (Smith, 2021: 241). Scholars have also employed terms like 'narrative' (Daly, 2022) or 'script' (Ellison and Munro, 2009c) to capture the structural context within which rape myths are embedded and operationalised. Theorising rape myths in this way compels both a socio-cultural understanding of rape myths and a contextualised examination of their application.

To illustrate this important point, let us look closely at one research study exploring how rape myths are mobilised in jury deliberations. Louise Ellison and Vanessa Munro have carried out several jury simulation studies, taking the form of acted mini-trial scenarios before mock juries followed by observation and analysis of the jurors' subsequent deliberations (Ellison and Munro, 2009a, 2009b, 2009c, 2010, 2013, 2015).[35] The object of the research

---

[34] Gavey (2019) adopts a broadly Foucauldian approach, harnessing the concept of discourse(s) to the production of a normative order which legitimises sexual violence. Other scholars, such as Hänel, for example, deploy the notion of ideology, arguing that rape myths are part of an ideological structure which renders certain forms of rape socially acceptable (2018: 13).

[35] In the first study, volunteer jurors were asked to watch one of nine mini rape trial reconstructions (lasting 75 minutes) and to deliberate for 90 minutes. The scenarios all presented variations of a disputed sexual encounter between work colleagues (Ellison and Munro, 2009a: 204–6). The second study took a broadly similar form, but the scenario enacted involved a sexual encounter between parties who had formerly been intimate (Ellison and Munro, 2013). Jurors were also asked to complete a questionnaire, inviting their views on the scenario both before and after deliberation.

was to gain a better understanding of if, and how, rape myths were relied upon by jurors with a view to developing practical strategies, for example the provision of better judicial guidance or more targeted juror education, to counter the justice-inhibiting effects of bias and prejudice. In the first study, involving an acquaintance rape scenario, Ellison and Munro analysed the texts of jury deliberations to explore how assumptions and beliefs relating to, for example, delayed reporting, lack of evidence of physical resistance, complainant behaviour and demeanour and so on featured in juror judgement and decision-making (2009a, 2009b, 2009c). The researchers found that jurors frequently drew upon 'scripts' to distinguish what they perceived to be 'normal' sexual seduction from rape.[36] The notion of script here was used to denote 'a mental representation of a situation which is crafted in such a way that enables the subject-matter to be explained as a incorporating a coherent sequence of events' (2009c: 293). Such scripts, Ellison and Munro theorised, derived from the interaction of cultural norms and expectations about sex with individual personal experience, producing an evaluative frame of reference for processing and interpreting the scenarios presented to the jurors (2009c: 295).

Ellison and Munro found multiple examples of reliance upon rape myths and gender stereotypes in the course of juror deliberations built into the scaffolding of the distinction between 'normal sex' and 'real rape', and evidenced in discussions about where and when 'normal' sex took place, how sexual communications were generally conducted and how responsibility for managing a situation of sexual risk ought to be assigned (2009c: 307; see also Herriott, 2023: 88). Crucially, this research revealed that rape myths did not necessarily manifest as firmly held and consciously articulated beliefs but emerged as architectural features of the sexual scripts in circulation. A particular consequence of this research finding is that studies based on abstract surveys or RMA tests alone, while not without value, are limited in their ability to account for the operation of rape myths in applied situations.[37]

In a second study conducted by Ellison and Munro (2013), the acted-out trial scenario presented to the mock jurors involved a complainant's

---

[36] Similar results have since emerged from Herriott's study, using jury simulation methods to examine how sexual history evidence features in juror deliberations (2023).

[37] This point also emerges in a study conducted by Tinsley et al (2021) in New Zealand, comprising post-verdict interviews with 18 jurors in real sexual offences trials which showed that 'cultural misconceptions' about rape continued to inform juror assessments of defendant culpability. Commenting directly on Thomas (2020), Tinsley et al observe: '[O]ur research suggests it might be problematic to assume that because real jurors in an attitudinal survey claimed not to believe misconceptions about sexual violence, culturally embedded beliefs will not impact on deliberations in actual trials' (2021: 469).

allegation that she had been raped by an ex-partner.[38] As with the previous study, a key research object was to shed better light on how (if at all) rape myths, particularly the 'real rape' myth, featured in juror deliberations. Again, the findings are interesting. First, Ellison and Munro observed that most participants were 'receptive in principle' to the idea that a woman could be raped by a man with whom she had previously been in a relationship (2013: 309). This awareness was evidenced by juror comments across the deliberations. Nevertheless, jurors remained concerned about the ambiguity that previous acquaintanceship or intimacy brought to the situation. To resolve the challenge this presented, jurors drew upon a range of 'scripts' about socio-sexual relations to gauge and measure the behaviour of both parties, scripts which included placing primary responsibility for sexual gatekeeping on women, and assuming the normalcy of male sexual initiation (2013: 310–11, 314). Jurors appeared to consider the risk of sexual miscommunication to be particularly high where the parties had previously been intimate, increasing the expectation that the complainant manage the situation in such a way as to leave no room for misunderstanding (2013: 312; see also Herriott, 2023: 92). Some jurors even speculated that in light of the prior relationship and the complainant's warm reception of her ex-partner, the defendant made an honest mistake in assuming her consent (2013: 313). Equally significant for some jurors was the absence of conclusive evidence of force or resistance, the reasoning being that a rape victim would feel more emboldened to resist a threat of force from an ex-partner and less likely to 'freeze' in fear than if the perpetrator were a stranger (Ellison and Munro, 2013: 315–16).[39]

Overall, the researchers concluded that the fact of prior intimacy between the parties 'created an opportunity for jurors to invoke and rely upon engrained expectations regarding resistance and sexual (mis)communication, which – when combined with persuasive strategies that interpreted the standard of proof as requiring nothing short of absolute certainty – mitigated against the likelihood of returning a guilty verdict' (300). Strikingly, the effect of deliberations appears to have heightened jurors' unwillingness to return a verdict of guilty (as gauged by pre- and post-deliberation surveys). In sum, the study confirms the findings of other studies that jurors struggle

---

[38] The alleged rape took place in the complainant's home after her ex-partner, who had previously lived there with her, called to collect some of his possessions. Some alcohol was consumed by both parties, and there was physical evidence of intercourse and some scratches and bruising (which a forensic examiner concluded was neither consistent or inconsistent with rape [Ellison and Munro, 2013: 304]).

[39] This was notwithstanding that there was evidence of scratching and bruising on the complainant's body although no internal vaginal trauma – again, a fact upon which some jurors placed considerable significance (Ellison and Munro, 2013: 317).

to convict in acquaintance/intimate partner rape situations, while also demonstrating how gendered socio-sexual expectations influenced their thinking in reaching a verdict.[40]

We have dwelled on the research on rape myths and jury studies at some length for a reason: it reveals something very important about how sexual history evidence features in rape trials, not necessarily demonstrated by research studies that focus on the operation and effectiveness of rape-shield laws. Ellison and Munro's work shows that once the fact of prior acquaintance between the parties becomes known to the jury, it provides an opening for the importation of a network of norms and expectations about how people (ought to) behave in normal sexual encounters. Acquaintance rape poses a problem for jurors, they posit, because of its 'many commonalities with a seduction script based around male-dominated, adversarial, sexual interaction' (Ellison and Munro, 2010: 794).

The implications of this finding are deeply troubling because they suggest that once the fact of prior acquaintance or intimacy enters the court record, the chances of acquittal increase, regardless of the nature and relevance of the evidence of the parties' prior acquaintance. To put it another way, even where sexual history evidence is introduced within the strict letter of legal requirements, its effect on trial outcomes is arguably much more extensive.

Sexual history evidence in the contemporary courtroom

When footballer Ched Evans was acquitted of rape in 2016 after new evidence of the complainant's sexual history with other men triggered an appeal against his conviction,[41] no major studies of the use of sexual history evidence in British courts had been published since the spate of studies conducted in the first decade of the century. One benefit of the public

---

[40] Other studies exploring how the fact of a prior relationship operates to preclude a finding of guilty include: Schuller and Hastings (2002) (Canadian study showing that where evidence of prior sexual relationship between complainant and defendant was introduced, mock jurors were less likely to find the complainant credible, more likely to find her blameworthy, and/or to have consented); Burgin and Flynn (2019: 14–17) (study of trial transcripts in Victoria, Australia, evidencing cross-examination strategy to establish implied consent/reasonable belief in consent where defendant and complainant had a prior relationship); Temkin and Krahé (2008: 81) (research participants invited to respond to questions on complainant/defendant responsibility/blame in a range of hypothetical sexual assault scenarios – the study found that the closer the relationship between the complainant and defendant prior to the alleged assault, the less blame was attributed to the defendant and the more blame attributed to the complainant for what had occurred).

[41] *R v Evans* [2016] EWCA Crim 452.

debate prompted by *Evans* was to fuel demand for fresh data on the use of sexual history evidence, particularly given the degree of contestation expressed in public fora about the extent to which such evidence actually featured in rape trials.[42] A range of studies have since emerged with more in train. This new body of evidence is characterised by many of the same features as the earlier studies. The methodological gold standard continues to be court observations, but surveys of, and interviews with, criminal justice stakeholders have also been conducted, as well as 'dip' sampling of case files. At the same time, debate about the extent to which sexual history evidence presents a problem of justice remains unresolved. Indeed, there is a striking divergence in the outcomes and conclusions of recent studies. On the one hand, we have a whole swathe of new studies, mainly conducted by researchers with an interest in addressing sexual violence, highlighting how sexual history evidence continues to be deployed in court in problematic ways. On the other hand, we have a set of studies, mostly conducted by or for legal professional bodies, which appear to confirm the view, strongly expressed by the Criminal Bar after *Evans*, that sexual history evidence is very restricted and only rarely features in trial processes. Acknowledging and accounting for these diverging outcomes is critical to understanding why the criminal justice system continues to fail victims of sexual violence.

Sexual violence research

One example of research problematising the use of sexual history evidence is Smith (2018). Smith observed a series of rape trials in Northumbria in 2010 and 2012, 28 trials in total.[43] She reported that sexual history evidence was routinely used in rape trials 'with all except two of the full trials discussing the survivor's sexual background in some form' (2018: 105). Frequently, evidence was introduced in ways that contravened the formal regulatory framework,[44] leading her to conclude that the '1999 YJCEA restrictions are unfit for purpose' (2018: 120). Smith drew particular attention to the way in which sexual history evidence was used by defence counsel, for example where the defendant and complainant had previously been in a relationship, by highlighting similarities between the disputed encounter and prior consensual sex (2018: 108–9). Sexual history evidence was also used to highlight inconsistencies in, and undermine the credibility of, the

---

[42] See further Chapter 1.

[43] All of Smith's trials involved adult complainants.

[44] In 90 per cent of trials where sexual history evidence was admitted, s 41 applications were made, usually during rather than in advance of trial. Applications were rarely challenged by the judge or prosecution, 'suggesting a general acceptance for the inclusion of sexual history evidence' (Smith, 2018: 105).

complainant's testimony (110–11). In some cases, too, sexual history evidence was included via the prosecution, usually because it had come up in pre-recorded police interviews and was part of the complainant's evidence-in-chief. Once in, however, the evidence provided the defence an opportunity to question the complainant about her sexual history by way of rebuttal (2018: 114–15). The overall picture of rape trials emerging from Smith's analysis is far from reassuring and her critique of the operation of section 41 nothing short of devastating.[45]

Another Northumbrian court study took place in 2015–16, in part prompted by Smith's. Acting in her capacity as Police and Crime Commissioner, Dame Vera Baird commissioned an observation study of a further 30 rape trials (including but not confined to adult complainants). The observers, who were lay volunteers, appointed and trained by the regional CPS, reported that, in 11 of the 30 trials, questioning or evidence relating to the complainant's sexual history was introduced. However, in only four cases did the procedural rules regarding the application of section 41 appear to be properly followed, with a number of applications to admit evidence made after the trial had commenced or not at all (Durham, 2017: 8).

The observers reported that efforts were made by several judges to stop inadmissible lines of questioning. However, prosecuting counsel did not tend to object where evidence was admitted late or in breach of the prescribed procedures[46] (Durham, 2017: 8). In one case, involving marital rape, the defence sought to introduce evidence of the complainant's alleged adultery as 'bad character' evidence, presumably under section 100 of the Criminal Justice Act (CJA) 2003. In another 'bad character' case, defence counsel made repeated references to the complainant's alleged infidelity while purporting to attack her credibility on grounds of a record of alcohol abuse. In yet another case, the jury was shown videos of the complainant and defendant – who had previously been in a sexual relationship – having apparently consensual sex to support a defence argument that the complainant, in a videotape

---

[45] See also Temkin et al's (2018) analysis of court observations in eight rape trials taking place in London and the South East in 2010, in which the complainant's prior sexual behaviour with third parties was introduced in four of the trials, all outside the scope of a valid section 41 application (213–14). Likewise, Williams (2020) found that in 16 of the 18 rape trials she observed, complainants were cross-examined about their sexual history (186). Williams records witnessing only seven s 41 applications, all taking place on or after the day the trial had begun, concluding that in at least some of the cases she observed, the evidence in question should not have been admitted (see generally Williams, 2020: 186–200).

[46] The Report recommended that prosecutors and judges make further, more robust objections/interventions when sexual history evidence is introduced outside the scope of prescribed procedures (11), though Hoyano (2018) argues that lay observers are not in a position to know if the correct procedures have been followed (26–7).

of the alleged rape, was engaging in role play by pretending to be asleep. Interestingly, the complainant testified that she was unaware that she was being videoed during sex (Durham, 2017: 9). Finally, observers also reported that in six of the 11 cases, the evidence introduced related to the complainant's sexual behaviour with other men (Durham, 2017: 10) and that the defence drew upon sexual stereotypes and assumptions to build the case for consent (14–15).

Hoyano (2018), who, as we shall see, has undertaken her own study of the use of sexual history evidence, has criticised the Northumbria study on a number of grounds including its use of lay volunteers rather than trained legal experts. She proceeds to detail the various ways in which, because of the lack of a 'thorough understanding of the adversarial trial, the rights of the defence, the legal framework of the Sexual Offences Act 2003, [or] of the relevant rules of evidence' (2018: para 19), the observers appear to have misread or misinterpreted trial proceedings. This seems a somewhat inapt argument to advance given that the ultimate decision-makers in a criminal trial are also lay observers, that is, juries. Moreover, it arguably misconstrues the nature of this particular study – which is surely to glean how trial proceedings are viewed and experienced by ordinary members of the public. Thus, although Hoyano criticises the Northumbria observers for apparently misunderstanding the roles of both prosecuting and defence counsel, she fails to see what this tells us about the public's expectations of the trial process, and how perhaps they differ from those of Hoyano herself. When Hoyano pronounces that '[t]he quality of the analysis of the data was impaired by a misunderstanding of the fundamental roles of prosecuting counsel and the trial judge to ensure that the defendant has a fair trial' (2018: para 21), one is immediately struck by how narrowly she perceives the justice issues at stake: it is the responsibility of both the prosecution and defence to ensure, she affirms, that the defendant has a fair trial. But who then is looking out for the interests of the complainant? And is it so surprising that members of the public are also asking that question?[47]

A quite different study, also criticised by Hoyano (again mainly on the grounds that the researchers did not properly understand the law), is the LimeCulture survey of ISVAs carried out in 2017. Unlike the Northumbria observation studies, which were concerned with the rape trial generally, the LimeCulture study focused directly on participants' views and experiences of the operation of section 41 of the YJCEA 1999. LimeCulture, an organisation

---

[47] There is a resonance here between the observations of the research participants in the Northumbria study and studies which reveal the breadth of the gap between complainant expectations of the criminal justice system and the traumatic realities of their involvement, particularly at the trial stage. See in particular Molina and Poppleton (2020).

which supports the work of organisations seeking to combat sexual violence, conducted an online survey of ISVAs to which 36 responded (all from England and Wales). The responses reflected a reasonable geographical spread, and the survey sought predominantly quantitative information from the responding ISVAs. Taken together, the experience of the 36 ISVAs spanned at least 550 trials over the previous two years.

The survey responses confirmed that questions about a complainant's previous sexual history continue to figure significantly in the trial process with only 25 per cent of ISVAs reporting that sexual history evidence had not been an issue in any of the cases in which they had been involved. Some 44.5 per cent of participants reported that sexual history featured in less than a quarter of cases they had worked, 19.5 per cent in less than a half, and 11 per cent reported that sexual history was a feature of more than three quarters of the cases they worked on (LimeCulture, 2017: para 15). Given the geographical spread of ISVAs across England and Wales, these data reveal, among other things, considerable regional variations in the application of section 41. The survey data also appeared to show that in a significant number of cases (again there were regional variations), the procedural rules governing the introduction of sexual history evidence and the requirement to provide advance information to the complainant were not being followed (LimeCulture, 2017: paras 17–24). Overall, the survey concluded that proper processes relating to section 41 were not being applied consistently across England and Wales and that, as with other studies, complainants were often unaware that questions would be put to them about their previous sexual behaviour.

Law-centred research

The studies just discussed are far more limited in design and scope than the widescale, triangulated research carried out by Kelly et al in 2006 and Burman et al in 2007. And, as we have seen, they have attracted some criticism, in terms of scope, evidentiary weight and methodological robustness. Arrayed against them are several studies taking a very different view of the effects and effectiveness of section 41, all prompted by the public and political furore unleashed by *Evans*.

An MoJ Review, commissioned in the wake of *Evans*, appeared to lend weight to claims that complainant sexual history evidence was not commonly invoked in rape trials. Of a sample[48] of 309 cases finalised in 2016,

---

[48] The study adopted a random dip sample methodology, selecting two files flagged as rape charges for each month in 2016 across 13 CPS areas, producing a sample database of 309 case files. For a critique of this methodology, see Hoyano (2018: 38) and McGlynn (2017b).

an application under section 41 was made in only 40 cases (13 per cent), while applications to admit evidence or questions about the complainant's sexual history were granted in only 25 cases, that is, 8 per cent of the total sample (although well over half of the cases in which a section 41 application was made). This allowed the study to conclude that 'in the overwhelming majority of cases analysed (92 per cent), no evidence of the complainant's sexual history was permitted to be introduced by the defence' (MoJ, 2017: 8), supporting the view expounded, inter alia, by the Criminal Bar that admission of sexual history evidence was 'exceptional' (MoJ, 2017: 11). Interestingly, in the majority of cases where a section 41 application was made, the evidence in question related to prior sexual behaviour with the defendant. In just under a quarter of applications granted, the evidence related to sexual activity with a person other than the defendant (MoJ, 2017: 8). In only 35 per cent of section 41 applications did the prosecution oppose the introduction of sexual history evidence (MoJ, 2017: 10).

The headline findings of this study have been challenged, not only because they are out of line with other studies (for example, Durham [2017] found that sexual history evidence was introduced in 11/30 trials, that is, over one third of the trials observed), but also because the scope of the study was confined to reviewing CPS files of rape cases to identify those in which a section 41 application was made. Obviously, this fails to take account of the possibility that sexual history evidence may feature in trials in which a section 41 application has not been made (McGlynn, 2017b). As we have seen, both Smith (2018) and Durham (2017) found instances of the use of sexual history evidence in trials in which no section 41 application had been made. There is also the fact that the prosecution can introduce evidence of a complainant's prior sexual history – and usually does where the complainant and defendant were in a relationship at the time of the alleged rape – without making an application.

Another study examining the operation of section 41 is Hoyano (2018). This study, commissioned by the Criminal Bar Association (CBA) of England and Wales, claims to be 'the largest empirical study of the use of previous sexual behaviour evidence in sexual offences trials' (2018: foreword). It was carried out in 2017, and as with the MoJ study, was prompted by public debate post-*Evans*. Taking the form of an online survey of CBA members, it invited both quantitative and qualitative responses relating to barristers' experiences of section 41 in the 24 months prior to November 2017. A total of 179 barristers responded,[49] producing a sample of 377 sexual

---

[49] This was from a membership base of 3,880, a response rate of 4.6 per cent. A total of 13 respondents were screened out on the grounds that they had not handled any sex offences cases in the previous 24 months (Hoyano, 2018: 41).

assault cases (across the spectrum of sexual offences) and 565 complainants. Most respondents had experience of prosecuting and defending sexual offences cases.

Hoyano's key findings include:

- Almost 60 per cent of respondents considered that section 41 was working in the interests of justice; only 27 per cent thought it was not working.
- There was a 'wide and thoughtful consensus among barristers that some restrictions on previous sexual behaviour evidence were warranted, to eliminate questions based on stereotypes and myths in sexual assault trials' (2018: 6).
- None of the respondents thought that section 41 should be made more restrictive, but a number expressed concerns that the legislation was already too restrictive.
- Only one respondent reported that trial judges were not always sufficiently rigorous in their application of section 41 (Hoyano, 2018: 6).

Hoyano's study also includes some useful data on the use and frequency of section 41 applications. She found:

- That of the 565 complainants in the sample, 144 applications were filed, of which 105 (73 per cent) were successful to some extent.[50] Thus, 18.6 per cent of complainants in the sample were the subject of section 41 agreements or orders.
- The most frequent gateways invoked in applications were 'that the evidence was relevant to an issue which was not an issue of consent'[51] (49 per cent) and that the evidence rebutted evidence already led by the prosecution[52] (25 per cent).
- In 35 per cent of applications, the defence filed the documents after the prescribed time limit of 28 days (2018: 8).

It is difficult to know what weight to place on Hoyano's findings. Hoyano herself maintains that they confirm the view, previously articulated by the CBA, that the admission of previous sexual behaviour evidence under section 41 remains 'exceptional' and that evidence is only admitted in so far as it complies with a legislatively prescribed relevant evidential purpose and is narrowly conceived (Hoyano, 2018: 9). The data also show, she argues, that

---

[50] Sixty-six applications were granted in full, 39 in part (n=105) (Hoyano, 2018: 54).
[51] YJCEA 1999 s 41(3)(a).
[52] YJCEA 1999, s 41(5).

judges and prosecuting counsel are vigilant in ensuring that the complainant is not subject to 'any unnecessary distress' (Hoyano, 2018: 9).

In various ways, these findings are out of line with other studies. Hoyano gauges that section 41 applications are made in just under one fifth of sexual offence trials, compared to Kelly et al's figure of just under a third in 2006. Strikingly, too, Hoyano's study reveals a higher level of section 41 applications than the MoJ study which identified applications in only 13 per cent of the sample case files.[53] One difference between Hoyano's study and Kelly et al is that Hoyano's case sample includes a range of sexual offences, not just rape. It may be that section 41 applications are more common in rape cases, although as Hoyano's data do not break down categories of offence, we have no real evidence to assume this. Interestingly, the data suggest that section 41 applications are far more likely to be made where the complainant is female: section 41 applications were made in respect of 5.4 per cent of male complainants and in 31.6 per cent of female complainants. As Hoyano notes, this finding invites further research (2018: 56). It also suggests another reason why the proportion of section 41 applications in Hoyano's study is lower than in some other studies. Because she has included all sexual offences, including a significant number of historic sexual abuse cases, the breakdown of male to female complainants is roughly one in four (52).

A further limitation of Hoyano's study is that her analysis is limited to the operation of section 41. She proceeds on the assumption that in so far as sexual history evidence falls within the remit of legislatively prescribed relevance, its use in the courtroom is not, and certainly ought not to be, an issue.[54] Hoyano is not necessarily wrong to cast her research gaze narrowly, but it does make it difficult to compare her findings with studies which probe the use of sexual history evidence beyond the scope of section 41. It also limits the extent to which one can extrapolate generally from her data. The claim for example that the admission of sexual history evidence under section 41 remains 'exceptional', while barely supported by her own data, tells us nothing about how sexual history evidence features in trial proceedings outside the formal remit of section 41 (and Hoyano makes only the barest

---

[53] Although Hoyano (2018) argues that because of difficulties presented by data counting, this percentage is likely to be an overstatement (2018: 55). Hoyano also acknowledges various limitations in the MoJ methodology, including the fact that the study assumes that no s 41 application has been made where it is not recorded in the CPS case file (and where there is no requirement that it should be) (2018: 38).

[54] Tucked away towards the end of Hoyano's report and not included in her headline findings, we come upon data which suggests that in up to 23 cases questions about the complainant's sexual experience were asked or permitted without the imprimatur of a successful section 41 application (70–2). Hoyano strives to minimise the significance of these data, but it is odd that she does not at least acknowledge them in her executive summary.

efforts to explore this [2018: 70–2]). For a fuller picture, we are reliant on court observation studies, and these tell a different story. It is true that by virtue of their time and labour-intensive nature, court observations tend to be more limited in sample size, but whether carried out by lay observers or legally trained academic researchers (as many are), these studies provide us with concrete examples of how sexual history evidence is actually being mobilised in the courtroom. In so doing, they allow us to glimpse the traumatic realities associated with testifying as a complainant in rape trials. A concern for complainants is almost wholly absent from Hoyano's study. Other than affirming the vigilance of judges and counsel 'to avoid causing the complainant *any unnecessary distress*' (our emphasis), Hoyano remains laser-focused on defendants' fair trial rights (2018: 9).

The same view emerges from participant responses, the majority taking the view that section 41 is 'working in the interests of justice' and that in so far as it is not, it is because its alleged strictness prevents defendants from adducing relevant evidence (Hoyano, 2018: 46–9). Much weight is placed by respondents on the 'safety valve' provided by *R v A (No 2)*, and there is support too for returning some measure of discretion to judges outside the scope of prescribed gateways (Hoyano, 2018: 47). Only one respondent reports experience of judges taking too relaxed a view to the legislative provisions (Hoyano, 2018: 75), allowing Hoyano to conclude that a broad consensus exists across the Criminal Bar as to the appropriateness of some limitations on the introduction of sexual history evidence, and that, subject perhaps to some tweaks and amendments, the section 41 framework is working well.

Conclusion

And there we have it. At best, the contemporary picture remains patchy, evidencing a clear need for more extensive, up-to-date data on the use of sexual history evidence in England and Wales. At worst, we confront a minefield of unresolved disagreement about the problem to be solved, the interests at stake and the underlying principles of justice that are, or ought to be, engaged in thinking and talking about this issue. Our analysis of the field has also highlighted the many difficulties associated with researching the use of sexual history evidence in trial settings. Researchers must confront: the range and relative effectiveness of different methods; practical and ethical difficulties accessing research subjects and fora; the sheer costs of gaining a comprehensive picture of how sexual history evidence features in criminal justice processes; and the need to manage and contextualise the diverging views and experiences of differently situated stakeholders.

What perhaps we can say, based on the evidence available, and taken in conjunction with studies carried out in other countries, is that there is little to warrant the full confidence of the legal establishment that the problem of the misuse of sexual history evidence has been largely resolved and enough to suggest that the mischief rape-shield legislation is designed to address remains at large. Moreover, when we take into account the insights which have emerged from jury simulation studies about how, in the context of jury deliberations, evidence relating to the complainant's sexual history interacts with culturally circulating, deeply gendered, socio-sexual scripts about responsibility and blame in sexual encounters, there continue to be real grounds for concern that sexual history evidence is working against rather than for the interests of justice, conceived broadly to include not just the right of the accused to a fair trial but the legitimate expectation of all citizens that the state will take effective steps to prevent sexual violence.

This then prompts another question. How do we account for the confidence in the current system displayed by judges and barristers? More broadly, how do we bring into serious conversation the apparently opposing concerns of sexual violence activists on the one hand and core legal professionals on the other? This is the point where we need to dig deeper, to probe and interrogate the continued attachment of the law of evidence to the use of sexual history evidence. It is time to confront the holy grail of relevance.

6

The Relevance of Sexual History Evidence

Introduction: the 'logic' of relevance

How do we *know* when a complainant's sexual history is relevant to the question of whether she was raped? The legal consensus is to view this is as a matter of logic and common sense. These are the concepts to which judges appeal when assessing claims of evidentiary relevance. They also surface repeatedly in legislative and policy debate. Logic and common sense are seen here as pathways to objectivity and truth. We *know* sexual history evidence is relevant when it helps to establish, objectively, what has occurred; when it has a *material bearing* upon the truth or falsity of what is alleged.

How though do we know that the evidence bears truthfully upon the facts? What intellectual processes prompt us to connect one factual claim, for example that the complainant consented to sex with the defendant on a previous occasion, with another, that is, that the complainant consented to sex with the defendant on the occasion forming the subject matter of the charge? This is precisely what the concept of relevance enables us to do, to connect disparate facts so that one has probative potency in relation to another. In his classic textbook, *Law of Evidence*, Ian Dennis (2020) breaks down the moves entailed in establishing relevance to reveal their logical base. At the heart of most relevance claims, he explains, is a form of deductive reasoning, whereby the truth of a proposition depends on applying a major premise ('all men are mortal'), to a minor premise ('Socrates is a man') to deduce a conclusion ('Socrates is mortal'). The minor premise and the conclusion are the 'facts' to be connected; the major premise provides the basis for connecting them. Determinations of relevance, Dennis explains, generally take this syllogistic form (2020: 3–003).

Of critical importance here is the role played by the major premise. Without the major premise, the minor premise and the conclusion are simply random, unconnected facts. From where do we get the major premise, and how do we know it is sound? This is where 'common sense' comes into play. The major premise is drawn from general experience, it is part of 'our common stock of knowledge about the world' (Dennis, 2020: 3–002). Behind determinations of relevance then are generalised assertions, the soundness of which depend on the extent to which they are seen to correspond correctly with the way things are. As Dennis points out, 'the background generalisations about the world' underpinning determinations of relevance are only 'authoritative to the extent that their truth is generally accepted' (2020: 3–002): we know the major premise is true because it is generally accepted as such, and, where it is not, and notwithstanding the correct application of deductive reasoning techniques, the conclusion it yields will be false.

Turning then to sexual history evidence, the process of connecting a complainant's prior sexual behaviour to present events will likely be predicated upon some generalisation about sexual behaviour widely accepted to be true. This is where the waters of logic become murky, generalisations about sexual behaviour, especially female sexual behaviour, being all too contestable. They are also likely to be historically contingent and contextually bound, drawing weight and authority from the norms and conventions that govern sexual relations at a particular place and time. Granted, there is also a logic involved in the process of generalising. It is a form of inductive reasoning, involving the collation and analysis of a body of data to reach some general conclusion or hypothesis. Lawyers are familiar with inductive reasoning as a common technique of doctrinal analysis. Legal scholars try to make sense of seemingly disparate judicial decisions by identifying a common thread or principle to bind cases together and render them coherent, as for example the neighbour principle (arguably) does for negligence. Inductive reasoning is also applicable to questions of fact, enabling us to observe and analyse common patterns in human behaviour and social interaction. These provide a basis for planning and decision-making and, sometimes, for ascribing responsibility. However, the soundness of any generalisation is only as good as the data on which it is predicated. If the data are flawed, skewed or in some way unrepresentative of the pool from which they are drawn, they will produce imperfect results.

This account of how knowledge of the world is formed and validated is familiar to us. It is located within an epistemological frame which presupposes that knowledge comprises representations of a reality external to us, and that valid knowledge – what we recognise as truth – is what most accurately represents that reality. There are conflicting accounts of how to test what passes for knowledge to ensure it corresponds correctly with the real. For Descartes (2005), true knowledge is acquired by deploying the faculties of the mind in abstract methodical fashion, applying a distinct set of reasoning techniques to the apprehension of natural and scientific phenomena. For

Locke (1998) and Hume (2008), knowledge is produced by experience, our sensory perceptions of the world yielding representations which, in turn, generate data from which empirically grounded conclusions may be drawn. Both accounts of knowledge presuppose the separation of reality from its representations (what epistemologists call 'representationalism'), and, more importantly, both accounts place the individual's apprehension of the external world at the heart of knowledge generation and validation (what is sometimes described as 'epistemological individualism'). Thus conceived, knowledge is the product of a knower's efforts to represent an objectively constituted world, an approach which stresses the need to isolate the knower from the context(s) in which knowledge is acquired so that the faculties of the mind can operate without interference. Hence Descartes (2005) placed great emphasis on the need to strip the mind of external influences so that reason could do its work. To access and adequately represent an objectively constituted world requires the adoption of a perspective which transcends the particularity of our subjective experience.

This depiction of knowledge acquisition and validation in terms of an individual subject who casts his isolated gaze on an objectively constituted world with a view to representing it exactly is philosophically crude but nevertheless broadly reflective of culturally prevalent understandings of knowledge. The rational subject strives to be objective, to pursue truth through the application of a detached dispassionate stance, harnessing recognised reasoning techniques – such as logic – to reach sound conclusions. In scientific enquiry, this approach is confidently believed to yield knowledge that is close to perfectly representative of the natural world. When it comes to human relations, however, scientific standards of objectivity are more difficult to attain, the social and subjective dimensions of human interrelations sometimes impeding the application of a wholly dispassionate stance. Hence the invocation of general acceptance to justify knowledge claims about social interactions in an evidentiary context. Our 'common stock of knowledge about the world' may not measure up to scientific standards of objectivity but, in so far as it reflects the agreement of a community of individuals, all of whom have reached the same conclusion through independent processes of thought and reflection, it is considered sufficient to ground claims of factual relevance.

This then is what we mean by 'common sense' and why it is thought to provide a foundation for applying generalised assumptions or beliefs to decision-making or dispute-resolution. Such assumptions or beliefs derive their justification from the fact that they are – or are said to be – commonly shared by a community. Moreover, it is not just that they are commonly shared, but that, *because* they are shared, they are likely accurately to represent the reality of matters – including, in the context of the rape trial, the 'reality' of how women behave in sexual situations.

The logic of the twin myths

To illustrate this point, consider, for a moment, two assumptions with a long operational history in rape trials, namely that unchaste women are more likely to consent to sex and are less worthy of belief. These 'twin myths' about women's sexual experience have frequently founded claims of evidentiary relevance, notwithstanding that, as Chapter 3 reveals, they were only ever partially inscribed into the formal doctrinal framework. Of their wide acceptance until recently in legal commentary, culture and practice, there can be little doubt, senior judges repeatedly acknowledging their pernicious influence on decision-making in rape cases historically.[1]

What logical processes underlie the historical invocation of these now discredited generalisations? Syllogistically speaking, the assumption that 'women who have consented to sex in the past are more likely to consent again in the future' is the major premise, an assertion of propensity based on a generalisation about women's sexual behaviour derived from our common stock of knowledge of the world. According to Liat Levanon, this assumption about women's sexual behaviour is a particular instance of a general 'assumption of repetition' – what she describes as 'the (scientifically valid)[2] assumption that human beings tend to repeat courses of conduct' (Levanon, 2012: 612). The assumption of repetition functions in the rape trial to connect the fact of a complainant's prior sexual behaviour with the facts under scrutiny. The nature of this connection is rarely presented as fully probative: the fact that the complainant has had prior sexual experience does not *prove* she consented to sex with the defendant. However, it does – the argument goes – increase the probability that she consented, because it shows a past propensity to consent to sex. This raised level of probability connects the two facts to one another in a relationship of relevance (Roberts and Zuckerman, 2010: 101).

As we have noted, nowadays, people are disinclined to accept the assumption that unchaste women are more likely to consent to sex, the scientific validity of the assumption of repetition notwithstanding.[3] 'The fact that a woman has had intercourse on other occasions', McLachlin J declares, 'does not in itself increase the logical probability that she consented to intercourse with the accused.'[4] Simply put, the underlying generalisation

---

[1]   See, for example, *Seaboyer* [1993] 1 LRC 464, 474 per McLachlin J and *R v A (No 2)* [2001] UKHL 25, [27] per L Steyn.

[2]   On scientific support for the assumption of repetition within the field of human psychology, see Levanon (2012: 626–8).

[3]   See Levanon's (2012) analysis of the limits of the assumption of repetition when applied to sexual history evidence and discussion later in this chapter.

[4]   *Seaboyer*, 474.

about the sexual propensities of unchaste women no longer commands general acceptance. The major premise has fallen away and can no longer found a claim of relevance.

The assumption that unchaste women are less credible than their virtuous sisters is now regarded as similarly suspect. Underpinning this assumption is/ was a belief that women with sexual experience are prone to tell untruths, especially about sexual matters. This is notwithstanding that, as McColgan observes, 'no evidence has ever been proffered in support [of the] notion that ... unchaste women are more likely to lie in relation to sexual offences, than are others' (1996: 281). In fact, as Roberts and Zuckerman remark, quite the opposite can be claimed, certainly where the complainant is in the business of selling sex:

> Over the years, some strange notions of relevance became embedded in the common law. For example, it was assumed that evidence of prostitution diminishes the credibility of a rape complainant and increases the probability that the intercourse was consensual, when on a dispassionate appraisal, one might expect prostitutes to be the last people to make false allegations of rape, since sending customers to gaol can hardly be good for business. (2010: 443)[5]

Historically, as we have seen, general evidence of a complainant's sexual reputation *was* believed by the courts to bear upon a witness's credibility. The close association of sexual and moral virtue in culturally dominant ideals of femininity enabled a connection to be made between lack of chastity and bad character, thereby bearing directly on the issue of a witness's credibility.[6] As norms of sexual behaviour have changed, the association of unchastity with immorality has weakened, almost to the point of non-existence: most people today would *not* regard lack of chastity as de facto evidence of bad character. Thus, the fact that a complainant has a sexual past should no longer suffice to support a claim of relevance relating to her credibility. This does not mean that such evidence, if introduced, does not influence how a complainant is perceived, particularly by jurors. As we saw in Chapter 5, notwithstanding the absence of any logical link between chastity and veracity, evidence of a complainant's prior sexual history continues to shape juror perceptions of complainants' moral standing. We return to the mechanisms which enable this dissonance later in the chapter.

---

[5]   There is some empirical support for this argument – see for example Flowe et al (2007) (psychological study showing that women with extensive sexual history are less likely to report rape or to make a false allegation of sexual assault).

[6]   See *R v Riley* (1887) QBD 481 discussed in Chapter 3.

Law, power and epistemology

The preceding discussion shows that the beliefs encapsulated in the twin myths no longer enjoy general acceptance. Therefore, they cannot serve as major premises for purposes of syllogistic reasoning. Indeed, it is precisely because their fallibility has been exposed – the sexist underpinnings and outmoded moralistic attitudes the twin myths encapsulate – that public policy attitudes to sexual history evidence have altered, leading multiple jurisdictions to restrict its use.

The historical operation of the twin myths, and their periodic recrudescence notwithstanding persistent legislative efforts to repress their use, nevertheless beg several questions: How did such now discredited generalisations gain sufficient acceptance to qualify as 'common sense' knowledge in the first place? Why did their questionable foundations escape the attention of judges and legal scholars for so long? Can we be confident that such assumptions and beliefs no longer operate to support claims of relevance in the rape trial? If they do not, what assumptions and beliefs *do* currently support claims of relevance?

To answer these questions, we need first to revisit the epistemological underpinnings of evidentiary claims of relevance. Let us suppose for a moment that the key premises underpinning the dominant epistemological model outlined earlier are open to question: *Is* knowledge best understood in terms of a strict demarcation of reality from representation which the individual knower strives to bridge through the application of internal cognitive processes in isolation from the broader context? The advent of postmodern sensibilities, and the accompanying rejection of key premises of the modernist/Enlightenment project, including epistemological premises, has thrown long-held assumptions about knowledge acquisition and validation into doubt. In place of the belief that reality exists independently of the knower, with subjects on one side and objects on the other side of the representation/reality divide, a view has emerged within epistemological thought which posits the relation between reality and representation differently. One aspect of what is sometimes described as 'social epistemology' is to regard the real as, at least in part, constituted by our representations. More importantly, our representations do not derive solely from within; they are not the outcome of the application of internal cognitive processes by isolated selves but are socially produced and mediated.

To grasp a conception of knowledge as social, we must move away from the idea of knowledge acquisition as a process of representation and instead view it as an interaction: knowledge comes from interacting with our environment rather than simply representing it. It is socially instituted practices, including language, which give shape, meaning and *value* to what and how we know (Hekman, 1990). We know, for example, that if someone offers to shake our hand, this is a mark of civility, a gesture of respect which we are expected to reciprocate. Outside the social network of norms, practices and meanings which frame this performance, however, we cannot apprehend the act other than in terms of the bare materiality of an extended limb. In the same way, our apprehension and assessment of sexual encounters is bound up with social and cultural expectations that give these encounters meaning and significance. Philosopher and rape survivor Susan Brison (2002) explains how, even as she was being raped, she sought to make sense of what was happening by drawing upon prefabricated cultural tropes and narratives of sexual violence. Her access to the reality of her rape, her sensory and emotional perception of what was occurring, comprised more than just the corporeal responses provoked by violent physical assault, but was significantly mediated by her internal efforts to classify the event linguistically and align that classification with its cultural meanings. In this way, the materiality of the act was rendered intelligible to her, both at its occurrence and in her later traumatic reflections.

If we accept that knowledge is to some degree socially constituted, then the social location of the knower assumes significance. To the extent that social practices are implicated in processes of knowledge formation, *social location* – understood in terms of roles, relations, identities and the social stratifications they produce – *matters epistemically*. Social location renders knowledge partial and contingent, comprising diverse perspectives which reflect knowers' different viewpoints. Significantly, some of these viewpoints tend to be better heard and affirmed than others. This is the point where the relation between knowledge and power becomes visible. Power confers authority, and with authority comes privilege, both political and epistemic. Notwithstanding a multiplicity of experiences of, and perspectives on, our social world, it is the experiences and perspectives of the powerful that are most likely to be heard and accepted as true or objectively real. This insight is at the heart of standpoint theories of knowledge which assert that unequal social relations – whether based on gender, race, class and/or other structures of social ordering – produce differing standpoints or angles of vision on the world, with the standpoint of the dominant group(s) assuming the status of universal truth (Harding, 2003). At the heart of standpoint theory, in its many variations, is recognition that what counts as (valid) knowledge is invariably mediated by relations of power.

The troubling effects of inequality on knowledge generation and validation are no less present in law than in other social institutions and go some way to explain why assumptions and beliefs which now seem plainly wrong held sway for so long in legal discourse and decision-making. In

1989, Carol Smart drew attention to the power of law to 'confer' truth, effectively to authorise what passes for knowledge of human experience and to 'disqualify' non-authoritative representations, including the lived experiences of women and/or racial minorities. More recently, Ngaire Naffine has proffered an eviscerating analysis of 'the man problem' in criminal law, arguing that the views of 'men of legal influence' – views which she shows to be saturated in sexism and misogyny – have become so thoroughly embedded in the conceptual and normative infrastructure of criminal law as to be difficult to displace (Naffine, 2019: 185). Her critique is a compelling exposé of the extent to which certain angles of vision become vested in the form and substance of legal doctrine, as well as of the way in which doctrinal norms and conventions are instrumentalised in the maintenance of such vesting. Her analysis cautions us not just to be suspicious of what has passed for legal knowledge in the past, but to continue to interrogate the bases upon which knowledge claims in law are made. This is especially so in contexts where social inequalities are likely to influence perceptions and assessments of social situations, as is undoubtedly the case when it comes to sexual matters.

Accepting that knowledge is mediated by power entails recognising that knowledge claims, in authoritative discourses such as law, are likely to draw upon, reinforce and formally inscribe social relations of inequality, including gender-based relations. That law is a discourse of tradition, drawing much of its present authority from its conformity to a perceived legal past, places further limits on its capacity to escape the historical roots of its becoming (Conaghan, 2013: 227–8). We see this repeatedly as efforts to overcome the patriarchal legacy of law, expressed, for example, in the purposes and contents of rape-shield legislation, come up against a discursive logic deeply rooted in the legal substrata. Critical to this discursive logic is its claim to objectivity, to represent a principled and wholly unbiased stance upon the trial process which is simultaneously premised upon the primacy of defendants' fair trial rights. What though if the framework supporting this justice ideal is inextricably entangled with the congealed remnants of law's patriarchal past? How do we go about the process of disentanglement? In what follows, we begin to probe the discursive logic of the relevance framework, paying particular attention to the (often unarticulated) underpinning generalisations about male and female sexual behaviour that continue to inform the use of complainant sexual history evidence in the rape trial and the social location(s) from which they derive.

The relevance framework

First, though, we outline the procedural and normative framework which determines how sexual history evidence finds its way into trial terrain.

Types of evidence

When making a claim of relevance, the first question to be asked is: Relevant to what? As previously noted, relevant evidence is evidence which has a material bearing upon the truth or otherwise of a disputed issue of fact. The issue of fact must relate to a 'proper object of proof' (Dennis, 2020: 1–003), that is, to a fact that needs to be proved for the prosecution of the charge to succeed. This obviously includes the elements of the offence – in the case of rape, proving that sexual intercourse took place, that consent was absent and so on (what are known as 'facts in issue'). Objects of proof may also include facts which, while not facts in issue as such, provide means of proof thereof. These are known as 'evidentiary facts' and may include, for example, evidence of motive and opportunity as well as physical evidence – fingerprints, DNA and the like. A third category of potentially relevant evidence bears upon the credibility of witness testimony. As we have seen, this kind of evidence frequently surfaces in the rape trial. Evidence relating to witness credibility commonly falls within the category of 'collateral evidence', that is, evidence which does not relate directly to the facts in issue but is contingently relevant in that it affects the weight accorded to witness testimony *about* facts in issue (Dennis, 2020: 1–012). A distinct framework of rules governs the use of such evidence, including the 'collateral finality rule' according to which, during cross-examination, answers to collateral questions (of which credibility is archetypal) should be taken as final.[7] The effect of this rule is to prevent the introduction of rebuttal evidence on questions of credibility subject to well-established exceptions, including where evidence is led to establish a general reputation for untruthfulness. This of course is a hook upon which the use of sexual history evidence to challenge a complainant's credibility has often been hung.

The role of probability

Evidence is relevant when it has some bearing on the truth or falsity of a disputed fact. The 19th-century English jurist James Fitzjames Stephen observed that two facts stand in a relationship of relevance where 'according to the common course of events, one, either taken by itself or in conjunction with other facts, *proves or renders probable* the past, present or future existence or non-existence of the other' (Stephen, 1948: article 1, our emphasis). Relevance then does not depend on establishing the truth or falsity of a disputed fact as a matter of certainty. It is enough that the *likelihood* of its truth or falsity is affected by the factual linkage.

---

[7] For further discussion of the collateral finality rule and exceptions thereto, see Roberts and Zuckerman (2010: 351–8).

Is some minimum or necessary level of probability required to satisfy evidentiary claims of relevance? This is a difficult question to answer in the abstract. Thomason insists that relevance is a binary concept – 'It makes no logical sense to refer to evidence as being more or less relevant to a particular issue; evidence either is or is not relevant to an issue' (2018: 345). In so far as this is the case, relevance sets a low bar for evidentiary admission as even the slightest increase in probability satisfies the relevance test. Yet, factual claims may be more or less probable, depending on the strength or weight of the evidence advanced. If even the slightest increase in probability is sufficient, relevance provides a worryingly weak filter.

For this reason, the *extent* to which evidence has a bearing, that is, its weight or probative value, is also important in law.[8] To be admitted, evidence needs to be *sufficiently* relevant, the extent to which it renders probable the disputed fact being judged to outweigh the anticipated costs of considering it, including variously, the time and resources occasioned by its admission, whether it aids or impedes jury deliberations, and its persuasive versus prejudicial value (see generally Dennis, 2020: 3–008). Relevance as operationalised in legal processes is not a 'fixed point on a scale'[9] which can be precisely charted. The weight and probative value of evidence will vary and be context dependent. Sometimes, too, as, for example when rape-shield laws are in place, the bar for the admission of relevant evidence is set at a higher level than otherwise. In England and Wales, as we have seen, sexual history evidence may only be admitted where 'a refusal of leave might have the result of rendering unsafe a conclusion of the jury or (as the case may be) the court on any relevant issue in the case',[10] while in New Zealand sexual history evidence is not admissible unless a judge is satisfied 'that the evidence or question is of such direct relevance to facts in issue in the proceeding ... that it would be contrary to the interests of justice to exclude it'.[11]

How do we assess whether evidence renders a disputed fact 'more or less probable'? To answer this question entails engaging in a process of comparison: one compares the likelihood that the disputed fact is true (or false) *without* the introduction of the evidence with the likelihood that the disputed fact is true (or false) *with* the introduction of the evidence. In the case of sexual history evidence, one compares the likelihood that the disputed fact, say the fact of consent, is true without the introduction of evidence of

---

[8]   There is a longstanding debate among evidence scholars about whether logical relevance and probative value should be combined within a single conceptual frame, that is, 'legal relevance', or kept analytically distinct. For discussion, see Thomason (2018: 345–6).

[9]   *Vernon v Bosley* [1994] PIQR P337, per Hoffmann LJ.

[10]   YJCEA 1999, s 41(2)(b).

[11]   Evidence Act 2006, s 44(2) (NZ).

the complainant's sexual history with the likelihood that the disputed fact is true *if* the evidence is admitted.

Do the facts of the complainant's prior sexual history make it more probable that she consented to sex with the defendant? Traditionally, as we have seen, the courts have been inclined to accept that they do – to view the fact that a complainant has had prior sexual experience as making it more likely that she consented to sex on the occasion forming the subject matter of the charge. The application of the assumption of repetition produces the generalisation – women who have consented to sex in the past are more likely to consent to it in the future – providing the major premise which connects the fact of the prior sexual relationship with the disputed fact of (non)consent.

Note how probability plays a double role here. First, it features in the general premise supporting the claim to relevance: in general, women who have consented to sex in the past are more likely to consent to sex again in the future (we put to one side for the moment the fact that the soundness of the underlying premise is now in doubt). Second, this probability-based generalisation about patterns of (female) sexual behaviour serves as the foundation for the assertion that the complainant was more likely to consent to sex with the defendant. Another way of stating this is to say that the complainant belongs to a class of women who, by virtue of their propensity to consent to sex in the past, are more likely to have consented to sex in the present instance than the class of women in general.

The relevance of a complainant's sexual history to her credibility

Having outlined the framework within which legal claims of relevance are made, we return to the link between lack of chastity and credibility. In *Seaboyer*, McLachlin J declares: 'There is no logical or practical link between a woman's sexual reputation and whether she is a truthful witness.'[12] This is true even if relevance is pitched at the most minimal of levels. Lack of chastity is no longer generally accepted as evidencing a propensity to tell untruths, whether regarding sexual matters or otherwise. Why then does sexual history evidence continue to feature in attacks upon a rape complainant's credibility? Part of the problem here, as we saw in Chapter 5, is the lack of correspondence between law in the books and its real-life materialisations. However, even within the formal parameters of legal regulation, there is a legal reluctance wholly to sever the thread which has traditionally connected a complainant's sexual history with her capacity for truthfulness. This reluctance is often attributed to the

---

[12] *Seaboyer*, 479.

commonly expressed view that, when it comes to sexual offences, complainant credibility is more than a collateral concern. As Dennis remarks:

> The traditional common law distinction between cross-examination as to the issue and cross-examination on collateral matters such as a witness's credibility is extremely problematic in the context of sexual matters. Where the complainant's testimony provides the only substantial evidence against the accused, her credibility effectively becomes the issue. (Dennis, 2020: 15–005)

Similarly, in *R v A (No 2)*, Lord Clyde observes: 'Issues of consent and issues of credibility may well run so close to each other as almost to coincide. A very sharp knife may be required to separate what may be admitted from what may not.'[13]

The effect of this blurring of lines is to elevate complainant credibility to unique evidentiary status in the context of the rape trial, bolstered by the widely shared perception that because, in cases of rape, the evidence usually amounts to no more than 'one person's word against another's', the credibility stakes are especially high. In fact, as Saunders (2018) argues, it is rarely the case that the evidence in a rape case is limited to the competing narratives of the complainant and defendant. There may well be additional evidence supporting the complainant's version of events, for example CCTV or medical evidence or even the testimony of independent eyewitnesses. Framing rape cases within a 'he says/she says' narrative is problematic precisely because it diverts attention away from collecting and/or considering evidence which might corroborate the complainant's account, while placing undue weight on factors, such as the complainant's sexual history, which are perceived to undermine it.

More significantly, undergirding this exceptionalist approach to complainant credibility is the unstated but nevertheless operative assumption that, in sexual offences cases, the risk of false allegations is greater than in other kinds of offence. It is this which justifies the aggressively sceptical approach to rape complainant testimony often adopted by defence lawyers. One does not have to dig too deeply into the substrata of evidence law before excavating Hale's mantra: '[Rape] is an accusation easily to be made and hard to be proved, and harder to be defended by the party accused though never so innocent' (1800: 635). Factually speaking, of course, Hale's statement is untrue (and probably was at the time of its first utterance). Rape is *not* an easy accusation to make. Rape complainants must surmount significant legal and cultural hurdles to be heard and believed, while the odds of being convicted of rape are notoriously low. As an underlying premise to support claims of evidentiary relevance, Hale's pronouncement

---

[13]   [2001] UKHL 25 [138].

lacks the necessary factual foundation. Indeed, most people, if asked, would likely acknowledge this. Research by Gunby et al (2013) shows that, when questioned, research participants agreed that false rape allegations were likely to be rare. Yet, concern about false allegations frequently arose in group discussion of hypothetical scenarios (2013: 95–7).

This dissonance between the practical reality and legal representation of rape complaints is a perfect example of how certain standpoints become embedded in the normative infrastructure of law, the particularity of their angle of vision cloaked in a mantle of truth or common sense. It also goes some way towards explaining the capricious stance law adopts regarding how sexual history evidence bears upon a complainant's credibility. Section 41(4) YJCEA 1999 states that 'no evidence or question shall be regarded as relating to a relevant issue in the case if … the purpose (or main purpose) for which it would be adduced or asked is to establish or elicit material for impugning the credibility of the complainant as a witness'.[14] On its face, section 41(4) is broad in scope, leaving little room for defence counsel to deploy sexual history evidence to challenge a complainant's credibility. This aligns with a legislative concern to decommission the second of the twin myths. In contrast, the stance of the courts has been to look for ways to limit the reach of section 41(4). One approach, already discussed, has been to probe the porosity of the boundary between credibility and consent, effectively to reconceive the evidentiary issue as consent rather than credibility.[15] Another strategy is to reconfigure the 'purpose' of the evidence so that it is not caught by the reference to 'purpose (or main purpose)' in the relevant legislative provision. This stratagem enabled the Court of Appeal in *R v Martin*[16] to hold that evidence that the complainant had made prior sexual overtures towards the defendant (which he had rejected) bore directly on the issue of her motive to fabricate a complaint.[17] As Dennis (2020: 15–012) observes, it is difficult to see how this is not evidence, the purpose of which is to impugn the credibility of the complainant. Yet the Court of Appeal determined 'that, on ordinary principles of interpretation, it was one purpose but not "the purpose" or "the main purpose" of the questions to impugn the credibility of the complainant'.[18] As an interpretative stance, this is unconvincing to say the least. Perhaps perceiving this, the *Martin* court also speculated – drawing

---

[14] Note that s 41(4) only applies to the gateways listed in section 41(3) and does not cover rebuttal evidence introduced under s 41(5) which, from an evidentiary perspective, makes sense given the purpose of rebuttal questioning.
[15] This approach was taken by the English courts to contain the effects of earlier restrictions in SO(A)A 1976, s 2. See discussion in Chapter 3 and Temkin (1993).
[16] [2004] EWCA Crim 916.
[17] Thus, falling within YJCEA 1999, s 41(3)(a): 'not an issue of consent'.
[18] *Martin*, [37].

on *R v A (No 2)*[19] – that the wording of section 41(4) be read in accordance with the defendant's right to a fair trial. The effect of the proposed reading would be to disallow sexual history evidence attacking the credibility of the complainant 'as a witness' (whatever that might mean), but to allow it in so far as it bore upon her credibility in relation to a fact in issue.[20] Dennis (somewhat faint-heartedly) commends this approach as 'a pragmatic device to ensure that the accused has a fair opportunity to present his defence' (2020: 15–012).

The approach of the *Martin* court to the facts of the case is of broader interest to us here. In evaluating the potential probity of the evidence, the Court of Appeal placed considerable weight on the fact that, according to the defendant's account – with which the complainant's substantially diverged – his rejection of her advances occurred immediately after she had performed oral sex on him. The Court felt the timing was particularly significant because rejection in such circumstances, they opined, would be more hurtful than rejection in non-intimate circumstances.[21]

What standpoint and assumptions underpin the Court's conclusions as to the significance of the alleged sexual rejection? One could perhaps agree that, assuming the truth of the defendant's account (which was very much in doubt), the 'fact' of rejection in the immediate aftermath of intimacy might indeed be more hurtful than in non-intimate circumstances. How though do we get from there to the assumption that rejection in such circumstances increases the probability that the hurt party would choose to fabricate a complaint of rape? The leap made is from hurt to malice, the underlying assumption being that sexual rejection commonly triggers malicious intent. Does it though? If a man is sexually rejected by a woman at or after a critical point of intimacy, would we think him more likely to make a false allegation of sexual assault? Or is this a reaction we are more inclined to attribute to women? How likely is it that anybody responds to sexual rejection by falsely reporting they were raped?

Therein lies the myth, painfully exposed: it is the stereotype of the vengeful woman, thwarted in love, that underpins the *Martin* court's decision, a stereotype powered by highly gendered perceptions of sexual behaviour. We have a major premise, that is, that women who suffer sexual rejection are (more) likely to seek revenge from the men who have spurned them by making a false allegation of sexual impropriety. This connects the minor premise (the 'fact' that the complainant was sexually rejected

---

[19]   [2001] UKHL 25.
[20]   The reasoning on this point is poorly expressed in the *Martin* judgment (at [38]) but see discussion in Dennis (2020: 15–012).
[21]   *Martin*, [35].

by the defendant) with the conclusion (the 'fact' that she sought revenge by manufacturing a false allegation). Even if we were to concede that, at the most minimal level of logical relevance, a woman who has suffered sexual rejection is more likely to fabricate a rape complaint than women in general, the 'truth' of the major premise depends on the most speculative of assumptions, shot through with a good dose of old-fashioned misogyny. Thus, any increased level of probability, bearing in mind that this is a generalisation wholly unsupported by reliable data, is likely to be modest at best. It is difficult to see how anyone could confidently assert that such evidence is 'substantially probative' of a motive to fabricate (Thomason, 2018: 346).[22]

Yet another way in which the courts have bypassed the seemingly wide scope of section 41(4) YJCEA 1999 has been to reclassify the evidence as other than 'sexual', placing it outside the protection of section 41 altogether. This approach has been adopted by the English courts in relation to evidence that the complainant has previously made a false rape allegation.[23] To understand how a prior rape allegation can affect the course of a later trial of a wholly unrelated sexual offence, we must consider how the provisions of YJCEA 1999 section 41 interact with the general legal framework governing the introduction of 'bad character' evidence. Since 2003, new legislative restrictions have been in operation in England and Wales to limit the introduction of evidence of a witness's bad character unless such evidence meets prescribed tests of relevance and probative value.[24] The legal trend towards tightening the rules governing attacks on the moral credibility of witnesses is general and reflects a policy concern to ensure that witnesses are not unduly deterred from testifying in criminal trials. The use of complainant sexual history evidence falls within and without this general trend. On the one hand, as we have seen, section 41(4) YJCEA 1999 precludes the introduction of any evidence of a complainant's sexual behaviour if it is reasonable to assume that its purpose (or main purpose) is to impugn the credibility of the complainant. On the other hand, evidence of a complainant's bad character, which while touching upon sexual matters is deemed to fall outside the scope of 'sexual behaviour' for purposes of section 41 protection, may be introduced if it satisfies the requirements of section 100 CJA 2003.

---

[22] Interestingly, and notwithstanding a finding that the evidence should have been admitted, the Court of Appeal in *Martin* declined to overturn the conviction on the grounds that the exclusion of the evidence did not render the conviction unsafe ([40–4]).

[23] See *R v T, R v H* [2001] EWCA Crim 1877.

[24] CJA 2003, s 100 requires that evidence of a witness's bad character can only be admitted if it has important explanatory value or has substantive probative value in relation to a fact in issue which is of substantial importance in the context of the case.

According to the courts, evidence that a complainant previously made a false allegation of sexual assault falls into this category.[25] Such evidence is considered relevant because it suggests a propensity to lie about sexual attacks, therefore increasing the probability that the complainant is lying. How does a court know that a complaint is false, particularly bearing in mind that many genuine rape complaints do not proceed because of well-documented failings in the criminal justice system? To guard against the risk that defence counsel might deploy the fact of a prior allegation to bypass the restrictions of YJCEA 1999, the Court of Appeal in *R v T*[26] ruled that evidence of a prior sexual assault allegation should only fall outside the scope of section 41 if the defence can provide a proper evidential base for asserting its falsity. Unfortunately, as Dennis notes, the courts are in some confusion as to what *counts* as a proper evidential basis, a considerable case law accumulating on the issue.[27] In *R v AM*,[28] the defendant sought to introduce evidence that, some years prior to the issue forming the subject matter of the charge, the complainant made an untrue rape allegation. The Court of Appeal overturned the trial judge's decision not to admit the evidence, holding that so long as the defendant could point to 'some material from which it could properly be concluded [by the jury] that the complaint was false', the evidence ought to have been admitted. This was so even if the factual foundation for the claim was 'less than strong'.[29] In considering the material from which an inference of falsity might be drawn, the Court considered, among other factors, the complainant's delay in reporting the earlier rape and the fact that she later declined to follow through on the complaint and urged the police not to pursue it. By contrast, in *Davarifar*,[30] the Court rejected the defendant's appeal against his rape conviction based on a failure to introduce evidence at trial of a prior sexual assault allegation which the complainant had made while she was a child in foster care.

An interesting feature of both these cases is the way in which the trial segues into a rehearsal of the weight and substance of prior sexual assault allegations made by the complainant, placing the legal focus at a spatial and

---

[25] Interestingly, Hoyano (2018) criticises what she perceives to be a confusing overlap between the YJCEA s 41 and CJA s 100, observing a growing tendency for defence counsel to apply under both provisions where any evidence of a sexual nature is involved (2018: para 114).

[26] [2001] EWCA Crim 1877: 'It would be professionally improper for those representing the defendant to put such questions in order to elicit evidence about the complainant's past sexual behaviour … such under the guise of previous false complaints' [41].

[27] See generally Dennis (2020: 15.012).

[28] [2009] EWCA Crim 818.

[29] *AM*, [22].

[30] [2009] EWCA Crim 2094.

temporal distance from the defendant's conduct and behaviour. Also striking is the Court's reliance on factors such as delayed reporting to evaluate the likelihood that a prior allegation was false. This is notwithstanding wide acknowledgement among criminal justice agencies that delayed reporting is not remotely indicative of the falsity of a complaint; indeed, such a belief is commonly cast in the legal and policy literature as a rape myth.[31]

These difficulties are recognised by some judges. In *R v Campbell*,[32] in which the defence drew upon delays in reporting, as well as the fact that the complainant was a Class A drug abuser, to bolster their claim that the complainant had previously made false allegations of sexual assault, the trial judge produced a carefully crafted judgment, taking proper account of section 41 YJCEA 1999 and section 100 CJA 2003, to reject an application to admit the evidence. Her decision was later affirmed by the Court of Appeal. The reference to the complainant's drug use[33] highlights another problem to which the focus on complainant character can give rise. On the one hand, serious drug abuse may contribute to inconsistencies in a complainant's account of her assault and the surrounding circumstances. On the other hand, serious drug users are likely more vulnerable to sexual assault, in which context a history of previously unresolved sexual assault allegations may be indicative not of a complainant's tendency to lie about sexual assault but of a pattern of failure on the part of key criminal justice actors to respond to sexual assault reports made by vulnerable complainants.

To be fair, the overall weight of this body of case law does lean in the direction of acknowledging the institutional difficulties that complainants face when making allegations of sexual assault. As Dennis concludes: '[I]t does ... seem to be clear that [when seeking to introduce evidence that a previous complaint was false] it is not enough ... to show that a complaint was raised but not pursued by the complainant, or that the police or the CPS decided not to prosecute' (2020: 15–012). At the same time, the very fact that a rape complainant may find herself required to answer questions about a previously unresolved, entirely independent rape allegation is troubling, and indeed adds to the many reasons why complainants might hesitate before reporting a sexual assault in the first place. Nor can we be sure, outside the formal contours of appellate rulings, what is happening on the ground. In *AM*, the Court of Appeal emphasised that decisions about admitting evidence of previous, allegedly false rape allegations were necessarily fact-sensitive,

---

[31] See, for example, CPS guidance on rape and sexual offences, available at Rape and Sexual Offences – Annex A: Tackling Rape Myths and Stereotypes | The Crown Prosecution Service (cps.gov.uk), available at https://www.cps.gov.uk/legal-guidance/rape-and-sexual-offences-annex-tackling-rape-myths-and-stereotypes [Accessed 14 December 2022].
[32] [2016] EWCA Crim 597.
[33] See also *R v All-Hilly* [2014] EWCA Crim 1614.

dependent on a full and thorough evaluation of the evidence by the trial judge.[34] A lot thus turns on the stance adopted by individual judges and the extent to which they are willing to recognise and give due weight to the legitimate concerns of rape complainants.

The relevance of a complainant's sexual history to consent

Playing the odds

We saw in Chapter 3 that, for purposes of establishing consent, specific evidence of a complainant's sexual activities with persons other than the defendant was not allowed at common law for a host of reasons, including the remoteness of such evidence, the administrative strain its introduction placed on the justice system, and unfairness to the complainant. On the other hand, evidence that the complainant had prior sexual relations with the defendant *was* permitted, indeed was often judged to be directly relevant to the question of consent.

The practical realities of the rape trial departed from this formal legal position. The picture presented by late 20th-century studies of trial proceedings in English courts was of aggressive and intrusive questioning about all aspects of a complainant's sex life by defence counsel, with little effort made by judges to moderate or restrict abusive practices (Adler, 1987; Lees, 1996). Undermining a complainant's moral credibility remained a critical defence strategy (Temkin, 2000) but of equal importance were efforts to harness the details of a complainant's sexual past, whether with the defendant or third parties, to the issue of her consent to sex with the defendant. At its crudest, this strategy involved the application of the first of the twin myths, namely that women who had previously consented to sex were more likely to do so again. In the 1969 case of *R v Bashir*,[35] the Court held that evidence that the complainant was a prostitute went directly to consent, allowing defence counsel to bypass the collateral finality rule which was concerned with issues of credit. In *R v Krausz*, the Court of Appeal went further, holding that evidence of a specific sexual encounter between the complainant and a third party was relevant to consent and should have been admitted at trial.[36] By showing that the complainant was 'a woman ... in the habit of submitting her body to different men without discrimination, whether for pay or not', the Court reasoned, the evidence lent support to the defendant's account that the

---

146

sex in question had been consensual, followed by a request for payment by the complainant.[37]

The introduction of rape-shield protections in England and Wales, first in 1976 and then in 1999, has done surprisingly little to limit the ability to deploy complainant sexual history to evidence consent. Indeed, in relation to sexual behaviour with third parties, the current legal regime is arguably more permissive than its common law predecessor. Although formally evidence going to consent must pass through one of the legislative gateways as well as meet prescribed requirements of probity and specificity, judicial interpretation of the gateways alongside the ECHR 'gloss' conferred by *R v A (No 2)*[38] has produced a legal regime in which arguments relating a complainant's sexual past with the question of her present consent can still be made.

Let us track the precise moves which allow a court, logically and legally, to conclude that a complainant's sexual history bears upon the question of her consent to sex with the defendant. To apply a standard argument of propensity, one must first place the complainant in the class of women with prior sexual experience. This class is then compared to the larger class comprising the general population of women. The assumption of repetition is then invoked to enable the conclusion that women in the first class are more likely to have consented to sex on the occasion in question than women in the second class.[39]

A particular difficulty with this comparison is that in the context of contemporary sexual norms, most women are likely to belong in the class of women with sexual experience, making comparisons with the general population somewhat otiose.[40] Indeed, the practical implication of the claim that sexually active women are more likely to consent to sex would be to support a claim of relevance regarding sexual history evidence in most rape cases. The class to which sexually active complainants belong, McColgan

---

[37] *Krausz*, 474–5. The Court of Appeal decision to overturn Krausz's conviction was notwithstanding substantial evidence of physical injury to the complainant as well as corroborating testimony from several witnesses.

[38] [2001] UKHL 25.

[39] To put it precisely, the proportion of women in the first class more likely to consent to sex is said to be greater than the proportion of women in the second class.

[40] In the late eighteenth century, when legal norms governing the regulation of sexual history evidence began to emerge, the proportion of women with sexual experience compared to the general female population may well have been much smaller. This highlights a temporal lag at the heart of contemporary claims of relevance. As Heilbron (1976) observes: 'There exists, in our view, a gap between the assumptions underlying the law and those public views and attitudes which exist today which ought to influence today's law' (para 131).

argues, is simply too large to allow any sensible inference to be drawn (1996: 285–6).

Redmayne (2003: 78) questions McColgan's position. While acknowledging that the probability margin produced by such a comparison is likely to be slender, this does not make the evidence *logically* irrelevant: even the slightest increase in probability is sufficient to establish relevance.[41] At the same time, Redmayne agrees that the minimal probative value of such a marginal increase in probability militates against its admission, even without the application of the probative value test in section 41(2)(b) YJCEA 1999 (which precludes the admission of sexual history evidence unless its exclusion might have the result of rendering unsafe a conclusion of the jury on any relevant issue in the case). Such an argument, without more, would not meet either of the prescribed gateways in sections 41(3)(b) and (c) in any event.

Interestingly, Redmayne posits the proposition that a complainant's sexual history might in fact be contra-indicative of consent. The more sexually active women are, he reasons, the greater the risk they will be exposed to a situation where they are vulnerable to sexual assault. In other words, the fact of their greater sexual experience places them in a class of women more likely to encounter sexual abuse than women in general (2003: 82–3). Starting with a different underlying premise enables Redmayne to connect the 'fact' of a complainant's prior sexual history to the 'fact' that she was raped, producing a logically defensible conclusion.

One could take Redmayne's argument further. Applying it directly to a complainant's past sexual experience with the defendant, one could speculate that evidence of a prior sexual relationship between the complainant and defendant is *particularly* counter-indicative of consent because, statistically, the majority of sexual offences take place between partners or ex-partners. Assume the following major premise: Women are more likely to be raped by a partner than by a stranger. State the minor premise: The complainant claims she has been raped by her partner. This places her in a class of women more likely to have been raped than the general population. Syllogistically speaking, we can conclude that the complainant was probably raped.

This discussion is troubling as it shows that while probability is clearly central to claims of evidentiary relevance, it is a far from reliable tool when it comes to determining the truth of past events. Much depends on the choice and soundness of the underlying assumption as well as the selection of classes for comparison. Moreover, the generalisations which launch the deductive process may derive from social locations inflected by gendered inequalities of power. A perspective which connects a woman's prior sexual behaviour

---

[41] Redmayne (2003), like Thomason (2018), uses a binary rather than scalar concept of relevance.

with the likelihood that she consented to sex and then denied it is very different, for example, from a perspective which links a woman's prior sexual behaviour to an increased risk of sexual harm in a gender-unequal society.

Situational specificity

We have seen that, in making probability calculations, there is room for divergence in the choice of who or what is compared. Likewise, the scope for prejudice and statistical inaccuracy to influence the production of the generalisations forming the basis of probability calculations about social behaviour is considerable, albeit obscured by the apparent application of mathematical processes. The more complex the factual scenario, the more strained and contingent the probability claims which may be made. This, of course, is a key difficulty with invoking general assertions of propensity regarding female sexual behaviour. Even if we accept, at an abstract level, that people are more likely to repeat courses of conduct, the evidentiary significance of this general premise to specific factual scenarios is another matter entirely.

Indeed, real difficulties arise when we seek to apply abstract propositions, particularly of a sexual nature, to specific social interactions. Let's concede for a moment that the assumption of repetition allows us to attribute to a complainant a propensity to engage in sex based on her past sexual behaviour. A propensity to engage in sex, like a propensity to drink tea, does not help to determine whether, when and with whom one chooses to have sex (or drink tea), bearing in mind that a partiality for sex or tea is realised in the moment and is dependent on a range of factors which help to produce the precise conditions for indulging one's partiality. Recognising this is of critical significance if we accept, as most criminal justice actors claim to do, that the purpose of rape law is to protect the sexual autonomy of individuals – to give meaningful effect to the right to choose when, where and with whom to have sexual relations. As Lady Hale famously remarked: 'It is difficult to think of an activity which is more person and situation specific than sexual relations. *One does not consent to sex in general.* One consents to this act of sex with this person at this time and in this place' (our emphasis).[42]

In fact, historically, the law *did* recognise the idea of consent to sex in general. This is what provided the basis for the marital rape exemption, which, until relatively recently, precluded the prosecution of husbands for rape of their wives.[43] The legal authority underpinning the marital rape exemption is the other Hale (Matthew) who, in his classic treatise in

---

[42] *R v C* [2009] UKHL 42, [27].

[43] For discussion of the marital rape exemption, see further Naffine (2019).

criminal law, proclaimed: '[T]he husband cannot be guilty of rape committed by himself upon his lawful wife, for by their mutual matrimonial consent and contract the wife hath given up herself in this kind unto her husband *which she cannot retract*' (Hale, 1800: 634, our emphasis). The legal effect of marriage was thus to confer upon a husband an irrevocable right of sexual access to his wife.

The idea of consent to sexual relations underpinning the marital rape exemption is quite distinct from our modern understanding of consent as 'an interior state that expresses sexual desire or rejection' (Farmer, 2016: 288). As noted in Chapter 2, in medieval and early modern law, consent was approached formally, its presence or absence 'read' from external signs and manifestations, in which context a prior relationship between the complainant and defendant would have been seen as a strong signifier of consent. Hence the view, expressed in the earliest criminal treatises, that a man could not be convicted of raping his own concubine, a woman's prior agreement to sexual relations creating an almost property-like right in her male partner to sexual access. The doctrine of *coverture* was the most extreme legal expression of this underlying patriarchal logic, transforming a woman's consent to marriage into the complete erasure of her legal personhood and conferring upon her husband extensive power over her physical person and property.[44] In this moral and legal universe, sexual relations were conceived less in terms of a woman's sexual inclination at a particular moment and more in terms of who had rights of sexual access to her – and who had not. Within this worldview, the idea that a sexually active woman was more likely to consent to sex was simply a way of signalling the substance and scope of her sexual accessibility.

Lady Hale's remarks, by contrast, express a very different understanding of sex, sexual consent and the purposes and principles underpinning sexual offences law. Few would disagree with the proposition that the protection of autonomy and personhood are at the heart of the ideological framework governing contemporary rape law, producing a corresponding understanding of sexual violence, particularly as legally realised, which accords central weight to the individual's capacity to choose whether, when and with whom to have sexual relations.[45]

For purposes here, two consequences flow from this shift in legal understanding. First, as Levanon (2012: 628) has noted, the modern emphasis

---

[44] The erosion of coverture can be dated in England and Wales to the end of the 19th century, although aspects of that doctrine were operational well into the late 20th century. See further Conaghan (2013).

[45] On sexual autonomy as the contemporary organising principle governing the category of sexual offences, see for example Farmer (2016: 264–94).

on sexual autonomy generates strong social and moral reasons against the mobilisation of abstract, statistically based generalisations retrospectively to determine the sexual choices of individuals. For similar reasons, there has long been a reluctance to admit into a criminal trial evidence of a defendant's bad character (Redmayne, 2015). To judge a defendant's innocence or guilt largely on the basis of his past actions, regardless of his actual role in the crime of which he is accused, is to curtail his moral agency, his capacity to choose (or avoid) a course of action; and while it is commonplace in our everyday assessments of how people are likely to behave to draw upon evidence of their past actions, there is far more at stake when ascriptions of criminal responsibility are involved.

However, just as it is critical that the defendant's autonomy and capacity are accorded full consideration in the criminal trial, it is also critical that our system of justice gives proper effect to the right to sexual autonomy. Applying abstract generalisations about how people are likely to act in sexual situations fits uneasily at best with recognising and respecting individual sexual autonomy. Indeed, it is not just sexual autonomy, the freedom to exercise choice about sexual matters, which is undermined by the application of ahistorical, decontextualised and mathematically indeterminate assumptions about sexual behaviour to the circumstances of a contested sexual encounter. The extent to which, by virtue of raising a complaint, a complainant faces the invasion of her privacy, denial of her dignity and intensification of her emotional and psychological trauma are equally important considerations. It is simply not compatible with the stated objects of criminal justice that the rape trial should necessarily function as a forum for the secondary victimisation of the already victimised. In sum, there are legitimate reasons, even where a technical connection of relevance can be established, to question the justice value of introducing evidence of a complainant's prior sexual history.

A second consequence flows from the shift in the legal understanding of consent, and more broadly sexual violence, one which speaks directly to relevance in the sense that it invites the recalibration of the probability calculations underpinning relevance claims. This is a position which argues against the application of propensity claims – probability assessments based on the application of generalisations about women's sexual behaviour to the complainant's sexual history – not just because such an approach undermines the core principle of sexual autonomy underpinning modern sexual offences law (let us call this the justice argument) but also because, by failing to give proper weight to the specificity of individual sexual encounters, it prompts inappropriate comparisons and incorrect probability calculations.

We can call this the fallacious logic argument. How exactly does it work? The general thrust is that the specificity or situatedness of sexual encounters, understood within a normative framework which conceives consent to sex as an internal state of mind that is of the moment and can alter at will, renders evidence of a general disposition to consent to sex based on a complainant's previous sexual history largely irrelevant. Recognising specificity entails framing comparisons differently. For example, asking whether a woman already in a sexual relationship with the defendant is more or less likely to consent to sex with him than with other men becomes the wrong question to ask, the wrong comparison to make. If there was some question as to the identity of the parties – if we wished to determine, for example, with whom, among a selection of possibilities, the complainant was most likely to choose to have sex – then the fact of the parties' prior relationship might be relevant. However, where a sexual encounter between the complainant and the defendant is conceded, and the only question is whether it was consensual, then comparing the complainant's choices with those of women in general is simply not on point.

An example of this fallacious reasoning may be found in a case commentary on *R v A (No 2)*,[46] published by eminent criminal evidence scholar J.R. Spencer in the *Cambridge Law Journal*. Commenting on the relevance of evidence of a prior sexual relationship between the complainant and the defendant, Spencer remarks: '[E]ven the most committed feminists presumably accept that a person more readily consents to sex with her regular sexual partner than with others' (2001: 453). This may well be true, and had the issue involved determining whether the complainant had consented to sex with the defendant or to sex with someone else entirely, the evidence might well have had some bearing on the facts. It did not, however – or certainly not by virtue of the fact of a prior relationship alone – have any bearing on the question of whether the complainant had consented to sex with the defendant on the occasion forming the subject matter of the charge.

To be fair to Spencer, their Lordships in *R v A (No 2)* were of much the same mind. It is inconceivable to them that the evidence sought to be admitted (the defendant's claim that he and the complainant had consensual sex on several prior occasions) did not fall within any of the gateways prescribed by section 41 YJCEA 1999. Hence, their insistence that section 41 should be interpreted in a manner compliant with Article 6 ECHR. Nor did their Lordships go to great efforts to explain why the evidence in question was so plainly relevant. While Lord Steyn confidently pronounced that 'only in the rarest cases'[47] could evidence of the complainant's sexual experience with other men be relevant, he took strong issue with the fact that evidence of the complainant's sexual experience with the defendant was placed by the legislation on the same footing.[48] He characterised this as

---

[46]   [2001] UKHL 25.

[47]   *R v A (No 2)*, [28].

[48]   *R v A (No 2)*, [30]–[31].

'prospectant evidence which may throw light on the complainant's state of mind'.[49] Lord Hutton also viewed evidence of prior sexual relations with the defendant as bearing upon the complainant's state of mind:

> Where there has been a recent close and affectionate relationship between the complainant and the defendant it is probable that the evidence will be relevant, not to advance the bare assertion that because she consented in the past she consented on the occasion in question, but ... [because] ... evidence of such a relationship will show the complainant's specific mindset towards the defendant, namely her affection for him.[50]

The assumption seems to be that because there is evidence that the complainant, at least in the past, was affectionately disposed towards the defendant, she was more likely to consent to sex with him. More likely than whom? One assumes, once again, women in general, but if there is no factual dispute as to the identity of the parties, how does such a comparison advance the analysis of relevance? Most wives are affectionately disposed towards their husbands but would strongly resist any suggestion that the fact of their affection bore upon the question of precisely when and in what circumstances they chose to engage in conjugal relations.

To put it another way, establishing that the complainant is more likely to consent to sex with the defendant than women who are not in a relationship with him and/or establishing that the complainant is more likely to consent to sex with the defendant than with other men does not tell us anything about her sexual inclinations towards the defendant at any particular moment. If we accept that sexual relations are indeed situation-specific, that one does not consent to sex in general but to sex at a particular time and place and with a particular person, then what is important for purposes of the criminal enquiry is the immediate context surrounding the disputed sexual encounter. This requires a shift from a broad enquiry into the complainant's general disposition to have sex to a narrower enquiry into the likelihood that the complainant agreed at a particular time and in a particular place to sex with the defendant.

The fact of the allegation

We come now to another factor which complicates comparisons between the complainant's past and present sexual behaviour. This is the fact that

---

[49] *R v A (No 2)*, [31].
[50] *R v A (No 2)*, [152].

the complainant claims she did not consent. Her account of the sexual encounter under scrutiny thus differs from previous encounters in which consent is undisputed by either party. As Levanon observes, the assumption of repetition is disrupted by the fact of the sexual assault allegation, placing the complainant and the sexual behaviour in a distinct class from those to which the assumption of repetition might otherwise apply (2012: 629–30). The fact of the allegation evidences a stance of opposition to any pattern of repetition which might otherwise be claimed.

It is possible (though factually unlikely) that the complainant's allegation is untrue; that, of course, is the point of the trial. However, the significance of the allegation *as a fact* cannot be discounted. Not only does it disrupt the assumption of repetition; it calls into immediate question any claim by the defendant that the complainant consented to sex because she was affectionately disposed towards him. The defence narrative might then be reconceived in terms of sexual rejection and vengefulness on the part of the complainant, but this is a quite different argument which depends upon making a link between the complainant's prior behaviour and the credibility of her testimony, a strategy which, as we have observed, is problematic for other reasons.

Interrogating the gateways

A particular consequence of the argument we have been making is to cast doubt on the decision in *R v A (No 2)*[51] to widen the scope of admissibility of sexual history evidence beyond the gateways prescribed in section 41 YJCEA 1999. Certainly, none of the arguments proffered by their Lordships really explain why the fact that the complainant and defendant had engaged in sexual relations on several occasions before the evening of the alleged rape was relevant to the defendant's claim that the complainant consented. The fact is that faced with the restrictions posed by section 41 YJCEA 1999, and powered by an unswerving confidence in their own good sense, the House of Lords chose to subvert parliamentary efforts to channel invocations of a complainant's sexual history into clearly articulated, legislatively circumscribed legal arguments. Unsurprisingly, other examples of this casual reasoning have followed. Take the case of *R v Mukadi*, involving an appeal against a decision of the trial court not to allow evidence that earlier on the evening of the alleged rape, the complainant, while wearing 'a short tight skirt which in parts could be seen through' got into an 'expensive looking car' driven by a man (not the defendant) 'a good deal older than the complainant'.[52] The trial judge ruled that the evidence constituted 'sexual

---

[51] [2001] UKHL 25.
[52] *R v Mukadi* [2003] EWCA Crim 2765, [2–14].

behaviour', falling within the scope of section 41 YJCEA 1999, and that it was inadmissible, having no bearing on the question of her consent to sex with the defendant. He said:

> [T]his evidence provides material that [the complainant] was prepared to engage in sexual behaviour of the getting to know you, the come on type [but] ... doesn't, in my judgment, begin to touch on the issue of whether she was prepared to permit sexual intercourse, as required by the definition of rape ... requiring some penetration of the vagina by the penis.[53]

The complainant in *Mukadi* agreed that she had returned to the defendant's flat to get to know him, and that they had engaged in some consensual sexual behaviour (kissing and so on). She denied however that she had consented to sexual intercourse. Indeed, after the alleged rape took place, she tried to escape the defendant's flat through his bathroom window and fell, fracturing both wrists and her kneecap.[54]

The Court of Appeal allowed the defendant's appeal, asserting that whether or not the evidence in question fell within the scope of section 41 (the Court felt it was unnecessary to express a view on this point), it was plainly relevant to the question of consent and should have been admitted. There is no mention of legislative gateways, probabilities, comparisons or anything else that might allow one to make sense of this decision. The Court suggests that had the jury heard the evidence about the incident with the car, they might have taken a different view of the evidence of the complainant's 'state of mind' in accompanying the defendant and 'consenting to such activity as she did consent to'.[55] On that point, the Court is undoubtedly correct. The jury most likely would have acquitted. That does not however make the case for relevance, nor, indeed, at any point, does the Court of Appeal.

Note that evidence of the complainant's sexual behaviour 'at or about the time' of the alleged rape is admissible within the scope of section 41(3)(b). This section allows evidence of the immediate context of the sexual encounter to be considered in so far as it can be shown to bear upon the issue of consent.[56] Section 41 therefore presented no barrier to the defendant in terms of giving an account of what had occurred when the complainant

---

[53] *Mukadi*, [15]

[54] *Mukadi*, [8].

[55] *Mukadi*, [16].

[56] The ability to introduce evidence of contemporaneous sexual behaviour is further supported by s 41(2)(c) YJCEA 1999 which excludes 'anything alleged to have taken place as part of the event which is the subject matter of the charge' from the scope of 'sexual behaviour' for purposes of s 41.

accompanied him to his flat. Interestingly, in *R v A (No 2)*,[57] their Lordships considered the possibility of stretching the temporal scope of section 41(3)(b) as a way of reading in evidence of prior sexual intimacy between the parties. While there was broad agreement among their Lordships that sexual behaviour taking place a week before the disputed event fell outside the scope of the provision (which was why the evidence in *R v A [No 2]* could not pass through the section 41(3)(b) gateway), their Lordships were reluctant to place precise limitations on section 41(3)(b), and their suggestions varied from a few hours to a few days.[58] The uncertain scope of section 41(3)(b) is troubling because, suitably stretched, it allows the admission of evidence inviting the jury to infer consent from the complainant's sexual behaviour during an unspecified time frame leading up to the alleged rape. It is difficult to see how this is compatible with the idea that consent is of the moment and can be made and withdrawn at will. At the same time, fairness to the defendant would surely lean in favour of a full account of the context surrounding the disputed event.

Let us think about this seemingly irresolvable justice dilemma for a moment. We would argue that it derives from a narrative construction about male and female sexual behaviour which Gavey (2019) describes as part of the 'cultural scaffolding of rape'. There should be no objection in principle to putting the factual context immediately surrounding the event which forms the subject matter of the charge before the court, including the behaviour of the parties. The difficulty is that the social norms of sexual behaviour built into our contemplation and assessment of events do not correspond with the moral and ethical principles that underpin modern sexual offences law. As multiple studies have shown, the behaviour of the parties tends to be read and interpreted through a sexual script which assigns to women the role of sexual gatekeepers (Ellison and Munro, 2013). It is primarily through their sexual behaviour that jurors are invited to make sense of what has occurred. The sexual behaviour of the defendant attracts far less scrutiny because the same sexual script that assigns women the role of gatekeepers attributes to men an irrepressible sexual appetite which naturally seeks satisfaction.

Neither modern sexual offences law nor modern sexual morals cohere with this sexual script, but it is so embedded in criminal legal discourse as to resist easy expulsion. The challenge here goes beyond tackling what Temkin and Krahé (2008) characterise as the 'attitude' problem in criminal justice, that is, the extent to which rape-supportive attitudes and gender-bias and stereotypes infuse judgements about sexual behaviour. What we confront when we look closely at the use of sexual history evidence in the rape trial

---

[57]   [2001] UKHL 25.
[58]   For further details, see Chapter 4.

is a series of grooves and pathways through which it is repeatedly admitted, grooves and pathways cast in gendered form and reliant upon gendered imaginaries. The irony then of rape-shield initiatives is that such efforts to detach law from its patriarchal past inadvertently reattach them.

To advance this argument, let's look at yet another way in which a complainant's sexual history is thought to be relevant to the question of consent. This involves an appeal to similarity. Similarity is more than the assumption of repetition, the thrust of the argument being not simply that because of the complainant's sexual experience (whether with the defendant or third parties) she is more likely to have consented to sex with the defendant, but that the correspondence between her past sexual behaviour and the defendant's account of her sexual behaviour on the occasion forming the subject matter of the charge is so similar as to tend to support his version of events.

Levanon (2012) tells us that appeals to similarity are an accepted feature of most rape-shield regimes: '[T]here is almost a complete consensus among legal scholars, legislatures and courts that evidence of sexual history which is sufficiently similar to the sexual interactions at issue is relevant to consent' (2012: 611). In fact, as McGlynn explains, the similarity exception is controversial, and several jurisdictions have declined to incorporate it, primarily because of difficulties in setting the degree of similarity required (2018: 11). In England and Wales, the relevant provision is section 41(3)(c) YJCEA 1999. We encountered this provision before in the case of the footballer Ched Evans.[59] It permits the admission of evidence of sexual behaviour if it is 'so similar' to the sexual behaviour of the complainant at or about the same time as the event forming the subject matter of the charge that 'the similarity cannot reasonably be explained as coincidence'.

Two related elements interact in section 41(3)(c): a high degree of similarity combined with an uncommon quality which places the similarity in behaviour beyond the scope of coincidence. Thus, it is not a complainant's general sexual history which is relevant, but those aspects of her prior sexual behaviour deemed *sufficiently similar* to the sexual encounter at issue as to bear upon the question of her consent. At the same time, run-of-the-mill sexual behaviour seems beyond the contemplation of section 41(3)(c) as it can be too easily written off as coincidence.

In *R v A (No 2)*, their Lordships reluctantly accept the limits which this provision impose. Section 41(3)(c) cannot be 'stretched' to encompass a claim which amounts to no more than that the complainant and defendant have on some previous occasion engaged in consensual sex. Keen to widen its scope nevertheless, their Lordships emphasise that the level of similarity required

---

[59] See Chapter 1.

is something less than identical and that the behaviour being compared need not be bizarre or unusual. How then to avoid an explanation of the similarity in terms of coincidence? In *Evans*, as we saw in Chapter 1, the sexual behaviour in question – doggie-style sex with the woman taking the sexual lead – was a lot closer to run-of-the-mill than unusual or bizarre. The similarity in the accounts of the two witnesses with Evans' original account of the complainant's sexual behaviour could quite easily be written off as coincidence.

Let's once again break down the moves which support a claim of relevance here. That the complainant had consensual sex with two witnesses, and then also with Evans, are the 'facts' to be connected. The assumption of repetition provides the major premise connecting them. Thus far, we have little more than a crude instantiation of the first of the twin myths. Yet there is more going on. It is not just that the complainant has engaged in sexual activities with other men, it is that the type of sex described by the witnesses is *similar* to that described by Evans.

What is the significance of the similarity? It is at this point that class comparisons play a role. The evidence of the witnesses places the complainant in a class of women who enthusiastically enjoy doggie-style sex. It is difficult to gauge how large this class is likely to be or how it compares with the general population of women, with whom the complainant's class is presumably being compared. As it turns out, this information is important as it goes directly to the issue of the significance of the similarity. If the type of sex all three men describe is fairly commonplace (suggesting the class of women within which the complainant falls is large), then little significance can be placed on the similarity of the accounts. Coincidence easily explains why commonplace accounts of sexual behaviour from different men correspond. If, however, the sexual behaviour is highly unusual, then the fact that the complainant falls into the small class of women who engage in it might be thought to assume some significance in gauging the weight to be placed on the similarity of accounts.

The risk here of course is that unless the similarity principle is tightly defined to highly unusual circumstances, then its application is likely to lead to the admission of irrelevant evidence – or barely relevant, assuming we give some credence to Redmayne's argument about the marginal increase in probability the assumption of repetition produces. This argument is persuasively made by Levanon, who draws upon Bayes' theorem[60] to support

---

[60] Bayes' theorem, deriving from the mathematics of probability, is concerned with conditional probability, broadly with the probable effect of introducing a new factor into an existing probability calculation. As a mathematical theorem, it is highly significant, although its application in evidence law is not uncontroversial. For explication and further discussion, see Levanon (2012: 635–7).

the restriction of the similarity principle to circumstances where the sexual behaviour attributed to the complainant by the defendant 'has characteristics that are rare and unique, as compared with common sexual practices, and where, at the same time, a random incident with those same characteristics is likely to be non-consensual' (2012: 639). In other words, if the sexual behaviour in question is so rare and unusual that it is most likely to occur in non-consensual contexts, then the introduction of evidence which shows the complainant is in the habit of consenting to such a practice might be accorded some significance.

There is an undeniably intuitive correspondence between Levanon's conceptualisation of a restricted similarity principle and section 41(3)(c). Consider, for example, *R v T*,[61] discussed in Chapter 1, in which the complainant alleged she had been raped inside a children's climbing frame. It could conceivably be asserted that this incident had characteristics so rare and unusual as to support a conclusion that, applied to the general population, it was likely to have been non-consensual. Another way to put it is to say that the similarity between the sexual behaviour under scrutiny and the evidence of sexual behaviour the defendant sought to admit (of previous consensual sex with the complainant inside the climbing frame) is so striking as not to be reasonably explained by coincidence.

Levanon's analysis goes some way to defend section 41(3)(c) but certainly not the decision in *Evans*.[62] The difficulty, as Levanon acknowledges, is with the uncertainties associated with applying even a restricted similarity principle. She notes that 'there may be cases where the court would regard some circumstances as unique and unusual and would therefore admit similar sexual history evidence and yet the court's evaluation would be statistically wrong' (2012: 642). She gives the example of sexual intercourse with strangers in dancing clubs, which a court might consider rare but which in reality 'is rather common' (2012: 642). A woman's enthusiastic enjoyment of doggie-style sex might be similarly, mistakenly characterised by a court.

The risk of such errors is such that the similarity principle, if it is to be applied at all, should only be invoked in the rarest of circumstances. In most contexts, we have simply no way of gleaning the necessary statistical evidence to enable us to make a defensible probability calculation. Cases like *Evans* run roughshod over the principle of sexual autonomy which rape law purports to enshrine. Indeed, even a disposition to have sex inside climbing frames can be applied to override a complainant's assertion of lack of consent only with some unease.

---

[61] (2004) 2 Cr App R 32.
[62] [2016] EWCA Crim 452.

Most importantly, and regardless of whether the case for admission of sexual history evidence is properly, legally made out, once this evidence is in, it does its own work. It assumes a significance and a potency far in excess of the circumscribed conditions set for its admission. It is like an out-of-control train which runs off the evidentiary rails to crash through the barriers of relevance and probative weight. Sexual history evidence is a power unto itself, and that power derives from, and continues to call upon, a patriarchal legacy which still resides in law, and is quintessentially expressed in the performance of the rape trial.

Conclusion

The argument presented in this chapter can be summarised as follows. The basis for introducing evidence of a complainant's sexual history turns first and foremost on questions of relevance. Relevance, it turns out, is not a straightforward concept and while logical in form and derivation, is only as sound as its underlying premises, which, as it also turns out, in the case of sexual history evidence, are all too fallible. Relations of power and inequality play a role in structuring the processes which construct and validate knowledge, creating the conditions for the adoption and promulgation of problematic gender-based assumptions in law and legal discourse. Recognising the patriarchal legacy of law has cast doubt on the legitimacy of traditional assumptions about the relevance of sexual history evidence. Legislatures have acted to restrict what are widely regarded to be improper uses of such evidence. Analyses have particularly critiqued the way in which abstract and often unfounded generalisations about female sexual behaviour have been applied to discredit the testimony of rape complainants. However, all this leaves open the question as to what circumstances, if any, the relevance of sexual history evidence can properly be claimed.

Our analysis has explored a range of circumstances in which sexual history is said to be relevant, paying particular attention to the operationalisation of rape-shield laws in England and Wales. We have shown that rape myths lurk beneath many of the cases which together set the legal standards of relevance. We have also shown that the twin myths, however publicly discredited, are not far from the thick of things either. Most importantly, we have sought to show that the arguments used to support the introduction of sexual history evidence derive from a particular angle of vision which is so thoroughly embedded in legal discourse and practice as to present as 'common sense'. As a consequence, the unsubstantiated factual assumptions upon which such arguments are often based, the fallacious logic which they often employ, and the unequal, socio-sexual relations and practices they express and advance, are too rarely challenged.

7

Sexual History Evidence
and Subjectivity

Introduction

In the previous chapter, we saw how relevance operates as an ideologically imbued intellectual construct that purports to manage the admission of sexual history evidence in the rape trial. We argued that the doctrine and discourse of relevance, in governing the use and admission of sexual history evidence in the rape trial, is just as infused with gendered assumptions as other aspects of the framework that governs rape law and policy. Recognising the ways in which so many elements of law, policy and practice that touch sexual violence are shot through with the patriarchal legacy we have been tracing in this book shows how even ostensibly neutral legal concepts like relevance are liable to corruption or perversion where sexual violence is concerned. In this chapter, we shift register slightly to consider what a feminist philosophical and psychoanalytic frame can tell us about the ways in which the 'patriarchal legacy' continues to feature in rape law and practice.

Feminists have frequently observed that rape law reflects the perspective of the perpetrator rather than the victim. As Catharine MacKinnon bluntly puts it: '[T]he fact that the law of rape protects rapists and is written from their point of view to guarantee impunity for most rapes is officially regarded as a violation of the law of sex equality, national or international, by virtually nobody' (2006: 25). Far from being neutrally drafted and applied, feminists have long pointed to burgeoning attrition rates and survivor narratives of trauma while engaging with the criminal justice system to evidence the claim that laws on rape simply do not work. Of critical importance here is the feminist insight that rape law and discourse mirror the offence itself by treating the victim of rape as an object rather than a subject, a designation which militates against their proper recognition before the court as a legal person. The operation of sexual history evidence in the rape trial further complicates this designation, disrupting the linearity of the story of violation a prosecutor might be trying to tell and often investing a complainant with a complex and contradictory form of agency.

In this chapter, we consider the construction of subjectivities in rape law discourse. We understand subjectivity for these purposes to signify the cultural construction of particular roles, positions and forms of consciousness, which are materially, symbolically or discursively supported, inter alia, by law. Our analysis here requires an exploration of the development of legal subjectivity as well a historical appraisal of the development of masculine and feminine 'sexuate subjecthood'. We use the term 'sexuate' to denote a mode of being or ontology irreducible to biology or birth-assigned gender (Irigaray, 2008: 142–3; Jones, 2011: 3–7). That which is sexuate will encompass sexuality but is not limited to sexual preference or desire. It designates the contours of our being and becoming as singular subjects, as well as the interaction of the body's morphology with its environment. Because our sexuate identity is necessarily always mediated and understood within the ideological lens or the metaphysical framework through which we view it, we are here analysing a projection of ideality on to materiality. In other words, in giving an account of sexuate subjecthood in its emergence through rape law and sexual history evidence, we are not making ontological claims about the essential nature of womanhood or manhood. We seek instead to observe the patterns that emerge when different bodies interact with rape laws, or are brought into being by legal discourse, to enable us to better understand the role sexual history evidence plays in reflecting and producing subjecthood and subjectivity.

Our analysis in this chapter is primarily informed by feminist philosophical and psychoanalytic frameworks, which help us draw out the symbolic meaning and function of sexual history evidence and explain its longevity and centrality to legal thinking on rape and rape law. Much of the feminist work that attempts to look deeply at what happens in the rape trial draws on this body of scholarship to understand how meanings as well as narratives come to be fixed on and around certain bodies and behaviours and how these meanings and narratives are reproduced, including by institutions like the criminal justice system (Naffine, 1994; Young, 1998; Bumiller, 2008; Du Toit, 2009; Russell, 2016, 2023). We are drawn to this body of thought as part of our multidisciplinary appraisal of sexual history evidence because it insists that we peer beneath the surface of what the law says about itself and the crime of rape, to reveal the invisible meaning-making mechanisms that give coherence to a legal construct like sexual history evidence. This is particularly important in trying to understand what law *does* to those party to the rape trial, including in relation to the making and unmaking of legal and sexuate subjectivity.

Legal subjecthood

There is a clear relationship in modern law between legal subjectivity and agency. In the criminal law, it is the subject with full control over their faculties and actions who commits the *actus reus* with the requisite *mens rea*, who is called before the law and calls for the law in their own defence. In Ngaire Naffine's classic formulation, the legal subject who arises from the process of modernisation is 'rational, self-determining, autonomous, perhaps most significantly, ... self-owning' (1998: 193). That is, the legal subject is fully agential, possessed of all relevant critical faculties and of themselves.

While the legal subject is certainly *subject to* the law, they are not necessarily *subjected to* law in the same way that someone with limited agency might be. An infant child for whom the court acts *in loco parentis* is a subject with rights, but it would be difficult to say that they have agency;[1] similarly, the 'mentally disordered' patient sterilised by order of the court,[2] or the 37-year-old man with impaired cognition prevented by court order from pursuing sexual relationships because he does not understand the meaning of consent.[3] Full agential legal subjecthood, therefore, is always contingent upon and placed in a relation with other important concepts, in particular, rationality and the capacity to act reasonably. And while these attributes are key components upon which our system of law proceeds, they are crucially also gateways to personhood. As Conaghan observes:

> Reason provides law both with an overarching frame and an internal disciplinary mechanism. It supports the presentation of law as ordering and systematic. It also positions law as benign and progressive by aligning it with a conception of human nature in which reason serves as a key indicator of human worth. (2013: 201)

As feminist philosophers have observed, gender has always played a central role in determining who can reason and therefore be considered a subject of law or interact with and access law. Indeed, the association of reason with masculinity reaches back to Aristotle and continues to feature in cultural discourse today. Hence Genevieve Lloyd's comment that throughout the history of Western philosophy, femininity 'was associated with what Reason supposedly left behind' (Lloyd, 1993: 2).

In her early excavation of Western metaphysics, Luce Irigaray exposed the ways in which psychoanalytic interpretations of ego formation were

---

[1]   *In Re A (Children) (Conjoined Twins: Surgical Separation)* [2001] 2 WLR 480.
[2]   *In Re F (Mental Patient: Sterilisation)* [1990] 2 AC 1.
[3]   *A local authority v JB* [2021] UKSC 52.

based upon a partial understanding of the development of self-hood (1985a). The 'mirror phase' that is said to propel subjectivity is dependent on the self being able to see an image represented back to itself in the external world, through which it can construct an 'I'. As the masculine imaginary proliferates, the male subject projects his ego as universal. Women come to stand in for the mirror or the 'matter' upon which the masculine subject relies to see himself as whole. Catherine Carol explains Irigaray's notion of masculine 'specularisation', or the process by which the masculine subject comes to stand in for the universal subject, erasing the possibility of a 'sexually different' feminine subject:

> Reflecting their own ideas, values, desires back to themselves, male subjects construct a world of sameness, so that 'woman never appears' fully 'as a subject or agent in her own right'. The mirror is a display of mastery, and difference cannot be seen in the mirror because it is a reflection of the self-same subject. (Carol, 2019: 238)

Masculine mastery is represented most clearly through the phallus as the unifying signifier in the governing symbolic order – the social world which we all inhabit, that determines the contours of language and communication, modes for interpreting intersubjective relationships, the basis for the development of knowledge, and of building consensus around law and the social contract.[4] Masculinity is associated with all the most valorised attributes, values and concepts, such that all dominant ways of being, knowing and thinking can be said to be 'phallocentric'. The masculine subject can find himself wherever he looks in myth, history and culture, furnishing men with a rich imaginary domain from which to construct their subjectivities. As Drucilla Cornell argues, without access to an imaginary domain, or a psychic space in which we can conceive of ourselves as whole, we 'cannot effectively get the project of becoming a person off the ground' (1995: 4). And so it is with femininity, symbolically coded as 'lack' or nothingness,[5] associated with the denigrated side of binary thinking, and in particular, with fluidity, waste and the body (Douglas, 1966; Kristeva, 1982).

In so far as the feminine deviates from the masculine universal, it lacks coherence in the dominant symbolic order. The chaos inherent in woman's plural morphology – its ebb and flow as well as its confounding generative

---

[4] We are working with a Lacanian understanding of the symbolic, in the context of its representation in the tripartite order of the imaginary, symbolic and the real (Lacan, 1966). See Jameson (1977) for a thorough discussion of the symbolic and its role in subject-making in Lacan.

[5] For a thorough discussion of femininity as castration and lack in the work of Lacan and Freud, see Moi (2004).

capacity – is seen to mirror the chaos and unpredictability of the natural world (Irigaray, 1985a, 1985b: 106–18). That chaos presents a symbolic threat to law's stability as a unitary discourse; as a source of truth, certainty and knowledge (Goodrich, 1990, 1995). One way then to conceive rationality in Western metaphysics is as a transcendence of the feminine.

As Conaghan explains in her 'topography' of legal reason, there is a long history in Western philosophy and jurisprudence of women being considered simply incapable of attaining fully developed rationality, because they are associated with nature and emotions, unable to rise above the particularities of family or their unruly bodies, or to comprehend abstract concepts and ideas (Conaghan, 2013: 204–10; see also, Lloyd, 1993). As with the mirror phase in psychoanalysis, the figure of woman in law served as the counterfactual against which the symbiosis between masculinity, rationality, reason and law ossified and came to be seen as natural and inevitable. This relationship is personified most clearly in criminal law in the figure of the 'rationalist legal person' (Naffine, 2011), otherwise known as the 'reasonable man'.

The rationalist's person in law can be traced to the Lockean concept of the person as a thinking, intelligent being capable of practical reason and possessed of the faculties necessary to make decisions according to, and within the bounds of, law (Naffine, 2011: 17). In the modern law-making nation state, the legacy of the nature/culture dichotomy aligned along gendered lines is most clearly transposed to the private/public divide. Traditionally, the problem of woman's nature was solved by absorbing her legal personality into that of her husband's, who was made the controller of his wife's mind and body (Blackstone, 1803). Confining women to the private sphere placed them largely outside law's purview, assigned to a 'standard legal category of inferior persons, along with servants, children and also lunatics' (Naffine, 2019: 49). We see the legacy of women's historic alignment with privacy in the framing of and response to crimes of sexual and intimate partner violence, of which women are the disproportionate target, where the designation of that violence as 'private' or 'domestic' has traditionally justified the state's reluctance to intervene or recognise certain behaviours as criminal (Smart, 1989, 1995; Graycar and Morgan, 1990; Kennedy, 1992).

It is against this backdrop in the modern lawscape that the transfer of legal personality or subjecthood to women as a class occurs. As we have seen in Chapters 2 and 3, the harm of rape is now attached to the woman as person, and she complains of rape as a legal subject in her own right, who asserts her claim to sexual autonomy. The eponymous 'reasonable man' has morphed into the 'reasonable person', thus endowing both men and women equally with the capacity for reason. However, as Naffine makes plain, while 'women bear personifying rights and responsibilities in much the same manner as men can as legal persons … it is far less clear that women, *as women*, are persons in law' (2011: 16). In other words, feminists remain unconvinced that the 'reasonable person' truly reflects in and to law the experience or perspective of the feminine subject and the 'reasonable person' is just the masculine subject masquerading as universal.

In the criminal law, the most 'successful' feminist intervention has been to modify or mitigate the rationalist legal person ostensibly to include the feminine subject; to 'cure the defect of woman by concessions to her frailty' (Russell, 2016: 296). So, the battered woman is a rational actor, except that she has 'learned helplessness',[6] or the rape victim is acting reasonably, except that she is frozen in fear (see further, Marx et al, 2008). These excuses or justifications, often filtered through medical diagnoses, then provide an explanation as to why a woman's reason is impaired in such situations; why they do not flee or 'fight back', as the reasonable person surely would. These interventions rely on 'fitting' women into the box occupied by the 'reasonable person' or the neutral universal subject of law. Criminal law continues to devise ever more elaborate ways to shroud the masculinity of the rationalist legal person with the proliferation of ostensibly neutralised concepts, and the inclusion of women's behaviour and experiences into frameworks that remain designed to cater for and respond to men's behaviour.[7]

Formal equality, then, has provided no guarantee that the old association of woman with unreason has been cast out of legal thinking. The problem, of course, is that whether referred to as a 'man' or a 'person', reason is an attribute that will more readily 'stick' (Ahmed, 2004) to subjects embodied as men. Including women in the category of rationalist legal person was always going to be problematic because reason relies on its privileging in the Cartesian duality and grounding in disembodiment. As long as women are predominantly associated with embodiment, they are necessarily outsiders to rationality (Grear, 2011: 41). Most significantly, while the continued association of the feminine subject with embodiment and irrationality might be present throughout the law, its consequences have become more difficult to ignore in cases of sexual violence, as these cases have feminine embodiment at their heart (Russell, 2016: 292). As we shall see, the continued association of the feminine subject with unreason engenders a curtailed and precarious legal subjectivity, one that has implications for the application of rape laws, including laws governing sexual history evidence.

---

[6]   For a critique of 'learned helplessness' and its application to victims of domestic violence, see Sheehy et al (1992); Kaganas (2002).

[7]   See, for example, Edwards' discussion of the 2009 reforms to the partial defence to murder of provocation/loss of control in England and Wales in the context of battered defendants who kill (2016, 2021).

Rationality, reason and rape law

How then has the 'rationalist legal person' or the 'reasonable person' manifested him or herself in rape law? How does the law conceive of the legal subject in the law of rape, and does this change depending on whether the person who is brought within its orbit is positioned as perpetrator/ defendant or victim/complainant? It is true, of course, that in much of the criminal law the reasonable person is invested with the common sense of the universal legal subject; this is not a problem that emerges only in rape law. However, we argue that reason(ableness) in its relation to subject-making takes on a conceptual and operational complexity in the rape trial not necessarily present elsewhere in the criminal law.

As noted in Chapter 2, section 1 of the SOA 2003 lays out the elements of the offence of rape as follows:

(1) A person (A) commits an offence if –
   (a) he intentionally penetrates the vagina, anus or mouth of another person (B) with his penis,
   (b) B does not consent to the penetration, and
   (c) A does not reasonably believe that B consents.
(2) Whether a belief is reasonable is to be determined having regard to all the circumstances, including any steps A has taken to ascertain whether B consents.

The *actus reus* of the offence is penile penetration of the anus, vagina or mouth, without consent, and the *mens rea* is intention in respect of the penetration and the lack of reasonable belief in consent. The meaning of consent is elaborated in section 74 of the same Act: '[A] person consents if he agrees by choice, and has the freedom and capacity to make that choice.'

In its modern iteration, the harm of rape is predominantly conceived in terms of a violation of sexual autonomy: the right to choose when, where and with whom one has sex. Transposed on to the bodily specifications of rape law, and the heterosexual imaginary which gives it meaning, the right to sexual autonomy tends to manifest as a limited form of agency in which the agentic scope of the penetrable party is limited to a right to grant or withhold consent.[8]

---

[8] The right may be even more limited than this. In its assessment of the nature of consent in a consultation paper that preceded the introduction of the SOA 2003, the UK Home Office concluded that 'consent was the essential issue in sexual offences, and that the offences of rape and sexual assault were essentially those of violating another person's *freedom to withhold* sexual contact' (Home Office, 2000: 14, our emphasis). See further Russell (2013).

In this formulation, it is the penetrating party (person A) who acquires consent and who is agential in the classic sense, and the penetrable party (person B) who exercises agency to the extent they can grant or refuse consent. What person B wants is relevant to this enquiry, to the extent that it has been outwardly manifest and in a way that person A can understand, in their capacity in SOA 2003 section 1 as the 'reasonable person' of criminal law.

How then does sexual history evidence make 'sense' within such a legal framework? A rationalist interpretation of section 1, combined with the notion of sexual autonomy enshrined in section 74, tells us that men cannot rely on an *expectation* of how a woman might behave as a proxy for actual consent in the moment. Consent must be sought, given and received afresh in each instance of sexual negotiation. As we have seen in Chapter 6, when the harm of rape is conceived in these terms, the relevance of sexual history evidence becomes problematic certainly to the issue of consent, because the evidential focus must surely be on the facts surrounding the event forming the subject matter of the charge. How then do we end up in the situation where the trial focus is able to shift, so smoothly and ineluctably, away from the defendant's conduct and towards the behaviour of the complainant at another time and place and even with another person? How is sexual history evidence – scripted by jurists and legislators as entirely natural, appropriate and indeed required by the interests of justice – allowed to impose its own (il)logic on the rape trial?

While we have seen a professed fealty to 'reason' and 'rationality' as the apotheosis of legal method throughout our analysis of rape law in this book, the relationship that criminal lawyers have to those concepts in practice is far from straightforward. As Norrie observes, a commitment among criminal lawyers to rationality or linear legal logic is both proclaimed and denied:

> Rationality is both a central legal virtue and an impossibility. Lawyers, both practising and academic, make their arguments on the assumption that logical reasoning is a central requirement, but in their moments of doubt, or when pushed to a position they do not accept, they jettison logic or insist on its limits. Yet those limits are never understood as I suggest they should be: as historical and social limits on a reasoning process that is necessarily contradictory. (Norrie, 2014: 12)

The willingness of the courts to jettison the principle underpinning most rape statutes that consent to sex is given in each case to a specific act, time and person by reference to certain interpretations of the law on sexual history evidence reveals this paradoxical relationship with rationality about which Norrie talks. This paradox is most stark when courts have gone out of their way to avoid the exclusionary rules in section 41, for example by reference to little more than 'common' or 'good sense'.[9] The substitute of linear legal logic for 'common sense' as the rational response to evidential relevance in cases of sexual violence is never understood, in Norrie's framing, as a social or historical limit on reason. Nor is it taken as indicative, as we would argue, of a gaping void at the heart of legal reason in its dysfunctional relationship with gender and, specifically, femininity. It is dismissed as an anomalous, yet necessary or even righteous, concession to 'justice' or 'rights' in their most esoteric sense,[10] rather than being seen as a pattern of unreason that indicates a profound contradiction at the heart of the criminal law. It is women's claims of violation that come to represent unreason in the rape trial, and which must be cured, erased and cast out so order can be restored, even where the application of rational legal logic cannot be relied upon to do so.

Where sexual history evidence is concerned then, it seems both to confound the rationality of legal logic and substitute into the rape trial its own system of logic. Sexual history evidence invokes a different kind of temporality for evidential relevance in the rape trial, which might take the relevant legal question outside the specific time and place of the act. It might even make the actions of other people relevant to the question of knowledge and consent, in the case of third-party sexual history evidence. Put otherwise, sexual history evidence offers a route to subvert the incoherence presented by women's access to sexual autonomy via laws prohibiting rape. In this sense, sexual history evidence can be reliably deployed to restore an old kind of rationality, in which masculine subjectivity is vindicated, and the illogic of women's agency rectified, via the mediating gaze of the legal judgment. If women exercising sexual autonomy is chaotic and irregular, sexual history evidence allows the court to refocus on what is reliably known to be true: women cannot be trusted with the full responsibility of legal subjecthood.

With this old rationality restored, sexual history evidence instinctively makes 'sense' even where rational legal logic, in its desire to vindicate women's subjecthood and autonomy through rape laws that specify the need for contemporaneous consent, has diverged from that view.

---

[9] See further Chapter 6.

[10] See Gotell (2006), pointing out that the right to a 'fair trial' has never meant that a defendant should be entitled to call any and all evidence in his defence. In Canadian jurisprudence, the 'fair trial' is to be conceived as one 'that does justice to all parties, including the complainant' and for that reason should recognise that the 'legal rights of the accused must not be allowed to distort the "truth-seeking" function of the trial process by employing discriminatory myths about rape victims' (Gotell, 2006: 759).

We turn now to consider in more detail the specific ways in which sexual history evidence problematises legal subjectivity in the rape trial. Our claim is that sexual history evidence wields a unique power to invert the subject positions of the parties to the trial such that it disrupts an already precarious story of violation a prosecutor might be trying to tell.

Sexual history evidence: subject or object?

The relationship between agency and subjectivity that we have been talking about is clearly of key importance in the criminal law in its attempt to establish the elements of offences and defences and attribute moral blameworthiness. As it manifests in rape law, the relationship between subjectivity and agency is slightly more difficult to pin down, and this is particularly so where sexual history evidence is concerned. The question of legal subjecthood and its relationship to agency is important for our purposes because it is the hinge point upon which so many of the problems with sexual history evidence that we have highlighted turn. If, as we have argued, women are not fully possessed of legal subjecthood as rape complainants, what then is their designation in law?

We have previously alluded to the feminist insight that rape law mirrors the act of rape itself by objectifying the victim of rape. In the law of rape, woman is the passive and consenting party who claims violation as a breach of sexual autonomy; she claims that she has been 'acted on' without consent. The harm of rape then is that one has been treated like an object, rather than a subject who is capable of choice and has the right to choose. Only a subject has agency; an object, by definition, cannot have agency or act as an agent. The process of objectification that occurs during the act of rape is a process of stripping the characteristics of person or self-hood (Du Toit, 2009), one of which is the capacity to act as an agent.

Feminists have theorised the objectification that occurs in the act of rape as existing on a continuum with 'just sex' (Gavey, 2019). The act of rape, so the argument goes, is merely the logical end point of the framework of permissible (hetero)sex: men are subjects, and women are objects; men take sex, and women give it; men penetrate, women are penetrated. Or, in MacKinnon's provocative formulation, men 'fuck' and women 'get fucked' (1982: 517). In MacKinnon's framework (1987, 1989, 2005, 2016), it is in the nature of heterosexual sex to be coercive because under male supremacy women's consent is exercised under the threat of force at all times. Male supremacy eroticises masculine dominance and feminine submission, and because of the centrality of the organisation of desire to gender, women's inequality in all spheres of life can be traced back to their gender. If women's vulnerability and capacity for violation is based in their sexuality, to be a woman is to exist in a latent or active state of victimhood.

Because it is in the rigid scripting of heterosexual sex that men are sexually acquisitive and women are sexually passive, and rape law can be seen to enshrine and reinforce this scripting, the relevant legal question in most cases of rape is to ascertain the point at which men's inherent sexual aggression becomes impermissible. Law's vast signifying power means it has a key role in reproducing the conditions under which the 'naturalness' of men's and women's roles in the negotiation of heterosexual sex solidify. It also means that the objectification of the rape complainant that occurs in the act of rape is reproduced in the rape trial itself. In the rape trial, women's bodies become the site of medical and juridic attention and interrogation; pored over and discursively dissected like cadavers as they watch on, still inhabiting that very body (Young, 1998; Bumiller, 2008). It is not 'just' therefore, that a victim is objectified by the rape trial; they are also abjected by the process (Diken and Laustsen, 2005), which requires the dis-integration of body and mind, and often involves the transformation of the body – for evidential purposes – into a penetrable meaty or fleshy mass that may operate independently of her will.

We do not want to contest the claim that rape law objectifies the rape complainant; there is more than enough evidence in the pages of this book to justify that claim several times over. However, we do want to slightly trouble the subject/object binary that is sometimes used as a shorthand for the treatment of men/women by the law of rape. We argue that the fixity of the subject/object binary becomes a problem where there is a slippage between those assigned positions during the trial.

A successful rape prosecution, more often than not, relies on presenting a linear or teleological narrative of violation in which a complainant is acted upon, objectified and stripped of her agency, expressed as a right to exercise sexual autonomy (to give or withhold consent). Agency has an important function here because it can affix itself to parties in the rape trial at different points, even those whose legal subjectivity might be called into question or who the prosecution might argue has been treated by the accused like an object. Sexual history evidence plays such an important role because one of its unconscious purposes and effects in the rape trial is to invert the binary: to make women agential subjects and men passive objects.

To return again to the facts of *Evans*, the prosecution's theory of the case in the second trial was that the complainant was so drunk that she was incapable of consenting to sex with Evans and he did not reasonably believe her to be consenting. Her evidence that she had no recollection of the event, coupled with the evidence of those who saw her entering the hotel with Evans' co-accused in the first trial, and exiting the hotel in the morning in a confused and upset state, as well as video footage on the night of the offence of her struggling to walk, was relied on to substantiate the claim that she had been raped by Evans. Evans, so the prosecution argued, was a sexual predator who was in the habit of 'picking up' drunk and vulnerable women for group sex with his friends, who took no steps to ascertain whether she was consenting or not and did not really care either way, in any case.

Watch how the narrative shifts once evidence of the complainant's sexual history with two other men is introduced into the trial. She is instantly endowed with a complex and contradictory form of agency. She gives instructions, she shifts positions and demands to be "fucked harder". And she did not just do this on this occasion: she is the sort of woman who does this often, and with men with whom she has only fleeting sexual relationships. In this account, Evans is simply following her instructions: the acquisitive sexual predator has gone. In its place is a man who has a fiancée and a baby (and wants to have another baby),[11] who had a decorated and promising career, who had adulterous sex that he very much regretted with a woman who was sexually voracious and demanding, who drunkenly berated and hassled men who did not want to be in relationships with her for sex;[12] a man who had just made a mistake. It is he, Evans, who has been victimised, it is he who is the object.[13]

It is this disorientating substitution of object for subject, and vice versa, that troubles the narratives we have available to us in rape cases. There is a logical and symbolic incoherence to the claim that a woman who might be an active and desiring sexual subject could also be the victim of rape. It is this incoherence that sexual history evidence brings to the surface in the rape trial and that is then exploited, consciously or unconsciously, by the defence in problematising the elements of consent or testimonial credibility.

In the final section of this chapter, we attempt to unpack this problematic further. It is not anomalous that at certain points in a situation at issue in the criminal law someone might shift between object and subject, passive and agential, depending on the circumstances. The very essence of the criminal defence of self-defence, for example, is that one can both be facing a perception of an imminent and serious threat of death or serious bodily harm and respond with defensive force. It is possible for the criminal law to recognise a person, therefore, in relation to a single event, occupying the position of both passive object who is acted upon, and agential subject who then acts in their own interests. What makes such a conceptual shift so difficult to manage in cases of sexual violence? And why is the role reversal

---

[11] *R v Evans*, Case No: T20167246, evidence of defendant (direct examination): 10 October 2016 (transcript on file with Russell).

[12] *R v Evans*, Case No: T20167246, evidence of complainant (cross-examination): 5 October 2016 (transcript on file with Russell).

[13] See also Herriot (2023: 102–5), in which mock jurors drew on sexual history evidence to posit a complainant as a deceptive or untrustworthy witness, while simultaneously reading the defendant as a *more* trustworthy and believable witness.

of man/woman subject/object via sexual history evidence such an effective tool for imputing doubt into women's narratives of violation?

We argue that this problem can be explained with reference to another important conceptual distinction that seems crucial to our understanding of the tenacity of sexual history evidence but is under-theorised in the feminist literature. That is the distinction between *legal* subjectivity on the one hand, and *sexuate* subjectivity on the other. A subject's sexuate subjectivity is historically and culturally contingent and shifts and intersects in its relationship with other modes of subjectivity. What interests us here is to trace the ways in which sexuate subjectivity and legal subjectivity come together and interact with one another in the rape trial space, and the role that sexual history evidence plays in shaping the contours of that relationship. Sexual history evidence, as a subjectivity destroying and constituting tool, wields the capacity to disrupt the stories of rape that the law is willing to accept as reasonable.

The sexuate subject of rape law

As we have seen, in the rape trial, woman as legal subject is always rubbing up against the woman as sexuate subject. Rape law and discourse has little room for the complexity of women's sexuate subjectivity outside the linear trajectory of violation it imagines. Sexual history evidence provides the route through which a woman complainant transforms from objectified victim of masculine sexual aggression and becomes a desiring sexuate subject in her own right. If women can only be thought as derivative, opposite or complement of men, as the mirror that reflects men back on to themselves and with no independent subject position of their own, the very notion of women as desiring and complex sexuate subjects becomes logically incoherent (Russell, 2013). Sexual history evidence mobilises that incoherence in the rape trial for the defence. Women can be seen as legal subjects possessed of rights like sexual autonomy that are capable of vindication, but only to the extent that their divergence from the position of the universal neutral subject is unsullied by the complexity of their sexuate subjecthood. As such, women are never fully possessed or in control of their legal subjectivity when it comes to sexual violence.

However, sexual history evidence does not just reveal the contingency of the feminine subject, it also serves to 'shore up' the masculine subject. Where an allegation or the taint of rape can strip a man of his access to the benefits conferred by masculine embodiment in the Western symbolic order, including uncomplicated access to legal and sexuate subjectivity, sexual history evidence can help make him 'whole' again. Who then is this sexuate subject that comes to interact with legal subjecthood and who arises differentially whether one is embodied as feminine or as masculine?

The feminine sexuate subject

Like all forms of subjecthood, the symbolic etymology of the sexuate subject is gender, race and class specific. We have seen in Chapter 3 how the historical emergence of various 'rape myths' justified and continue to sustain the relevance and usefulness of sexual history evidence to rape law, and how these were entwined with particular understandings of a woman's nature. This discussion helps us build a picture of the feminine sexuate subject, or at least of the one that is mobilised in the rape trial.

The centrality of chastity to feminine virtue is a thread that connects the past to the present in our consideration of sexual history evidence. As we have seen, in the Victorian era, the ideal feminine subject had no sexuality at all, or at least none outside that which was tightly proscribed. To the extent that women were permitted to have sex, it was within marriage for the purpose of reproduction, and the stain of the sex act was covered over or cured by her designation and role as 'mother'. Because of the chaos inherent in the female body, while a woman could certainly take steps to mitigate her sexuality, any variation from the ideal feminine sexuate subject involved some level of risk. For example, being alone with a man who was not your husband, being outside the home at the wrong time (Clark, 1987) or drinking alcohol (Lees, 1996: 67) all had the potential to put a woman's chastity as risk. Engaging in 'risky behaviour', even where that might have been by coincidence or happenstance, was likely to impact on the level of control a woman could have over her body, and thus the likelihood that it might send a message to a man who could mistakenly interpret it.

We can see the legacy of this way of thinking in modern courtrooms in which the messages that women's bodies send out become detached from the sender or seem to operate on a plane of their own. In her observation of rape trials in Victoria, Australia, in the late 1990s, Alison Young notes the ways in which metonymic aphasia, invention and fantasy operate to rescript a woman's actions, her clothing and her body as inviting sex (1998). A woman who attended a beach-themed party dressed in a swimsuit was remembered by a trial witness as wearing only lingerie. Another woman's naked body was seen by the defendant to reveal itself from underneath a transparent singlet, which the complainant insisted was completely opaque (Young, 1998: 449–51). Young's point is not, or not only, that a woman's body sends messages that can be misconstrued. Rather, in the disaggregating process of the criminal rape trial where will and matter separate, a woman's body is there to be interpreted by those who imagine her as interpretable:

[N]o message is ever simply launched by the woman's body to be decoded by the male audience. No matter what the woman's intentions may be, she is the projection of a projection: her bodily surface is a text to be interpreted by the one who imagines her as textual. The surfaces of her body are constituted as planes to be made plain ... The dynamic of projection therefore constructs the woman's surfaces as making what is inside or underneath appear to the man who is on the outside. (Young, 1998: 450)

So powerful is the collective fantasy of women's uncontrollable sexuality that reason, as it is usually understood, completely escapes through the nearest window. In its place is a 'projection of a projection'. While women are endowed with the rights of men as legal subjects in law, their subjecthood lacks symbolic coherence on its own terms because they lack the imaginary force behind the masculine subject, a designation that endows a natural alignment of one's subjecthood with truth, knowledge and rationality. What is often left then in the rape trial is the masculine projection of women as always already sexually available.

While some women may just lose control over their sexuality through circumstance or 'risky behaviour', the paradigmatic feminine sexuate subject lurking behind every woman who makes a complaint of rape is the woman who *did* have control over the power of her own sexuality and chose to wield it for malign purposes. This woman lures unsuspecting men for sex and then lies about it to try to save her virtue and to ruin good men. It is this figure who generates the most fear in men and in law, and against whom sexual history evidence is designed to guard. So powerful is this mendacious and vindictive woman's capacity to destroy the foundations of male supremacy and, by implication, the order of society, that law must be vigilant in ensuring she is never allowed to succeed.

As well as being generally chaste and in control of her chaotic sexuality, the ideal feminine sexuate subject is also able-bodied, cis-gendered, heterosexual, middle class and white. The further away she is from that ideal, the more precarious her access to legal subjectivity, and the more likely she is to be overwhelmed by the vicissitudes of her sexuate subjectivity. There is a significant body of empirical literature in the United States, for example, that attests to the ways in which Black women are disproportionately affected by the circulation and mobilisation of rape myths in the courtroom (Donovan and Williams, 2002; Konradi, 2007; Flood, 2012; Hlavka and Mulla, 2021). This research demonstrates how Black women's accounts of violation are habitually rescripted as consensual sex by depicting them as always already hyper-sexualised and promiscuous (Davis, 1981; Wriggins, 1983; Collins, 2004; McGuire, 2011). This erasure of Black women's realities occurs of course against a backdrop of chattel slavery in the United States, during which white men possessed 'an incontestable right of access to Black women's bodies' (Davis, 1981: 158). As Davis makes clear, sexual coercion formed an integral part of the logic of slavery as the 'right to rape' underpinned the economic status of Black people as white property (Davis, 1981: 158). Historically, Black women served as the counterfactual against which the purity of white women as the 'reservoirs of patrimony' at home was constructed and maintained, as well as contributing to the 'positive interpellation of whiteness as a signifier of value' (Hom, 2022: 201).

The afterlife of slavery, in which Black women were reduced to objects or to their bare functions, can be seen in the modern US rape trial through reliance by defence attorneys on tropes like the 'welfare queen', or by linking Black women to ambiguous and contradictory notions of mothering and motherhood (Collins, 2000: 76–106), further undermining their testimonial credibility (Powell et al, 2017: 472–4). What little comparable empirical research there is in the UK on race and sexual violence bears out the literature in the United States and elsewhere,[14] illustrating how intersecting vulnerabilities connected with being racialised as non-white put some women at greater risk of sexual violence and impact on the reliability of service provision including from the criminal justice system (Hester et al, 2012; Walker et al, 2021).

There is a sense then in which 'just being' can preclude a woman's access to legal subjectivity – the chance to have her 'right' to sexual autonomy vindicated in the rape trial – and tarnish her with the worst attributes of the masculine projection of feminine sexuate subjectivity. 'Just being' in the wrong place, or a place in which the law is unwilling to protect you, or 'just being' racialised as non-white, an immigrant (Sharma and Gill, 2010: 229–30; Gangoli et al, 2020), poor (Phipps, 2009) or mentally unwell (Ellison et al, 2015; Hester and Lilley, 2018; Walker et al, 2021). The feminine sexuate subject then is partial, contingent and a mass of contradictions. Sexual history evidence reminds us of those contradictions, sullying the neutral legal subjectivity endowed on women by reminding the court of the truth of women's nature.

How then does the feminine sexuate subject interact with her masculine counterpart? As we have seen, material, affective and symbolic values accumulate in and around the masculine subject, which buttress him from the wild contingency that the feminine subject experiences. The robustness of that selfhood, however, does not accrue equally to all men.

The masculine sexuate subject

In contrast with women rape complainants, men accused of rape seem to retain their legal subjectivity even where their sexuate subjectivity is at issue. Sexual behaviour that is predatory or criminal is often rescripted in

---

[14] See, for example, the discussion in the South African literature: Scully (1995); Gqola (2015); Graham (2015); Buiten and Naidoo (2016).

our cultural milieu as merely mistaken, bad manners or 'boys being boys' (Murnen et al, 2002; Weiss, 2009). In other words, it is in the nature of masculine sexuality to be aggressive; the job of rape law is to distinguish between sexual aggression that is good, and that which is bad (MacKinnon, 1989). As with the feminine sexuate subject, however, the further away the masculine subject gets from the ideal, the more readily his masculinity may be called into question. Indeed, the further away that the masculine subject gets from the able-bodied, cis-gendered, heterosexual, middle-class, white man, the less likely he is to see himself reflected back as whole within the dominant symbolic order. Masculine sexuate subjectivity as it relates to and intersects with sexual violence and the law has its own genealogy, which space precludes us from investigating fully, but which it behoves us to acknowledge as a complex, ever-shifting and historically contingent construction.

In his genealogy of the liberal subject of governmentality, Miguel de Beistegui notes how discourses around instincts and perversion came to be mobilised in different historical periods through understandings of the rationality of desire (2018). While the idea of behaviour or characteristics as instinctual has a long historical lineage, de Beistegui notes how, with Darwin in the 19th century, instinct had become naturalised and associated with the reproductive success of individuals who were possessed of it (2018: 94). The framing of desire as sexual instinct gives way to a clinical discourse in which a perversion of the sexual instinct was categorised as 'functional disease'. By being inscribed within the binary of normal and pathological, and by being understood as natural, albeit prone to deviation, sexual instinct came to be situated as a subject of medical and psychological expertise and to inform the construction of the liberal subject (de Beistegui, 2018: 96). An example of this type of discourse and expertise around sexual instinct can be seen through the development of the 'psycho-hydraulic' model of masculine sexuality, which emerged during the Enlightenment in 18th-century France and England. During that period, the idea that affects and impulses were fluids that could be cathartically purged from the body animated literature and popular culture and came to inform medical and psychological discourse (Hewitt, 2018: 25). During the same period, physicians and anatomists began to reconceive the sexual anatomy of men and women, which had previously been understood as largely similar, albeit inverted:

By the latter half of the 18th century, some were arguing that the vascular system responsible for transmitting and ejaculating semen was responsible for forming a man's emotional character. The physician and occultist Ebenezer Sibly stressed how 'spermatic liquor' was the elixir of life, 'an elaborate tincture' on which men's bodily health depended. Whereas he considered women to be cool and 'vegetative', Sibly reasoned that masculine 'strong' emotions such as 'anger and joy' were created by the dynamic and 'expulsive force' of fluids throughout the male body. Obstructed ejaculations led to a dangerous rise in fluid and psychological pressure, followed by haemorrhages and violent explosions of bodily fluids and tempers. (Hewitt, 2018: 26)

Andrew Jackson Davis, the influential American spiritualist, explains the accepted wisdom surrounding the conundrum of masculine sexuality in his 1874 book *The Genesis and Ethics of Conjugal Love*. While men were situated as 'the crowning glory of the whole organic harmony' in which the conjugal relation takes place (Davis, 1874: 17), they were very much at the mercy of a cycle in which their bodies would build up an excess of sexual energy – a 'charge to repletion, even to the verge of uncontrollable violence' (Davis, 1874: 28) – that required urgent release. As we have seen in Chapter 2, this understanding of men's rapacious and instinctual sexuality provided one compelling explanation for rape in 18th- and 19th-century legal discourse. It also necessitated the substitution of the middle-class white man for the middle-class white woman as the guardian and representative of the moral order, tasked with the responsibility of managing and mitigating men's uncontrollable sexuality, thus providing fertile ground for development of the mythology around victim precipitation of rape (Sanyal, 2019: 17).

A quote from a deliberating juror in one of Ellison and Munro's mock rape trial studies illustrates the remarkable longevity of this idea that men are possessed of a powerful phallic sexual energy that needs to be managed by women who come into contact with them: "[A] woman can stop right up to the last second … a man cannot, he's just got to keep going, he's like a train, he's just got to keep going" (2009a: 298). This logic was used by mock jurors in Ellison and Munro's study to generate sympathy for a defendant who was seen to be at the mercy of the 'natural' expression of his sexuality, which was 'driven by a different force' than a woman's (2009a: 299). The authors concluded that this type of reasoning about the nature of masculine sexuate subjectivity, in our terms, operated 'to normalize the excesses of male sexuality and to absolve the defendant of any responsibility to harness the apparently irrepressible power of his sexual arousal' (Ellison and Munro, 2009a: 299).[15]

---

[15]   The law reports too are littered with this type of reasoning to excuse and mitigate men's sexual violence. For example, in an infamous sentencing decision in Victoria, Australia, in 1992, the presiding judge imposed a heavily mitigated sentence on the defendant, who had been convicted of the rape and attempted murder of a 16-year-old girl. The defendant had 'grabbed' the victim off the street while she walked home from school, threatened her with a knife and dragged her down an embankment. When she had struggled and tried to take the knife, he had punched her in the face until she was unconscious and raped her. After the rape, he slit her throat. The judge suggested that one reason mitigation of

Importantly, for our purposes, the understanding of men as at the mercy of an uncontrollable sexuate subjectivity does not appear to compromise their legal subjectivity when it comes to cases of rape. By outsourcing responsibility to manage a man's natural sexual appetites to a precipitating woman, as long as he had not transgressed other symbolic boundaries that we go on to explore below, women appear to serve as a mediating buffer protecting men's legal subjectivity from contamination by their avaricious sexuate subjectivity. Sexual history evidence is one important tool that can be used to activate that mediating buffer: to refocus a court away from the wayward masculine sexuate subject and on to the woman, who can be seen to have 'caused' the train of masculine sexuality to derail.

While this medico-juridical discourse was developing around the 'nature' of masculine sexuality in 18th- and 19th-century Europe, the British Empire was expanding and consolidating at home and abroad. Considering the legacy of the British imperial period on, in particular, the development of the white, middle-class, masculine sexuate subject is important because, as María Lugones reminds us, sex and gender are fundamental ordering concepts and disciplinary tools in the colonial process (2007). Ann Stoler's painstaking research into the development of bourgeois sexualities in the context of European imperial expansion illustrates how crucial understanding the production of the sexuality of the racialised other was to that process (1995, 2010). In Stoler's argument, metropolitan bourgeoisie do not simply create their own sexuality and then measure racialised others against that standard. Instead, bourgeois sexuality is co-produced alongside racialised discourses of abnormal sexuality (Stoler, 1995; see also, Collins, 2004: 30). In her rereading of Foucault's *History of Sexuality* (1990a, 1990b), Stoler notes that while he was 'undoubtedly right' that the affirmation of the body was 'one of the primordial forms of class consciousness' (Foucault, 1990a: 126), Foucault underestimated the extent to which bourgeois understandings of their own sexuality were entwined with a developing consciousness around class, hygiene and the civilising mission of empire, which was always measured in racial terms: 'Sexual promiscuity or restraint were not abstract characteristics attached to any persons who exhibited those behaviors. But as often post-hoc interpretations contingent on the racialized class and gender categories to which individuals were already assigned' (Stoler, 1995: 115). Bourgeois bodies were perceived to be sexually distinctive then, particularly when compared to the 'barrage of colonial representations' of the racialised other as 'savage' and 'licentious' (Stoler,

---

sentence was needed was that the defendant was suffering at the time from 'pent-up lust', having 'unsuccessfully made sexual advances to a former lover' before the rape occurred. *R v Stanbrook* (Supreme Court of Victoria, O'Bryan J, 10 November 1992, unreported). See further, Kaspiew (1995: 362–7).

1995: 128), 'at once desired and repugnant, forbidden and subservient' (Stoler, 1995: 192). In this age of empire, argues Stoler, the question of who would be 'subject' or 'citizen' 'converged on the sexual politics of race' (1995: 133), and the politics of sexual desire informed networks of power and 'tangled with racial exclusions in complicated ways' (1995: 190). The implication of these complicated relations and networks in the colony was soon to reach the metropole and manifest notably in the discourse of the 'Black Peril': the fear of miscegenation and of the sexual assault of white women by Black men (Stoler, 2010: 58). Stoler points out how the narrative of 'Black Peril' drew on a host of concerns connected to sexual threats as well as the 'fear of insurgence and of perceived non acquiescence to colonial control more generally' (2010: 58). The discourse of 'Black Peril' served the continued construction of white bourgeois masculine sexuate subjectivity too by entrenching the need for constant vigilance and defence of community, morality and white male power (Stoler, 2010: 59; see also, Rutherford, 1997).

The masculine sexuate subject in the UK continues to bear the marks of the historically exclusionary politics of empire. A good example of this legacy activated in the present is the rhetoric around 'Muslim grooming gangs', which arose in the UK after the 7/7 terrorist attacks in London in 2005 (Cockbain, 2013; Tufail, 2015; Tufail and Poynting, 2016; Cockbain and Tufail, 2020). The discussion of 'Muslim grooming gangs' crystallised around two cases of sexual abuse that occurred in the towns of Rotherham in South Yorkshire in 2010 and Rochdale in Greater Manchester in 2012. In these cases, multiple male defendants of South Asian background were convicted for sexual offences committed against socially marginalised and vulnerable minors. Media reporting as well as official reviews of the cases (Jay, 2014) focused on the race, ethnicity and religion of those accused and highlighted the fact that several of their victims were young, white girls. The reporting around these cases at the time activated a moral panic characterised, in particular, by the fear of miscegenation, which served to obscure the violence done to non-white victims, and by white perpetrators, as well as the multiple state failures of safeguarding that were evident in the cases (Tufail, 2015). Understood against a long history of colonial othering of racialised Muslims, we can more readily see how the reconstruction of sexually perverted South Asian men as the new 'folk devils' who present an enduring threat to the British nation and its citizens occurs (Gill and Day, 2020). This process was clearly precipitated or accelerated by the events in the United States post-9/11, during which Islamophobia was 'globalised' (Morgan and Poynting, 2012) via the spectre of the external threat posed by the disaffected racialised other previously kept at bay, coming home. Importantly, the post-9/11 racialised 'Muslim terrorist' was also heavily coded with a perverse sexuality, which helped to crystallise that figure into a threat to the safety and security of citizens and to justify interventions both at home and abroad (Puar and Rai, 2002; Puar, 2007). The figure of the monstrous racialised sexual predator, then, is a constant presence throughout history and in the post-colonial context in which it serves a dual purpose of 'shoring up' the boundaries of the nation state as 'racial state' (Goldberg, 2002) and acting as a counter factual against which a particular form of white middle-class masculine sexuate subjectivity is normalised.

Given what we know about the centrality of race to our understandings of sex/gender and sexuality, coupled with the overwhelming evidence of disproportionate representation of Black and other minority ethnicities at all points of the criminal justice process (Angiolini, 2017; Lammy, 2017; Shankley and Williams, 2020), it should be little surprise so see these patterns reflected in current sexual offence data. Noah Uhrig's 2016 analysis of UK Home Office, Office of National Statistics, CPS and courts data, for example, found that Black and Asian men were significantly more likely to be arrested for sexual offences compared to white men (Uhrig, 2016: 21).[16] While Uhrig found that convictions for sexual offences for both Black and Asian men in his sample were either lower than or proportionate to white men, convicted Black and Asian men were about twice as likely as white men to be given custodial sentences at magistrates' court and were disproportionately represented in the prison population for these offences (Uhrig, 2016: 21).

What then do we take from this (albeit brief) discussion of race, empire and masculine sexuate subjectivity, and how is it relevant to our discussion of sexual history evidence and the rape trial? The claim we make here is that while sexual history evidence may compromise a rape complainant's claim to neutral universal legal subjectivity by activating the masculine projection of feminine sexuate subjectivity to undermine or compromise her claims of violation, masculine subjects are positioned to experience the benefits of sexual history evidence at multiple levels. While men clearly benefit from the ways in which sexual history evidence can call a complainant's consent or credibility into question, they also benefit from the conscious (Herriot, 2023: 102–5) and unconscious power of sexual history evidence to make them whole again where an allegation of rape may have damaged their subjecthood. Because the masculine subject *is* the legal subject – he stands in for the universal neutral subject of law – the robustness of that designation is not so readily compromised when it comes into contact with problematised

---

[16] Black men were 3.7 times more likely than white men to be arrested for sexual offences, while Asian men were about 1.8 times more likely (Uhrig, 2016: 45–6). The Home Office and ONS data used in this study was from 2013/14, while the CPS and courts data was largely from 2014 (Uhrig, 2016: 31–3).

aspects of his sexuate subjectivity. Even where his subjecthood may be called into question by an allegation of rape or the inference of sexual perversity, the masculine subject has a clearer route back to full subjecthood and will be better able to activate the network of material, ideological and symbolic benefits available to him in the rape trial than the feminine subject. While the route back necessarily relies on the denigration of the feminine subject, it also relies on activating the rich imaginary domain available to those embodied as men to help rebuild their subjecthood where it may have been tainted by the allegation of rape. Notwithstanding these points, the availability of the route back to subjecthood for the man accused of rape is always contingent on intersecting cleavages and its relationship to the feminine. While sexual history evidence can provide a route back to wholeness for the masculine sexuate subject, like Evans, where he is positioned to receive those benefits, for other differentially positioned subjects, those benefits will not equally accrue. As we noted earlier, in Evans' second trial his defence lawyer spent some time establishing Evans as a fiancée and father who had a history and a future, and whose only real (albeit 'immoral' and 'immature')[17] mistake was choosing the wrong woman with whom to have adulterous sex. By asserting Evans to be 'a man effectively of good character', when a jury heard him claim in his evidence that "I would never hurt a girl. I would never take advantage of a girl who has not consented. I would never treat a girl that way", they could be sure that he was someone who was, therefore, 'more capable' of belief than, presumably, the complainant.[18] By reference to the 'compelling' and 'important' claims of the two men who gave evidence of their experiences of sex with the complainant, during which she 'took charge' and demanded to be "fucked harder", Evans positions himself as more than being capable, of being *entitled* to the jury's belief and to be made whole again. This type of defence strategy may not work as well when a defendant cannot rely on a motif, like dedicated fatherhood, for example – where that role might be used as a touchstone for imputing other stereotypes around race and class – to establish himself as someone capable of and entitled to a jury's belief and to the reconstitution of his subjecthood as whole (Hlavka and Mulla, 2021: 212–46).

When we situate sexual history evidence as a tool in the wider toolbox upon which the law draws to reproduce and maintain particular understandings of both men and women's sexuate and legal subjectivities, which are also and necessarily imbued with intersecting factors like race and class, we can

---

[17] *R v Evans*, Case No: T20167246, closing submission for the defence, 13 October 2016 (transcript on file with Russell).

[18] *R v Evans*, Case No: T20167246, closing submission for the defence, 13 October 2016 (transcript on file with Russell).

better understand how that toolbox might remain resilient and resistant to change. So deeply embedded are the working presumptions about how men and women do and should behave sexually and otherwise, so central are they to the psychic and material machinery of not only the person, but the state and its law, that sexual history evidence seems to fulfil a constitutive role within and outside the rape trial. Excising the discussion of sexual history evidence from the context in which it is activated allows the precise contours of its activity – what it actually *does* in the rape trial – to remain largely hidden and, therefore, operative. In this sense, sexual history evidence as it functions in the rape trial is one part of a bigger story of inequality and social injustice, the roots of which are far deeper than many of us care to imagine, but that we must surely reckon with if we are to come to terms with its impact and effects.

Conclusion

In this chapter, we have engaged in a theoretically informed discussion to try to understand what happens at both conscious and unconscious levels in the rape trial when sexual history evidence appears. Sexual history evidence is a useful and extraordinarily effective specular tool in the rape trial, affecting a double movement by redirecting the court's attention away from the defendant and activating the masculine projection of feminine sexuate subjectivity in order to undercut the story of violation a prosecutor might be trying to tell. Feminine legal subjectivity in the rape trial is profoundly contingent on its relationship both to the masculine subject and to the extent to which a tool like sexual history evidence can be deployed to invoke the stereotypes and tropes associated with feminine sexuate subjectivity. Masculine subjectivity too plays a key role in the rape trial, and sexual history evidence has the capacity to make male subjects 'whole' again, where the allegation of rape may have called the coherence of that subjecthood into question.

When we understand the baggage that the embodied sexuate subject brings to the rape trial, we are perhaps better able to situate the role and function of sexual history evidence, not just as a liberal legal construct that serves a narrow purpose in the criminal trial (to ensure a 'fair trial' for men accused of rape), but as existing within a network of symbolic, material and ideological meanings and narratives that circulate within the trial and far outside it. These insights necessarily impact too on how we situate ourselves and our intervention into the broader discussion of rape law as feminist legal scholars called on to answer the question: What *should* we do about sexual history evidence? It is to that question we now turn in the final concluding chapter of this book.

8

Conclusion: What Is to Be Done about Sexual History Evidence?

Rape, law and justice revisited

The image that adorns the cover of this book is a reproduction of 'Susanna and the Elders' by the Flemish Renaissance painter Vincent Sellaer, thought to have been composed in the first half of 16th century. Susanna's story is one to which we were drawn because it is a story of sexual violence and law, in which several of the motifs we discuss in this book surface. The story, which appeared first in the Old Testament Apocrypha and is thought to have been written around the 2nd century BC (Moore, 1977: 92), is set in Babylon during the Exile. Susanna was the wife of a prominent Jewish community member and was observed bathing by two passing elders, who accosted her when she was alone, having been overcome by their lust for her. The elders threatened her with humiliation by publicly accusing her of adultery if she denied their requests for sex. Susanna 'courageously refused to commit this sin against God', and when the elders carried through with their threats, she was arrested, tried, convicted and sentenced to death (Bohn, 2001: 260). Susanna was never asked for her version of the events, and she never volunteered it (Glancy, 1993: 115; Bohn, 2001: 260). Before Susanna's sentence could be carried out, the future prophet Daniel interceded on her behalf, testifying to her virtue and demanding that the elders be cross-examined. The inconsistencies in their testimony, drawn out by Daniel's questioning, revealed their lies, and Susanna was exonerated. The elders were stoned to death in Susanna's place. As the biblical scholar Babette Bohn points out, Susanna's story is usually understood as one that situates the importance of fidelity, both to God and the bonds of marriage, and illustrates the value and efficacy of prayer (Bohn, 2001: 260). However, it is also a story about law, gender and justice.

While there are many artistic representations of Susanna and her story in period artwork, we were drawn to this image in part for its composition and colours, but also because it captures the oppressive essence of this part of Susanna's story (the attempted rape or 'seduction'),[1] and of what we perceive it must be like to be a rape complainant giving evidence in the courtroom. The elders loom over Susanna, appearing to whisper into either ear their entreaties for her to surrender her virtue and satiate the desire that observing her naked body has evoked in them. She covers her modesty with one hand, her right breast and stomach exposed, her other hand immobile by her side. The elder's hand on the right of the image looks like a claw going to paw at Susanna's body. The artist has rendered her in this scene with her eyes downcast, indicating her virtue and fidelity, her face otherwise expressionless. We know Susanna will successfully resist the elders' advances and have her virtue vindicated in court when they falsely accuse her. We know that Daniel and the law will ultimately come to her rescue, save her from humiliation and social and literal death. What would she have done if Daniel had not been there to speak for her, to testify to the truth of her chastity and speak to her narrative of violation where she could not? What if there was no law, no protective patriarch to save her from condemnation as an adulteress? Susanna's story can be read as a legal success story, one that shows us the importance of law working as it should to flush out the truth via the adversarial procedure and dispense justice. However, what it also shows us is the contingency and fragility of legal justice, particularly where women's narratives of sexual violation are concerned.

The nature and meaning of justice has long been a concern of feminist scholars and activists who study and write about sexual violence and advocate for victim/survivors. In the last ten years especially, feminist disillusionment with the existing criminal justice approach to crimes of sexual violence has led to a burgeoning and creative discussion around different and alternative approaches to justice, informed by the experiences, perceptions and wishes of victim/survivors. Some of this work seeks to displace the centrality of criminal justice to responding to sexual violence (Powell et al, 2015), including eschewing the criminal courts for the civil process instead (Godden, 2011, 2012). Other work looks to restorative approaches (McGlynn et al, 2012; Zinsstag and Keenan, 2017; Keenan and Zinsstag, 2022), or to notions of justice as 'kaleidoscopic' or as existing on a continuum to guide law and policy making (McGlynn and Westmarland, 2019; McGlynn, 2022). There is a focus too on procedural justice (Hohl et al, 2022), and on envisioning a response to sexual violence that corresponds with a broader notion of justice as 'transformative' (Kim 2018, 2021; ackhurst et al, 2022; Engle, 2022).

---

[1]   See further Bohn (2001: 260 at n 5) arguing that while the elders' actions are usually euphemistically referred to as 'seduction', they bear the characteristics of, and are therefore more properly described as, attempted rape.

One of the insights of this broad body of literature is that it exposes or calls into question the narrow conception of justice embedded within the norms and conventions of criminal law and of the criminal trial. Importantly also, it is often informed by a sense that we are all of us immersed within a powerful and operative network of material, ideological and discursive signifiers and narratives about gender, as well as other intersecting cleavages like race and class. The criminal justice apparatus and the law itself is far from immune from the effects of these intersecting signs and narratives; in fact, they have a key role in upholding and promoting them. We situate ourselves and our contribution in this book within this body of work. While our focus has been the discrete, in many ways, legal construct of sexual history evidence, what our analysis has revealed is that the import, meaning and reach of sexual history evidence is far wider. To return to the image of law as a toolbox, sexual history evidence is but one tool that is drawn upon in the rape trial to invalidate the experiences and voices of women and to shore up the status quo, in which men's symbolic world is protected and their understanding of themselves as whole reflected back on to them via their ready access to women's bodies. What we should *do*, therefore, about the problem of sexual history evidence must take into account those broader implications, and it is here that we situate ourselves in this final reflection.

Feminist research and the problem of rape and law

That the law often inflicts serious harm on those who call on it for justice is an insight upon which critical scholars of law have repeatedly insisted. Feminist scholars studying rape are frequently driven to despair by what they see when they look at the criminal justice process and talk to victims. Pratiksha Baxi understands the violence with which rape trials inscribe extreme indignity and humiliation on women's bodies as a 'public secret' in which an 'active not-knowing' is operationalised to ignore the effects of law on rape complainants (2013: 341). Rebecca Campbell makes this point even more stridently, arguing that the criminal justice system in its interaction with rape complainants is inherently and deliberately oppressive:

> It is active work – oppression – and police make time and devote energy to this work. They do not expend time and energy to investigate rapists. They do not submit rape kits for forensic testing. They do not utilize the results of that testing to find rapists and to refer for criminal charges. It is active work to NOT investigate rapists. It is active work TO denigrate victims. This is how the system works. (Campbell, 2022: 23, emphasis in original)

There is a redefinition or recalibration of subjectivity in the subject's encounter with the law during the criminal justice process in the aftermath of rape. Baxi (2013: 347) describes this redefined subjectivity as characterised by '[deep] wounding', and Russell (2023: 299) argues that the rape trial has its own 'deathly logic' with the capacity profoundly to stunt a complainant's being and becoming. The overwhelming evidence of the impact of the secondary victimisation of rape complainants who interact with the criminal justice apparatus, and in particular the rape trial, has clear ethical implications for feminist researchers. While our analysis in this book has extracted itself in parts from the affective vicissitudes of the law to engage with the doctrine on its own terms, we take Campbell's reminder well that emotions can and should be a guiding source of feminist research (2022: 23). So too the careful and 'slow scholarship' we have sought to enact as feminist method in our writing of this book (Mountz et al, 2015).

From all we know about sexual violence in our research into rape law for this book and elsewhere, it is hard to argue with the conclusion of many that the system that purports to prevent and respond to the problem of sexual violence is broken beyond repair. Indeed, as Horvath and Brown note in their recent retrospective on rape law and practice, the more one learns about the system, the less likely one is to want much to do with it: '[A]lmost all rape researchers we asked told us that if they were raped, they would not report to police' (2022: 288). Reflecting on their extensive multi-year ethnography of rape trials in Milwaukee, Hlavka and Mulla (2021) found themselves inevitably drawn to abolitionism: the position that advocates for justice outside state institutions and the movement away from, and/or defunding of, police and prisons (see further, Davis, 2005; Davis et al, 2022; Gilmore, 2022). The criminal justice system, Hlavka and Mulla conclude, is structurally and fundamentally unable to account for the violence it inflicts or even to make that violence legible to itself, let alone provide justice to those harmed through sexual violence (2021: 40–1).

The fact remains, however, that complainants do choose to engage with the criminal justice system, and it is the imperative represented by a desire to help those men and women that drives many legal scholars of sexual violence to continue to seek justice through law and the institutions of the state. The central conundrum posed by the realities of sexual violence and the continuing and catastrophic failures of governments, legislators and policy makers to improve the situation in any real way must inform, however, a thorough-going understanding of the limits of law as a means to achieving justice.

Those limits tend to reveal themselves without much digging. A crippling paradox that faces law and policy makers engaged in trying to increase rape prosecution numbers, for example, illustrates the circular logic of many of the immanent strategies on offer for addressing attrition. Prosecutors restrict the cases that are taken forward to trial because they fail the 'realistic prospect of conviction' test (CPS, 2018: 7) when the evidence available is assessed by reference to the full suite of rape myths and presumptions likely to be deployed by a jury or exploited by defence counsel. When objections are raised to how the evidential test for prosecution is being applied because so few cases are being put forward, prosecutors are encouraged to get their numbers up by bringing forward cases which do not necessarily conform to the 'real rape' paradigm. However, these cases frequently fail (as so many rape prosecutions inevitably do), thus reinscribing the initial paradigm that only very few rape cases will have a 'realistic prospect of conviction'. Trapped within a cycle in which only those cases within a very narrow frame will be taken forward, and in which resources are tight and diminishing, rape prosecutions continue to founder, and the 'real rape' paradigm remains intact.

Systemic failures like these are often explained away in neutral terms. Rape cases are so difficult, so the saying goes, because they involve the intractable 'he said/she said' paradox. Where a case is 'one person's word against another', how are any of us to know what really happened? This logic hides, of course, the myriad and intersecting ways that all the meanings and narratives we have been discussing in this book arise and make themselves known in cases of rape. The refrain that rape cases are just 'one person's word against another' serves to erase the symbolic reality in which tropes about *how women are* and *what women do* are put to work in the service of reducing the force of their words to a whisper. Leigh Gilmore draws out the paucity of 'both sides' logic in a discussion of the circulation of narratives of doubt of women's stories in law in literature:

> The locution 'no one knows what really happened' is less a position of reasoned and reasonable skepticism than an active, reflexive, and ultimately political feeling that women cannot be trusted to say what harm has befallen them. All too often, a short-circuiting of credibility appears as a unique fault of specific women rather than a predictable product of rape discourse; that is, of many cultural mechanisms working together to produce doubt. (Gilmore, 2017: 142)

To work in the area of sexual violence and law often involves the nagging feeling of being perpetually 'gaslighted' by (so we are told) the only system through which we can look to make sense of the problem and to find a way out. While the law might not be perfect, the story goes, if we can just calibrate it right, it will work as it should, dispensing justice equally and without fear or favour. Limited to a horizon of piecemeal and incremental reform within a system the primary goal of which is its own protection, it usually turns out that all along, we were treading against a tide that was always going out. At the heart of the problem is the fact that the criminal law confines the conceptualisation of rape to a problem of individual pathology, rather than an expression of gendered social relations, the consequence of which is entrenched and self-perpetuating inequality. There has long been a strong correlation between rape-prone and unequal societies (Sanday, 1981), and we know that those who experience the most inequality are also most at risk of sexual violence (Davis, 1981; Phipps, 2009; Nagy, 2015). Inequalities that concentrate around designations like gender are not just about identity, therefore; they organise, dictate and inhabit social structures, institutions and practices. Law cannot be extracted from these relations by fiat, method or principle, or just because we want it to be so. Strategies that eschew or ignore this reality are destined for failure, or to be slowly co-opted or absorbed by the status quo.

Normatively embedded 'laws as tactics'

We recognise that many of those reading this book may be looking to us for a neat set of legal or policy recommendations around which a programme for change or reform could be initiated to ameliorate, at the very least, the myriad problems with sexual history evidence we have catalogued in this study. Unfortunately, there is no panacea to be offered here, no ten-point plan to fix what is broken. The challenges we face with sexual history evidence, as with sexual violence more broadly, are unlikely to be solved through more police or prosecution targets, or fewer exceptions to evidential gateways in the rape trial. This is a problem of equality and social justice at the heart of which is the relationship between law and gender. It is here that we have to start.

What we can offer is a reflection on some options, as we see them, while trying to keep in mind the pitfalls involved with different strategies. Another important contribution we can make is methodological. We find ourselves at the end of this analysis intent on refusing the discourse of law reform on its own terms, or the 'policy cycle' we observed in Chapter 4, by which the linear path of our analysis is supposed to 'lead' us to a set of recommendations within the frame or horizon as set, along with requirements that it be delivered according to the appropriate form, in the right language, and in a specified time period. The work that has gone into this book has taken place over a period of about five years, which is how long it takes to investigate a problem like sexual history evidence from multiple angles, with the care and rigour necessary to generate meaningful insights. We are sure we have missed things, which we hope those who engage with our work will draw out so the conversation can continue. This 'slow scholarship' we are describing has revealed, among other insights, that we have to see legal and policy work in historical context and draw this context through to the present as a way to help us unpick the patterns of discourse and the legal constructs, like relevance, for example, that are rarely called into serious question but do such important work in maintaining the status quo. We need also to appreciate that the symbolic context in which sexual history evidence operates interacts seamlessly with the material context in which it is enacted in and outside the courtroom.

To accept all these foregoing points is not to say that nothing can be done to address sexual history evidence through and with law, but that we need to accept that change takes time and commitment, and we might need to start in a different place if we are to see the change we want. If we continue to engage with law without simultaneously questioning its capacity to deliver us from the scourge of sexual and other forms of violence, we will end up reproducing the same logic in which we are currently mired. In her analysis of the possibilities for decertifying legal gender, Davina Cooper evokes the concept of 'slow law' to elaborate or understand the contours and temporalities of radical proposals for legal change (2023: 28): ' "Slow law" is experimental law. But it is not teleological. It assumes the conditions, interests and agendas driving action will change. It also recognises that the rhythms of prototyping reform will fluctuate – accelerating, slowing down, and reversing as the political context evolves.' 'Slow law' may also be useful, asserts Cooper, where 'new subjectivities' are called for: it may enable us to mobilise existing categories through which we understand subjecthood where political goals and individual interests align, while simultaneously allowing us to hold open the possibility for more radical change in which the structure that buttresses the current system is fundamentally called into question. Where there is resistance to a movement away from, for example, the view that it is simply 'common sense' that sexual history evidence is relevant to questions of consent or complainant credibility in the criminal rape trial, 'slow law' may provide the 'legal tempo' (Cooper, 2023: 28) for the eventual realignment of that 'common sense'. As Cooper puts it, 'an important feature of "slow law" … is that it allows political aspirations to be articulated that stretch beyond what is presently viable, confronting both the obstacles and building blocks that need to be in place' (2023: 28).

While we are not here 'prototyping reform' in the sense Cooper is in her work on decertification, there are important lessons to be learned from a methodological approach to law and legal change which seeks to upend or problematise the taken-for-granted conditions under which we assume reform *must* take place, while keeping an eye to ever-changing immanent conditions. We make a similar move here in suggesting that we need to take a normatively embedded approach to law that matches the aspirations of the imaginary domain, through which we continue to envision the equality and social justice we want to see (Cornell, 1995). The task, therefore, is to enact a cautious and evidence-based engagement with law, always with an eye to the ways in which these strategies impact on and connect to broader movements for equality and social justice, given what we know about how sexual and other forms of violence flourish in conditions of inequality. In taking up this approach, we follow Dean Spade (2011) in seeking to engage with law tactically, taking it up where it makes sense to and can serve us, but without believing that what law says about us or itself is necessarily true. Amia Srinivasan neatly distils the political and affective dexterity and reflexivity that such an approach requires:

> There is no settling in advance on a political programme that is immune to cooption, or that is guaranteed to be revolutionary rather than reformist. You can only see what happens, then plot your next move. This requires being prepared – strategically and emotionally – to abandon ways of thinking and acting to which you may have become deeply attached. (2021: 176)

We also take seriously the need for 'feminist accountability' in thinking carefully about the implications of what we say and what we do, recognising that we are all implicated in networks of power and privilege, the impacts of which are differentially experienced (Razack, 1998; Russo, 2018). With all these important provisos in mind, let us have a look at what is to be done about sexual history evidence.

What is to be done about sexual history evidence?

There are three broad options for 'dealing' with the problem of sexual history evidence, as we see it.

Expunge sexual history evidence from the rape trial altogether

The first option is an outright ban on the admission of sexual history evidence in the rape trial, codified in legislation and robustly defended in the courts. As we have seen in Chapters 5 and 6, once sexual history evidence is admitted in the trial, it does its own work regardless of the narrowness of its relevance to the charge at issue. Defence lawyers instinctively know this, which is why they are so keen to protect defendant access to routes to admission.

The reader can probably rehearse the objections to this approach, foremost of which is that it is unlikely to have any political viability. The reader will recall from Chapter 4 that the claim that there is a problem at all with sexual history evidence in the rape trial is one that is continuously contested. The overwhelming evidence of secondary victimisation of the rape complainant in the trial, much of which occurs because of the introduction of sexual history evidence,[2] is a key driver in initiating the policy cycle of review and reform we observed in Chapter 4. Even those who object to the idea that the law that governs sexual history evidence is not working as it should or needs reform acknowledge the reality of secondary victimisation. The difference, however, is that those who assert the law is working as it should, explicitly or implicitly accept secondary victimisation of the complainant as an unfortunate, but unavoidable, cost of protecting an accused's right to a 'fair trial'. In other words, the perception that the law is working as it should is premised on an ideological acceptance of the legitimacy of the system and its collateral costs, the tolerance of which is ultimately a political choice. As long as that tolerance exists among the political and judicial class, crystallised in the case law and popular discourse as 'common sense', and supported by the hierarchy of 'rights' as they currently exist in the criminal trial, sexual history evidence is bound to continue in some form or another.

A central objection to the argument for total expungement of sexual history evidence from the rape trial is that it will prevent the jury from gaining a full and rounded picture of the narrative precipitating the disputed act. Surely, it is argued, no one can object to the 'bare fact' of a prior relationship between the parties being presented as 'background evidence' that frames the events leading up to the alleged rape. In principle of course this is true, and there is a sense of artificiality in giving an account in which some of the background information is necessarily withheld. At the same time, and as we have repeatedly observed, the introduction of such evidence, even merely as part of the background narrative, can have a devastating effect on the outcome of the trial, an effect, moreover, which impedes rather than advances criminal justice.

At the same time, we believe that further restrictions on the introduction of sexual history evidence may compound rather than alleviate the problems we have identified. This is partly because such a move might further 'fetishise' complainant sexual history, that is, confer a weight and meaning to such evidence which might reinforce rather than undermine its current evidentiary significance. More importantly, however, we are sceptical of such a measure because it will not solve the problem of how a complainant's sexual history is culturally perceived, nor thwart interpretations of facts based on problematic socio-sexual scripts which accord to women the role of sexual gatekeepers. In this sense, the 'problem' of sexual history evidence lies beyond the courtroom, in the cultural scaffolding of rape (Gavey, 2019)

---

[2]   The spectre of sexual history evidence being introduced or dredged through as part of an investigation into a rape allegation is one of the most frequently cited reasons women give for declining to report or support the prosecution of allegations of rape (Kelly et al, 2006; McGlynn, 2018).

which legal norms and processes undoubtedly reinforce but which is not exclusively legal in its forms or manifestations. Notwithstanding these points and keeping in mind the 'slow law' discussed earlier, if sexual history evidence, as we have argued, has such a profoundly negative influence on criminal and other forms of justice, then it makes sense to want it completely excised from the criminal rape trial. Ultimately, our capacity to imagine or bring into being a shift of such magnitude in which the *irrelevance* of sexual history evidence might come to align more closely with what currently passes for 'common sense', in both its juridic and popular uses, depends on our capacity to influence or shift the normative frame via which we have these conversations.

Continued reform of the legislative frameworks governing sexual history evidence

There are clearly areas in which changes can still be made to existing legal frameworks with a view to dealing with some of the more egregious problems with sexual history evidence we have observed. We drew out several of these possibilities in our jurisdictional review in Chapter 4 and will observe the monitoring of the new provisions in New Zealand with some interest, given the nature of the changes to the Evidence Act 2006, enacted in December 2021. The extension of the 'heightened relevance' requirement to sexual experience with the defendant, and to sexual disposition evidence, is an interesting development in that jurisdiction, notwithstanding the limitations to relevance as a concept highlighted in Chapter 6. So too will it be interesting to see how or whether the 'mere fact' exception to the heightened relevance test in the New Zealand provisions will be exploited as a proxy gateway for the continued admission of evidence that is otherwise now excluded. However, and again, the capacity for reforms such as these to shift the current situation in any meaningful way is limited by the frame through which they are channelled and perceived. There is very little evidence in any of the jurisdictions we reviewed in Chapter 4 that any one calibration of law and policy in this area represents a 'gold-standard' or offers a panacea. And which system works best depends on who you are asking and how that person, institution or body of actors might measure success; as we have seen, not everyone involved in responding to sexual violence is aiming for the same outcomes.

Procedural options

Ironically, given the limits we observed in Chapter 4, it is procedural adjustments that we see as holding the most potential for changing the discursive and operational context within which sexual history evidence currently features. The scope for procedural change exists on a continuum from options that may seem quite radical, to those which are already in train but are worth drawing out so that we can see how their potential impact 'fits' with our vision of meaningful change.

There is promise in a strategy such as ILR for rape complainants, where is it adequately resourced and implemented (Jillard et al, 2012). This is so not just for improving outcomes where the admission of sexual history evidence is concerned, but also for disrupting the normative schema around which the existing rights-based approach to the adversarial trial operates. As discussed in Chapter 4 and following Lise Gotell's thoughtful discussion on this point (2006), the existing discourse tends to pit the accused's right to a 'fair trial' against a complainant's right to (or interest in, depending on the jurisdiction in question), dignity or privacy in her capacity as witness for the prosecution. These rights/interests are then relied upon to object to defence attempts to admit sexual history evidence or other information like counselling or medical records, but often and necessarily give way to the defendant's rights. The current approach to dealing with this problem is to try to 'force' the court to take better account of the rights of the complainant through, for example, a 'heightened relevance test' (New Zealand), or by having them constitutionally and legislatively enshrined (Canada). In our view, the crux of the shift that is required regarding the rights-based approach is a normative one with the end goal of challenging the conflation of the vindication of the defendant's rights through the admission of sexual history evidence with the 'fair trial' per se. One of the positive effects of ILR has been to expose the complainant's lack of voice and participation in the criminal justice process, creating a policy agenda which compels the articulation of her interests as a key stakeholder. This in turn unbalances the neat presentation of criminal justice as a contest between the state and the accused, in which the latter is positioned as the exclusive rights-bearer. It is in disrupting this unnecessarily constricted expression of criminal justice that we see the most potential for ILR. Where more time or discursive attention is paid to the complainant's rights and interests, via their increased visibility in the trial through a dedicated advocate, for example, ILR has the potential to shift the weight of those rights, or to open space for the 'emptiness' or 'nothingness' of a right like privacy to be given some content (Gotell, 2006: 753).

As we argued in Chapter 7, women are never fully possessed of legal subjecthood in the rape trial, which is what makes them so vulnerable to the ideological, discursive and material force of sexual history evidence. The liberal rights-based approach to cure a problem like this remains, in many ways, mired within the history we have been investigating in this book, in which equality means increased access to the rights of the universal (masculine) legal subject, rather than as rights-holders as singular and independent subjects in their own right (Irigaray, 1991; Cornell,

1995; Russell, 2013). Notwithstanding these very real limitations, we do have a discourse of rights open to us through which complainants' status as rights-bearing citizens can be developed and reinforced. ILR for rape complainants as standard throughout the entirety of the rape trial, or criminal justice process, is a realistic goal for advocates (Smith and Daly, 2020), and certainly always where the admission of sexual history or other confidential information is at issue.

Outside ILR, there are several other procedural changes that have the potential to shift this normative schema we have been talking about. Some of these have more political and public support than others. The use of specialist 'rape courts', where rigorously trained lawyers, judges and other participants are sequestered to deal with these cases, is a possibility that several scholars and others are investing their time in advocating (Dripps, 2009; Smith and Skinner, 2015). The establishment and use of such courts is a logical next step from the sexual assault referral centres, currently in operation in several jurisdictions, in which specially trained police and lay personnel trained as ISVAs can support and advise complainants in the aftermath of sexual violence (Stern, 2010: 102–6). These facilities and practices have the aim of limiting the exposure of rape complainants to those who may draw upon 'rape myths' and other problematic assumptions and stereotypes in dealing with complainants or making decisions about their cases (Hester and Lilley, 2018; Rumney et al, 2020).

Another area in which a flurry of research is being done, and which implicates the normative schema that supports the status quo, are initiatives that involve the (re)education of judges and juries around sexual violence. In most jurisdictions, there is some provision for the education of judges who will or may sit on sexual offence cases. In England and Wales, to get a 'sex ticket', judges are required to attend a course which covers topics such as rape trauma, medical and forensic science and legal and procedural issues, with an expectation that they will continue to attend such a seminar every three years (Stern, 2010: 93; Judicial College, 2022: 10–11). Similar programmes are provided in New Zealand, for example, where Te Kura Kaiwhakawā, the Institute of Judicial Studies, provides continuing education resources and training for judges that includes education in and around the dynamics of sexual violence. There is a clear need for more research on this type of strategy with judges, including on its efficacy in relation to decision-making on sexual history evidence (Rumney and Fenton, 2011). In respect of juror education, some jurisdictions, including England and Wales, have required the use of judicial directions on 'counterintuitive' evidence in rape trials where 'such directions [are] crafted with care and [always] discussed with the advocates in advance'.[3] While current research

---

[3]   *Crown Court Compendium, Part 1*, 20–1 Sexual Offences, para 13 (June 2022). See further, *R v D* [2008] EWCA Crim 2557; *Miller* [2010] EWCA Crim 1578.

suggests that the efficacy of juror education around sexual violence is patchy at best (Ellison, 2019; Tinsley et al, 2021; Hudspith et al, 2023), researchers continue to pursue these strategies as a way to excavate and disrupt the gendered norms about sexual violence embedded in the law and which are taken up and mobilised both by advocates and decision-makers (Herriot, 2023: 167–9). We need to be realistic about the efficacy of expending significant time and energy on these types of strategies where the impact may be marginal. The seductive weight of sexual history evidence – its place in the cultural and social imaginary and what it evokes in finders of law and fact in the rape trial – is simply no match for a few pages of judicial guidance to juries, testimony from an expert witness or two-day training sessions with judges, all of which can seem more like taking an umbrella out in a hurricane rather than a sincere attempt to address the problems that present in these cases. Many scholars and activists have rightly highlighted these limitations, and advocate for much broader educative initiatives in schools, for example, with sex education and young people's understandings of consent.[4] There is less discussion of the need to rethink legal education or the law curriculum, not just as a way to diversify what is taught, but to embed a thorough-going critical engagement with or displacement of the standard account of legal history and doctrine (MacKinnon, 2003; Kennedy, 2007). The movement to 'decolonise the curriculum' has been slow to enter the law school (Adébísí, 2020, 2023), and criminal and evidence law are long overdue their decolonial reckoning (Aliverti et al, 2023). That is to say, we need to embed a discussion of the precepts upon which 'criminal justice', for example, proceeds, and not just as an 'add on' to the back end of a unit or module on criminal law, but as a foundational question for interrogation. All these considerations feed into the development of the lawyers, judges and jurors of tomorrow, who need to be equipped with the skills and capacity to pause and reflect when faced with legal constructs like evidential relevance or uncritical appeals to 'common sense' where something like sexual history evidence is concerned.

More generally, evidence gathering in the area of sexual violence, and the operation of sexual history evidence specifically, remains crucial, and most of this needs to be done independently of state institutions to protect its integrity. We desperately need more empirical research into the experiences and treatment of racialised complainants in England and Wales. This will require multi-year and major funding commitments so that we can have a

---

[4]   See, for example, the Schools Consent Project in the UK that seeks to 'empower young people aged 11–18 in England, Wales & Northern Ireland with the skills, confidence and knowledge they need to make safe, healthy choices around sexual consent'. https://www.schoolsconsentproject.com/ [Accessed 5 June 2023].

better sense of how complainants from these communities are treated and experience the criminal justice process when it comes to sexual violence.

Final reflection

A key aspect of our professed commitments to 'laws as tactics' and 'feminist accountability' means reflecting on the externalities involved with any sort of engagement with the criminal justice apparatus, including those we have highlighted in this final chapter. What does it mean to have access to a more normatively embedded right to privacy, for example, without a more thorough-going understanding of what justice means in cases of rape? And justice here necessarily refers to a broader concept that considers interconnected movements for social, racial and economic justice, all of which are implicated and touched by the mechanisms of the criminal justice system. It is difficult to imagine ourselves outside the conditions under which we currently live, in which gross inequality engenders and produces epidemic levels of violence and harm, without recourse to those tools of criminal justice that we have been told are there to protect us. It is simply impossible for many people to conceive of an imaginary of justice without police, courts and prisons at its centre. And yet, once we countenance the possibility that the mechanisms of criminal justice are not only failing us but might be making things worse, we are quickly confronted by the paradox that reliance on criminal justice generates and the inability of these structures to keep us safe (Kaba, 2021; ackhurst et al, 2022; Aaron, 2023; Ievins, 2023). The state and its agents are directly or indirectly the cause of a lot of violence, whether that be the violence of decades of austerity, the direct violence of policing and prisons, or the subtle but no less potent violence of apathy, inaction or ambivalence. To quote Srinivasan again: '[A] feminist politics which sees the punishment of bad men as its primary purpose will never be a feminism that liberates all women, for it obscures what makes most women unfree' (2021: 170).

The implication of accepting what is at stake in working in and with the state and of attempting to think with and through a broader notion of justice might be to shift from where we start or from where we focus in our efforts to build momentum for change. It might mean resisting being drawn into directing all our time and resources into advocating for ILR, for example, when there are other avenues for our energy and skills which better reflect the vision of justice we have in mind. In this way, we might see advocating for ILR across rape trials as standard as one part of a feminist anti-rape politics that includes decolonising sexual violence and the law (Coetzee and Du Toit, 2018; Du Toit, 2019), and centring indigenous women's and women of colour's knowledge and practices (Kim, 2021; Russell, 2021). It might also include attempting to build capacity for systems for community accountability or for different kinds of restorative practices outside the criminal justice system proper. In this way then, when thinking about feminist anti-rape politics and strategy, we have to build towards a vision of the world we want, accepting that we will likely make mistakes on the way, but hoping that things will be better in the end, and not just for rape complainants who face the admission of their sexual history evidence in the rape trial, but for all those to whom justice is owed.

References

Aaron, N. (2023) 'Bringing the failings of "criminal justice" and embodiments of sexually violent figures into the frame of feminist approaches to tackling sexual violence', Unpublished PhD thesis, Bristol: University of Bristol. Copy on file with the authors.

ackhurst, m., Brazzell, M., Day, A.S., Tomlinson, K. and Fowler, Y.R. (2022) 'Creative and transformative approaches to justice', in M. Horvath and J. Brown (eds) *Rape: Challenging Contemporary Thinking – 10 Years On*, London: Routledge, 268–82.

Adébísí, F. (2020) 'Decolonising the law school: presences, absences, silences … and hope', *The Law Teacher*, 54(4): 471–4.

Adébísí, F. (2023) *Decolonisation and Legal Knowledge: Reflections on Power and Possibility*, Bristol: Bristol University Press.

Adler, Z. (1982) 'The intention of Parliament and the practice of the courts', *Modern Law Review*, 45: 664–75.

Adler, Z. (1987) *Rape on Trial*, London: Routledge.

Ahmed, S. (2004) *The Cultural Politics of Emotion*, New York: Routledge.

Aliverti, A., Carvalho, H., Chamberlen, A., and Sozzo, M. (eds) (2023) *Decolonizing the Criminal Question: Colonial Legacies, Contemporary Problems*, Oxford: Oxford University Press.

Anderson, M. (2002) 'From chastity requirement to sexuality licence: sexual consent and a new rape-shield law', *George Washington Law Review*, 70: 51–162.

Angiolini, E. (2017) 'Report of the Independent Review of Deaths and Serious Incidents in Police Custody'. Available from: https://assets.publishing.service.gov.uk/government/uploads/system/uploads/attachment_data/file/655401/Report_of_Angiolini_Review_ISBN_Accessible.pdf [Accessed 3 April 2023].

Archbold, J.F. (1822) *A Summary of the Law Relative to Pleading and Evidence in Criminal Cases*, London: R. Pheney, S. Sweet & R. Millikin.

Baird, V. (2020) '2019/2020 annual report: Victim's Commissioner for England and Wales', HC 625.

Bashar, N. (1983) 'Rape in England between 1550–1700', in London Feminist History Group (eds) *The Sexual Dynamics of History*, London: Pluto Press, 28–42.

Baxi, P. (2013) *Public Secrets of Law: Rape Trials in India*, New Delhi: Oxford University Press.

Beattie, J.M. (1986) *Crime and the Courts in England 1660–1800*, Princeton: Princeton University Press.

Beattie, J.M. (1991) 'Scales of justice: defense counsel and the English criminal trial in the eighteenth and nineteenth centuries', *Law and History Review*, 9(2): 221–67.

Berger, V. (1977) 'Man's trial, woman's tribulation: rape cases in the courtroom', *Columbia Law Review*, 77: 1–103.

Birch, D. (2002) 'Rethinking sexual history evidence: proposals for fairer trials', *Criminal Law Review*, 531–53.

Blackstone, W. (1803) *Commentaries on the Laws of England, Book IV: 'Of Public Wrongs'* (14th edn), London: Cadell and Davies.

Blair, I. (1985) *Investigating Rape: A New Approach for Police*, London: Croom Helm.

Bohn, B. (2001) 'Rape and the gendered gaze: Susanna and the elders in early modern Bologna', *Biblical Interpretation*, 9(3): 259–86.

Bohner, G., Eyssel, F., Afroditi, P., Siebler, F. and Tendayi Viki, G. (2009) 'Rape myth acceptance: cognitive, effective and behavioural effects of beliefs that blame the victim and exonerate the perpetrator', in M. Horvath and J. Brown (eds) *Rape: Challenging Contemporary Thinking*, Tavistock: Willan Publishing, 17–45.

Bohner, G., Eyssel, F. and Süssenbach, P. (2023) 'Modern myths about sexual aggression: new methods and findings', in M. Horvath and J. Brown (eds) *Rape: Challenging Contemporary Thinking – 10 Years On*, Abingdon: Routledge, 159–71.

Bowers, T. (2011) *Force or Fraud: British Seduction Stories as the Problem of Resistance*, Oxford: Oxford University Press.

Bracton, H. (1210–68) *De Legibus et Consuetudinibus Angliae* ('On the Laws and Customs of England'), [online]. Available from: http://amesfoundat ion.law.harvard.edu/Bracton/ [Accessed 31 May 2023].

Brewis, B. and Jackson, A. (2020) 'Sexual behaviour evidence and evidence of bad character in sexual offence proceedings: proposing a combined admissibility framework', *Journal of Criminal Law*, 84: 49–73.

Brison, S. (2002) *Aftermath: Violence and the Remaking of a Self*, Princeton: Princeton University Press.

Brown, B., Burman, M. and Jamieson, L. (1992) 'Sexual history and sexual character evidence in Scottish sexual offences trials', Edinburgh: Scottish Office.

Brown, D., Farrier, D., McNamara, L., Steel, A., Grewcock, M., Quilter, J. et al (2020) *Criminal Laws: Materials and Commentary on Criminal Law and Process of NSW: 7th Edition*, Sydney: The Federation Press.

Brown, O. (2016) '"Team Ched" shows just how sick football culture in Britain is', *The Telegraph*, [online] 14 October. Available from: https://www.telegraph.co.uk/football/2016/10/14/team-ched-show-just-how-sick-football-culture-in-britain-is/? [Accessed 2 September 2022].

Brundage, J.A. (1990) *Law, Sex and Christian Society*, Chicago: University of Chicago Press.

Burgin, R. and Flynn, A. (2019) 'Women's behavior as implied consent: male "reasonableness" in Australian rape law', *Criminology & Criminal Justice*, 21(3): 334–52.

Buiten, D. and Naidoo, K. (2016) 'Framing the problem of rape in South Africa: gender, race, class and state histories', *Current Sociology*, 64(4): 535–50.

Bumiller, K. (2008) *In an Abusive State: How Neoliberalism Appropriated the Feminist Movement against Sexual Violence*, Durham, NC: Duke University Press.

Burman, M., Jamieson, L., Nicholson, J. and Brooks, O. (2007) *Impact of Aspects of the Law of Evidence in Sexual Offence Trials: An Evaluation Study*, Edinburgh: Scottish Government Social Research.

Burman, M. (2009) 'Evidencing sexual assault: women in the witness box', *Journal of Community and Criminal Justice*, 56(4): 379–98.

Cairns, D.J.A. (1998) *Advocacy and the Making of the Adversarial Criminal Trial*, Oxford: Oxford University Press.

Campbell, R. (2022) 'Revisiting *Emotionally Involved*: the impact of researching rape; twenty years (and thousands of stories) later', in M. Horvath and J. Brown (eds) *Rape: Challenging Contemporary Thinking – 10 Years On*, London: Routledge, 12–27.

Campbell, L. and Cowan, S. (2017) 'The relevance of sexual history and vulnerability in the prosecution of sexual offences', in P. Duff and P.R. Ferguson (eds) *Scottish Criminal Evidence Law: Current Developments and Future Trends*, Edinburgh: Edinburgh University Press, 67–96.

Carol, C. (2019) 'Luce Irigaray on women and natural law', in J. Crowe and C.Y. Lee (eds) *Research Handbook on Natural Law Theory*, Cheltenham: Edward Elgar Publishing, 236–52.

Cassidy, M. (2021) 'Character, credibility and rape shield rules', *Georgia Journal of Law & Public Policy*, 19: 145–76.

Catty, J. (1999) *Writing Rape, Writing Women in Early Modern England*, London: Palgrave Macmillan.

Cavallaro, R. (2019) 'Rape shield evidence and the hierarchy of impeachment', *American Criminal Law Review*, 56: 295–314.

Centre for Women's Justice, End Violence Against Women coalition, Imkaan and Rape Crisis England & Wales (2020) 'The decriminalisation of rape: why the justice system is failing rape survivors and what needs to change'. Available from: Decriminalisation+of+Rape+Report,+CWJ+EVAW+IMKAAN+RCEW,+NOV+2020.pdf (squarespace.com) [Accessed 31 May 2023].

Chalmers, J. (2014) 'Independent legal representation for complainers in sexual offence cases', in J. Chalmers, F. Leverick and A. Shaw (eds) 'Post-corroboration safeguards review report of the academic expert group', Edinburgh: The Scottish Government, 185–9.

Chalmers, J., Leverick, F. and Munro, V. (2021) 'Why the jury is and should still be out on rape deliberations', *Criminal Law Review*, 9: 753–71.

Chambers, G. and Millar, A. (1983) 'Investigating sexual assault', Edinburgh: Scottish Office Central Research Unit.

Clark, A. (1987) *Women's Silence, Men's Violence: Sexual Assault in England 1770–1845*, London: Routledge & Kegan Paul.

Cockbain, E. (2013) 'Grooming and the "Asian sex gang predator": the construction of a racial crime threat', *Race & Class*, 54(4): 22–32.

Cockbain, E. and Tufail, W. (2020) 'Failing victims, fuelling hate: challenging the harms of the "Muslim grooming gangs" narrative', *Race & Class*, 61(3): 3–32.

Cockburn, J.S. (1977) 'The nature and incidence of crime in England 1559–1625: a preliminary survey', in J. Cockburn (ed) *Crime in England 1550–1800*, Princeton: Princeton University Press, 49–71.

Coetzee, A. and Du Toit, L. (2018) 'Facing the sexual demon of colonial power: decolonising sexual violence in South Africa', *European Journal of Women's Studies*, 25(2): 214–27.

Coke, E. (1629) *The Third Part of the Institutes of the Laws of England concerning High Treason and Other Pleas of the Crown, and Criminal Causes*, [online]. Available from: http://lawlibrary.wm.edu/wythepedia/library/CokeThirdPartOfTheInstitutesOfTheLawsOfEngland1644.pdf. [Accessed 31st May 2023].

Collins, P.H. (2000) *Black Feminist Thought: Knowledge, Consciousness, and the Politics of Empowerment* (2nd edn), New York: Routledge.

Collins, P.H. (2004) *Black Sexual Politics: African Americans, Gender, and the New Racism*, New York: Routledge.

Conaghan, J. (2013) *Law and Gender*, Oxford: Clarendon Press.

Cooper, D. (2023) 'Crafting prefigurative law in turbulent times: decertification, DIY law reform, and the dilemmas of feminist prototyping', *Feminist Legal Studies*, 31(1): 17–42.

Cornell, D. (1995) *The Imaginary Domain: Abortion, Pornography and Sexual Harassment*, New York: Routledge.

Cowan, R. (2021) 'Asking for it: how rape myths can prejudice trials and potential solutions', in R. Killean, E. Dowds and A. McAlinden (eds) *Sexual Violence on Trial: Local and Comparative Perspectives*, London: Routledge, 85–96.

Cowan, S. (2010) 'All change or business as usual? Reforming the law of rape in Scotland', in C. McGlynn and V. Munro (eds) *Rethinking Rape Law: International and Comparative Perspectives*, London: Routledge, 154–69.

Cowan, S. (2019) 'Sense and sensibilities: a feminist critique of legal interventions against sexual violence', *Edinburgh Law Review*, 23: 22–51.

Cowan, S. (2020) 'The use of sexual history evidence, bad character evidence and "private data" in Scottish sexual offences trials', Edinburgh: Equality and Human Rights Commission.

Craig, E. (2016) 'Section 276 misconstrued: the failure to properly interpret and apply Canada's rape shield provisions', *La Revue du Barreau Canadien*, 94: 45–83.

Craig, E. (2018) *Putting Trials on Trial: Sexual Assault and the Failure of the Legal Profession*, Montreal and Kingston: McGill–Queen's University Press.

Crown Prosecution Service (2018) 'The code for Crown prosecutors', [online]. Available from: https://www.cps.gov.uk/sites/default/files/documents/publications/Code-for-Crown-Prosecutors-October-2018.pdf [Accessed 1 April 2023].

Crown Prosecution Service (2023) 'CPS data summary quarter 2, 2022–23', [online]. Available from: https://www.cps.gov.uk/publication/cps-data-summary-quarter-2-2022-2023 [Accessed 31 May 2023].

Daly, E. (2022) *Rape, Gender and Class: Intersections in Courtroom Narratives*, Cham: Palgrave Macmillan.

Daly, E., Smith, O., Bows, H., Brown, J., Chalmers, J., Cowan, S. et al (2023) 'Myths about myths: a commentary on Thomas (2020) and the question of jury rape myth acceptance', *Journal of Gender-Based Violence*, 7(1): 189–200.

Davis, A.J. (1874) *The Genesis and Ethics of Conjugal Love*, Boston: Colby & Rich.

Davis, A.Y. (1981) *Women, Race, and Class*, New York: Random House.

Davis, A.Y. (2005) *Abolition Democracy: Beyond Empire, Prisons, and Torture*, New York: Seven Stories Press.

Davis, A.Y., Dent, G., Meiners, E.R. and Richie, B.E. (2022) *Abolition. Feminism. Now*, Chicago: Haymarket Books.

De Beistegui, M. (2018) *The Government of Desire: A Genealogy of the Liberal Subject*, Chicago: University of Chicago Press.

Dennis, I. (2020) *The Law of Evidence* (7th edn), London: Sweet & Maxwell.

Dent, N. and Paul, S. (2017) 'In defence of section 41', *Criminal Law Review*, 8: 613–28.

Descartes, R. (2005) *Discourse on Method and the Meditations*, Harmondsworth: Penguin.

Diken, B. and Laustsen, C.B. (2005) 'Becoming abject: rape as a weapon of war', *Body & Society*, 11(1): 111–28.

Donovan, R. and Williams, M. (2002) 'Living at the intersection: the effects of racism and sexism on Black rape survivors', *Women and Therapy*, 25(3/4): 95–105.

Douglas, M. (1966) *Purity and Danger: An Analysis of Concepts of Pollution and Taboo*, London: Routledge.

Dowds, E. (2020) *Feminist Engagement with International Criminal Law: Norm Transfer, Complementarity, Rape and Consent*, Oxford: Hart Publishing.

Dripps, D. (2009) 'After rape law: Will the turn to consent normalise the prosecution of sexual assault?', *Akron Law Review*, 41: 957–80.

Du Toit, L. (2009) *A Philosophical Investigation of Rape: The Making and Unmaking of the Feminine Self*, New York: Routledge.

Du Toit, L. (2019) 'Towards a slow decolonisation of sexual violence', *The Philosophical Journal of Conflict and Violence*, 3(1): 35–54.

Duff, R.A. (2018) *The Realm of Criminal Law*, Oxford: Oxford University Press.

Dunn, C. (2012) *Stolen Women in Medieval England: Rape, Abduction and Adultery 1100–1500*, Cambridge: Cambridge University Press.

Durham, R., Lawson, R., Lord, A. and Baird, V. (2017) 'Seeing is believing: the Northumbria Court Observers' panel report on 30 rape trials', copy on file with the authors.

Durston, G. (2005) 'Rape in the Eighteenth-Century Metropolis: Part I', *British Journal for Eighteenth Century Studies*, 28: 167-179.

Durston, G. (2007) *Victims and Viragos: Metropolitan Women, Crime and the Eighteenth-Century Justice System*, Bury St Edmunds: Arima Publishing.

East, E. (1803) *A Treatise of the Pleas of the Crown*, London: A. Strahan.

Easteal, P. (2011) 'Sexual assault law in Australia: contextual challenges and changes', in N. Westmarland and A. Gangoli (eds) *International Approaches to Rape*, Bristol: Policy Press, 13–24.

Edelstein, L. (1998) 'An accusation easily to be made? Rape and malicious prosecution in eighteenth century England', *American Journal of Legal History*, 42(4): 351–90.

Edwards, S. (1981) *Female Sexuality and the Law*, Oxford: Martin Robertson.

Edwards, S. (2016) 'Loss of self-control: when his anger is worth more than her fear', in A. Reed and M. Bohlander (eds) *Loss of Control and Diminished Responsibility*, London: Routledge, 79–96.

Edwards, S. (2021) 'Women who kill abusive partners: reviewing the impact of section 55(3) "fear of serious violence" manslaughter – some empirical findings', *Northern Ireland Legal Quarterly*, 72(2): 245–70.

Ellison, L. (2019) 'Credibility in context: jury education and intimate partner rape', *The International Journal of Evidence & Proof*, 23(3): 263–81.

Ellison, L. and Munro, V.E. (2009a) 'Of "normal sex" and "real rape": exploring the use of socio-sexual scripts in (mock) jury deliberation', *Social & Legal Studies*, 18(3): 291–312.

Ellison, L. and Munro, V.E. (2009b), 'Reacting to rape: exploring mock jurors' assessments of complainant credibility', *The British Journal of Criminology*, 49(2): 202–19.

Ellison, L. and Munro, V.E. (2009c) 'Turning mirrors into windows? Assessing the impact of (mock) juror education in rape trials', *The British Journal of Criminology*, 49(3): 363–83.

Ellison, L. and Munro, V.E. (2010) 'A stranger in the bushes, or an elephant in the room? Critical reflections upon received rape myth wisdom in the context of a mock jury study', *New Criminal Law Review*, 13(4): 781–801.

Ellison, L. and Munro, V.E. (2013) 'Better the devil you know? "Real rape" stereotypes and the relevance of a previous relationship in (mock) juror deliberations', *International Journal of Evidence & Proof*, 17: 299–322.

Ellison, L. and Munro, V.E. (2015) 'Telling tales: exploring narratives of life and law within the (mock) jury room', *Legal Studies*, 35: 201–25.

Ellison, L., Munro, V.E., Hohl, K. and Wallang, P. (2015) 'Challenging criminal justice? Psychosocial disability and rape victimization', *Criminology & Criminal Justice*, 15(2): 225–44.

Engle, J.C. (2022) 'Sexual violence, intangible harm, and the promise of transformative remedies', *Washington and Lee Law Review*, 79: 1045–92.

Estrich, S. (1987) *Real Rape*, Cambridge, MA: Harvard University Press.

Farmer, L. (2016) *Making the Modern Criminal Law: Criminalization and Civil Order*, Oxford: Oxford University Press.

Farmer, L. (2018) 'Innocence, the burden of proof and fairness in the criminal trial: *Woolmington v DPP* (1935)', in J.D. Jackson and S.J. Summers (eds) *Obstacles to Fairness in Criminal Proceedings*, Oxford: Hart Publishing, 57–73.

Finch, E. and Munro, V. (2005) 'Juror stereotypes and blame attribution in rape cases involving intoxicants', *British Journal of Criminology*, 45(1): 25–38.

Fletcher, A. (1995) *Gender, Sex and Subordination in England 1500–1800*, New Haven: Yale University Press.

Flood, D.R. (2012) *Rape in Chicago: Race, Myth, and the Courts*, Chicago: University of Illinois Press.

Flowe, H.D., Ebbesen, E.B. and Putcha-Bhagavatula, A. (2007) 'Rape-shield laws and sexual behaviour evidence: effects of consent level and women's sexual history on rape allegations', *Law and Human Behaviour*, 31(2): 159–75.

Foucault, M. (1990a) *The History of Sexuality: An Introduction*, trans R. Hurley, New York: Vintage.

Foucault, M. (1990b) *The Use of Pleasure*, trans R. Hurley, New York: Vintage.

Galvin, H.R. (1985) 'Shielding rape victims in the state and federal courts: a proposal for the second decade', *Minnesota Law Review*, 70: 763–916.

Gangoli, G., Bates, L. and Hester, M. (2020) 'What does justice mean to Black and minority ethnic (BME) victims/survivors of gender-based violence?', *Journal of Ethnic and Migration Studies*, 46(15): 3119–35.

Gavey, N. (2019) *Just Sex? The Cultural Scaffolding of Rape* (2nd edn), New York: Routledge.

Geis, G (1978) 'Lord Hale, witches, and rape', *British Journal of Law & Society*, 5: 26–44.

Gerger, H., Kley, H., Bohner, G. and Siebler, F. (2007) 'The acceptance of modern myths about sexual aggression (AMMSA) scale: development and validation in German and English', *Aggressive Behaviour*, 33: 422–40.

Gill, A.K. and Day, A.S. (2020) 'Moral panic in the media: scapegoating South Asian men in cases of sexual exploitation and grooming', in S. Ramon, M. Lloyd and B. Penhale (eds) *Gendered Domestic Violence and Abuse in Popular Culture*, Bingley: Emerald Publishing, 171–97.

Gillen, J. (2019) 'Report into the law and procedures in serious sexual offences in Northern Ireland', Belfast: Department of Justice.

Gilmore, L. (2017) *Tainted Witness: Why We Doubt What Women Say about Their Lives*, New York: Columbia University Press.

Gilmore, R.W. (2022) *Abolition Geography: Essays towards Liberation*, London: Verso Books.

Glancy, J.A. (1993) 'The accused: Susanna and her readers', *Journal for the Study of the Old Testament*, 18(58): 103–16.

Godden, N. (2011) 'Claims in tort for rape: a valuable remedy or damaging strategy?', *King's Law Journal*, 22(2): 157–82.

Godden, N. (2012) 'Tort claims for rape: more trials, fewer tribulations?', in J. Richardson and E. Rackley (eds) *Feminist Perspectives on Tort Law*, London: Routledge, 163–78.

Gold, S. and Wyatt, M. (1978) 'The rape system: old roles and new times', *Catholic University Law Review*, 47: 695–727.

Goldberg, D.T. (2002) *The Racial State*, Oxford: Blackwell Publishing.

Goodrich, P. (1990) *Languages of Law: From Logics of Memory to Nomadic Masks*, Cambridge: Cambridge University Press.

Goodrich, P. (1995) *Oedipus lex: Psychoanalysis, History, Law*, Berkeley: University of California Press.

Gotell, L. (2006) 'When privacy is not enough: sexual assault complainants, sexual history evidence and the disclosure of personal records', *Alberta Law Review*, 43(3): 743–78.

Gqola, P.D. (2015) *Rape: A South African Nightmare*, Johannesburg: MFBooks.

Graham, L.V. (2015) *State of Peril: Race and Rape in South African Literature*, Oxford: Oxford University Press.

Graycar, R. and Morgan, J. (1990) *The Hidden Gender of Law*, Sydney: Federation Press.

Grear, A. (2011) ' "Sexing the matrix": embodiment, disembodiment and the law – towards the re-gendering of legal rationality', in J.A. Jones, A. Grear, R. Fenton and K. Stevenson (eds) *Gender, Sexualities and Law*, Oxford: Routledge, 48–61.

Green, S.P. (2020) *Criminalizing Sex: A Unified Liberal Theory*, Oxford: Oxford University Press.

Greenwald, A.G. and Banaji, A.R. (1995) 'Implicit social cognition: attitudes, self-esteem and stereotypes', *Psychological Review*, 102(1): 4–27.

Gregory, J. and Lees, S. (1999) *Policing Sexual Assault*, London: Routledge.

Groot, R.D. (1988) 'The crime of rape temp, Rich I & John', *Journal of Legal History*, 9: 324.

Gunby, C., Carline, A. and Beynon, C. (2013) 'Regretting it after? Focus group perspectives on alcohol consumption, non-consensual sex and false allegations of rape', *Social & Legal Studies*, 22(1): 87–106.

Haddad, R. (2005) 'Shield or sieve: *People v Bryant* and the rape shield law in high profile cases', *Columbia Journal of Law and Social Problems*, 39: 185–221.

Hale, M. (1800 [1736]) *Historia Placitorum Coronae Vol 1*, London: Sollum Emlyn.

Hänel, C.H. (2018) *What Is Rape? Social Theory and Conceptual Analysis*, Bielefeld: Transcript Verlag.

Harding, S. (ed) (2003) *The Feminist Standpoint Theory Reader: Intellectual and Political Controversies*, New York: Routledge.

Harris, H. and Grace, S. (1999) *A Question of Evidence? Investigating and Prosecuting Rape in the 1990s*, London: Home Office Research Study 196.

Harvey, A.D. (1994) *Sex in Georgian England*, London: Duckworth.

Hawkes, E. (2007) 'Preliminary notes on consent in the 1382 rape and ravishment laws of Richard II', *Legal History*, 11: 117–32.

Hawkins, W. (1716) *Treatise of the Pleas of the Crown*, [online]. Available from: http://lawlibrary.wm.edu/wythepedia/library/HawkinsTreatiseO fThePleasOfTheCrown1716Vol1.pdf [Accessed 31 May 2023].

Hay, D. (1989) 'Prosecution and power: malicious prosecution in the English courts, 1750–1850', in D. Hay and F. Snyder (eds) *Policing and Prosecution in Britain 1750–1850*, Oxford: Oxford University Press, 343–95.

Heath, M. (2005) 'The law on sexual offences against adults in Australia', *Issues*, 4 (June), Australian Centre for the Study of Sexual Assault.

Heilbron, R. (1976) 'Report of the advisory group on the law of rape', Cmnd 6352, London: HM Stationery Office.

Hekman, S. (1990) *Gender and Knowledge: Elements of a Postmodern Feminism*, Boston: Northeastern University Press.

Henderson, E. (2016) 'Best evidence or best interests? What does the case law say about the function of cross-examination?', *International Journal of Evidence & Proof*, 20(3): 183–99.

Henning, T. and Bronitt, S. (1998) 'Rape victims on trial: regulating the use and abuse of sexual history evidence', in P. Easteal (ed) *Balancing the Scales: Rape, Law Reform and Australian Culture*, Sydney: Federation Press, 76–93.

Herbert, I. (2016) 'There are no winners as rape case drags football down to its darkest depths', *The Independent*, [online] 15 October. Available from: https://www.independent.co.uk/sport/football/news/ched-evans-rape-case-not-guilty-verdict-no-winners-compensation-a7362306.htm [Accessed 31 May 2023].

Herriott, C. (2023) *Sexual History Evidence in Rape Trials: Is the Jury Still Out?*, London: Routledge.

Hester, M., Williamson, E., Regan, L., Coulter, M., Chantler, K., Gangoli, G. et al (2012) 'Exploring the service and support needs of male, lesbian, gay, bi-sexual and transgendered and Black and other minority ethnic victims of domestic and sexual violence', Bristol: University of Bristol. Available from: https://core.ac.uk/download/pdf/29026619.pdf [Accessed 4 January 2023].

Hester, M. and Lilley, S.J. (2018) 'More than support to court: rape victims and specialist sexual violence services', *International Review of Victimology*, 24(3): 313–28.

Hewitt, R. (2018) 'Do "animal Fluids move by Hydraulick laws"? The politics of the hydraulic theory of emotion', *The Lancet Psychiatry*, 5(1): 25–6.

Hlavka, H.R. and Mulla, S. (2021) *Bodies in Evidence: Race, Gender, and Science in Sexual Assault Adjudication*, New York: NYU Press.

HMCPSI (2002) 'A report on the joint inspection into the investigation and prosecution of cases involving allegations of rape', London.

HMCPSI (2019) 'A thematic review of rape cases by HM Crown Prosecution Inspectorate', London: HMCPSI Publication no CP001:1267.

HMICFRS/HMCPSI (2022) 'A joint thematic inspection of the police and Crown prosecution response to rape: phase 2 post charge'. Available from: https://www.justiceinspectorates.gov.uk/hmicfrs/publications/a-joint-thematic-inspection-of-the-police-and-crown-prosecution-services-response-to-rape-phase-two-post-charge [Accessed 5 June 2023].

Hohl, K., Johnson, K. and Molisso, S. (2022) 'A procedural justice theory approach to police engagement with victim-survivors of rape and sexual assault: initial findings of the "Project Bluestone" pilot study', *International Criminology*, 2(3): 253-26.

Hom, S. (2022) 'White supremacist miscegenation: Irigaray at the intersection of race, sexuality, and patriarchy', in R.C. Kim, Y. Russell and B. Sharp (eds) *Horizons of Difference: Rethinking Space, Place, and Identity with Irigaray*, New York: SUNY Press, 191–214.

Home Office (2000) 'Setting the boundaries: reforming the law on sex offences', London: Home Office.

Home Office (2021) 'The end-to-end rape review report on findings and actions', HM government, June.

Horvath, M.A.H. and Brown, J.M. (2022) 'Setting the scene: the challenges of researching rape', in M. Horvath and J. Brown (eds) *Rape: Challenging Contemporary Thinking – 10 Years On*, London: Routledge, 3–11.

House of Commons Home Affairs Committee (2022) 'Investigation and prosecution of rape, eighth report of session 2020–21'. Available from: https://publications.parliament.uk/pa/cm5802/cmselect/cmhaff/193/summary.html [Accessed 5 September 2022].

Hoyano, L. (2018) 'The operation of YJCEA 1999 section 41 in the courts of England and Wales: views from the barristers' row', Available from: https://www.criminalbar.com/wp-content/uploads/2018/11/REPORT-PROVIDED-FOR-CBA-WEBSITE-.pdf [Accessed 5 June 2023].

Hudspith, L.F., Wager, N., Willmott, D. and Gallagher, B. (2023) 'Forty years of rape myth acceptance interventions: a systematic review of what works in naturalistic institutional settings and how this can be applied to educational guidance for jurors', *Trauma, Violence & Abuse*, 24(2): 981–1000.

Hufton, O. (1995) *The Prospect before Her: A History of Women in Western Europe Vol 1 1500–1800*, New York: HarperCollins.

Hume, D. (2008) *An Enquiry concerning Human Understanding*, Oxford: Oxford University Press.

Ievins, A. (2023) *The Stains of Imprisonment: Moral Communication and Men Convicted of Sex Offenses*, Berkeley: University of California Press.

Iliadis, M. (2020) 'Victim representation for sexual history evidence in Ireland: a step towards or away from meeting victims' procedural justice needs?', *Criminology & Criminal Justice*, 20(4): 416–32.

Iliadis, M., Smith, O. and Doak, J. (2021) 'Independent separate legal representation for rape complainants in adversarial systems: lessons from Northern Ireland', *Journal of Law and Society*, 48: 250–72.

Irigaray, L. (1985a) *Speculum of the Other Woman*, trans G.C. Gill, Ithaca: Cornell University Press.

Irigaray, L. (1985b) *This Sex Which Is Not One*, trans C. Porter, Ithaca: Cornell University Press.

Irigaray, L. (1991) 'How to define sexuate rights?', in M. Whitford (ed) *The Luce Irigaray Reader*, Oxford: Blackwell, 204–12.

Irigaray, L. (2008) *Conversations*, London: Bloomsbury Publishing.

Jacob, G. (1729) *Law Dictionary*, sv 'Rape', [online]. Available from: http://lawlibrary.wm.edu/wythepedia/library/JacobNewLaw-Dictionary1729.pdf [Accessed 31 May 2023].

Jameson, F. (1977) 'Imaginary and symbolic in Lacan: Marxism, psychoanalytic criticism, and the problem of the subject', *Yale French Studies*, 55/56: 338–95.

Jay, A. (2014) 'Independent inquiry into child sexual exploitation in Rotherham', Rotherham: Rotherham Metropolitan Borough Council. Available from: https://www.rotherham.gov.uk/downloads/download/31/independent-inquiry-into-child-sexual-exploitation-in-rotherham-1997---2013 [Accessed 5 June 2023].

Jillard, A., Loughman, J. and MacDonald, E. (2012) 'From pilot project to systemic reform: keeping sexual assault victims' counselling records confidential', *Alternative Law Journal*, 37: 254–8.

Jones, R. (2011) *Irigaray: Towards a Sexuate Philosophy*, London: Polity.

Jordan, J. (2004) *The Word of a Woman: Police, Rape and Belief*, Basingstoke: Palgrave Macmillan.

Judicial College (2022) 'Judicial College prospectus March 2022–April 2023'. Available from: https://www.judiciary.uk/wp-content/uploads/2022/06/Judicial-College-Prospectus-2022-23.pdf [Accessed 31 May 2023]

Kaba, M. (2021) *We Do This 'til We Free Us: Abolitionist Organizing and Transforming Justice*, Chicago: Haymarket Books.

Kaganas, F. (2002) 'Domestic violence, gender and the expert', in A. Bainham, S. Day Sclater and M. Richards (eds) *Body Lore and Laws*, Oxford: Hart, 105–26.

Kahneman, D. (2011) *Thinking Fast and Slow*, New York: Farrar, Straus and Giroux.

Kaspiew, R. (1995) 'Rape lore: legal narrative and sexual violence', *Melbourne University Law Review*, 20: 350–82.

Keane, E.P.H. and Convery, T. (2020) 'Proposals for independent legal representation for complainers where an application is made to lead evidence of their sexual history or character', Edinburgh: Rape Crisis Scotland. Available from: https://www.research.ed.ac.uk/en/publicati ons/proposal-for-independent-legal-representation-in-scotland-for-com [Accessed 31 May 2023].

Keenan, M. and Zinsstag, E. (2022) *Sexual Violence and Restorative Justice*, Oxford: Oxford University Press.

Kelly, H.A. (1997) 'Statutes of rape and alleged ravishers of wives', *Viator: Journal of Medieval and Renaissance Studies*, 28: 361–419.

Kelly, L., Temkin, J. and Griffiths, S. (2006) 'Section 41: an evaluation of new legislation limiting sexual history evidence in rape trials', Home Office Online Report 20/06. Available from: https://webarchive.nationalarchives. gov.uk/ukgwa/20130128103514/http://www.homeoffice.gov.uk/rds/pdf s06/rdsolr2006.pdf [Accessed 31 May 2023].

Kennedy, D. (2007) *Legal Education and the Reproduction of Hierarchy: A Polemic against the System*, New York: NYU Press.

Kennedy, H. (1992) *Eve Was Framed: Women and British Justice*, London: Random House.

Kibble, N. (2001) 'The relevance and admissibility of prior sexual history with the defendant in sexual offences cases', *Cambrian Law Review*, 32: 27–63.

Kibble, N. (2005a) 'Judicial perspectives on sexual history evidence and the operation of s 41 Youth Justice and Criminal Evidence Act 1999: four scenarios (part one)', *Criminal Law Review*, 190–205.

Kibble, N. (2005b) 'Judicial discretion and the admissibility of prior sexual history evidence under section 41 of the Youth Justice and Criminal Evidence Act 1999: sometimes sticking to your guns means shooting yourself in the foot (part two)', *Criminal Law Review*, 263–74.

Kibble, N. (2008) 'Uncovering judicial perspectives on questions of relevance and admissibility in sexual offences cases', *Journal of Law and Society*, 35(4): 91–107.

Killean, R. (2021) 'Legal representation for sexual assault complainants', in R. Killean, E. Dowds and A. McAlinden (eds) *Sexual Violence on Trial: Local and Comparative Perspectives*, London: Routledge, 174–86.

Killean, R., Dowds, E. and McAlinden, A. (eds) (2021) *Sexual Violence on Trial: Local and Comparative Perspectives*, London: Routledge.

Kim, M.E. (2018) 'From carceral feminism to transformative justice: women-of-color feminism and alternatives to incarceration', *Journal of Ethnic & Cultural Diversity in Social Work*, 27(3): 219–33.

Kim, M.E. (2021) 'Transformative justice and restorative justice: gender-based violence and alternative visions of justice in the United States', *International Review of Victimology*, 27(2): 162–72.

King, R.F. (1998) 'Rape in England 1600–1800: trials, narratives and the question of consent', Unpublished master's thesis, Durham University. Available from: http://etheses.dur.ac.uk/4844/ [Accessed 31 May 2023].

Kittel, R. (1982) 'Rape in thirteenth century England: a study of the common law courts', in D. Kelly Weisberg (ed) *Women and the Law: The Social Historical Perspective Vol 2*, Rochester, VT: Schenkman Books, 101–15.

Konradi, A. (2007) *Taking the Stand: Rape Survivors and the Prosecution of Rapists*, Santa Barbara: Praeger.

Kristeva, J. (1982) *Powers of Horror*, trans. L.S. Roudiez. New York: Columbia University Press.

Lacan, J. (1966) *Écrits*, Paris: Editions du Seuil.

Lacey, N. (2016) *In Search of Criminal Responsibility: Ideas, Interests and Institutions*, Oxford: Oxford University Press.

Lammasniemi, L. (2020) ' "Precocious girls": age of consent, class and family in late nineteenth-century England', *Law and History Review*, 38(1): 241–62.

Lammy, D. (2017) 'The Lammy Review: an independent review into the treatment of, and outcomes for, Black, Asian and minority ethnic individuals in the criminal justice system'. Available from: https://assets.pub lishing.service.gov.uk/government/uploads/system/uploads/attachment_ data/file/643001/lammy-review-final-report.pdf [Accessed 3 April 2023].

Langbein, J.H. (1996) 'Historical foundations of the law of evidence: a view from the Ryder sources', *Columbia Law Review*, 96: 1168–202.

Leahy, S. (2014) 'Whether rules or discretion? Developing a best practice model for controlling the admissibility of sexual experience evidence in sexual offence trials', *Irish Journal of Legal Studies*, 4(1): 65–91.

Leahy, S. (2021) 'The realities of rape trials in Ireland: Perspectives from practice', Dublin Rape Crisis Centre. Available from: https://www.drcc. ie/assets/files/pdf/leahyrealitiesreport.pdf [Accessed 20 March 2023].

Leahy, S. and Fitzgerald O'Reilly, M. (2018) *Sexual Offending in Ireland: Laws, Procedures and Punishment*, Dublin: Clarus Press.

Lees, S. (1996) *Carnal Knowledge: Rape on Trial*, London: Hamish Hamilton.

Levanon, L. (2012) 'Sexual history evidence in cases of sexual assault: a critical re-evaluation', *University of Toronto Law Journal*, 62: 609–51.

Leverick, F. (2020) 'What do we know about rape myths and juror decision-making?', *International Journal of Evidence and Proof*, 24(3): 255–9.

LimeCulture Community Interest Company (2017) 'Application of section 41 Youth Justice and Criminal Evidence Act 1999: a survey of independent sexual advisors'. Copy on file with authors.

Lloyd, G. (1993) *The Man of Reason: 'Male' and 'Female' in Western Philosophy*, New York: Routledge.

Locke, J. (1998) *An Essay Concerning Human Understanding*, Harmondsworth: Penguin.

Lord Justice Clerks' Review Group (2021) 'Improving the management of sexual offences: final report', Scottish Courts and Tribunals Service.

Lugones, M. (2007) 'Heterosexualism and the colonial/modern gender system', *Hypatia*, 22(1): 186–219.

MacKinnon, C.A. (1982) 'Feminism, Marxism, method, and the state: An agenda for theory', *Signs: Journal of Women in Culture and Society*, 7(3): 515–44.

MacKinnon, C.A. (1987) *Feminism Unmodified: Discourses on Life and Law*, Cambridge, MA: Harvard University Press.

MacKinnon, C.A. (1989) *Toward a Feminist Theory of the State*, Cambridge, MA: Harvard University Press.

MacKinnon, C.A. (2003) 'Mainstreaming feminism in legal education', *Journal of Legal Education*, 53(2): 199–212.

MacKinnon, C.A. (2005) *Women's Lives, Men's Laws*, Cambridge, MA: Harvard University Press.

MacKinnon, C.A. (2006) *Are Women Human? And Other International Dialogues*, Cambridge, MA: Harvard University Press.

MacKinnon, C.A. (2016) 'Rape redefined', *Harvard Law & Policy Review*, 10: 431–77.

Marsh, L. and Dein, J. (2021) 'Serious sex offences in England and Wales: defending the indefensible', in R. Killean, E. Dowds and A. McAlinden (eds) *Sexual Violence on Trial: Local and Comparative Perspectives*, London: Routledge, 46–58.

Marx, B.P., Forsyth, J.P., Gallup, G.G. and Fusé, T. (2008) 'Tonic immobility as an evolved predator defense: implications for sexual assault survivors', *Clinical Psychology: Science and Practice*, 15(1): 74–90.

Mason, R. (2016) 'Law concerning use of sexual history in rape trials "could be reformed"', *The Guardian*, [online] 27 October. Available from: http://www.theguardian.com/law/2016/oct/27/law-concerning-use-of-sexual-history-in-trials-could-be-reformed [Accessed 3 April 2023].

McCallum, M. and Ng, G. (2020) 'A toolkit for navigating section 276 and 278 Criminal Code matters as complainant counsel in criminal proceedings', Vancouver: West Coast Leaf.

McColgan, A. (1996) 'Common law and the relevance of sexual history evidence', *Oxford Journal of Legal Studies*, 16: 275–307.

McDonald, E. (2020a) *Rape Myths as Barriers to Fair Trial Process: Comparing Adult Rape Trials with Those in the Aotearoa Sexual Violence Court Pilot*, Christchurch: Canterbury University Press.

McDonald, E. (2020b) 'Submission on sexual violence legislation bill 2019'. Available from: https://ir.canterbury.ac.nz/bitstream/handle/10092/102410/Submission%20on%20Sexual%20Violence%20Legislation%20Bill%202019.pdf?sequence=2 [Accessed 1 April 2023].

McDonald, E. (2023) *Prosecuting Intimate Partner Rape: The Impact of Misconceptions on Complainant Experience and Trial Process*, Christchurch: Canterbury University Press.

McGlynn, C. (2010a) 'Feminist activism and rape law reform in England and Wales: a Sisyphean struggle?', in C. McGlynn and V. Munro (eds) *Rethinking Rape Law: International and Comparative Perspectives*, London: Routledge, 138–53.

McGlynn, C. (2010b) 'R v A (No 2)', in R. Hunter, C. McGlynn and E. Rackley (eds) *Feminist Judgments: From Theory to Practice*, Oxford: Hart Publishing, 211–27.

McGlynn, C. (2017a) 'Rape trials and sexual history evidence: reforming the law on third party evidence', *Journal of Criminal Law*, 81: 367–92.

McGlynn, C. (2017b) 'Why laws on sexual history evidence still need reform', Huffington Post, [online] 17 December. Available from: https://www.huffingtonpost.co.uk/entry/why-laws-on-sexual-history-evidence-still-need-reform_uk_5a33b187e4b0e1b4472ae56d [Accessed 3 April 2023].

McGlynn, C. (2018) 'Challenging the law on sexual history evidence: a response to Dent and Paul', *Criminal Law Review*, 3: 216–28.

McGlynn, C. (2022) 'Challenging anti-carceral feminism: criminalisation, justice and continuum thinking', *Women's Studies International Forum*, 93, doi: https://doi.org/10.1016/j.wsif.2022.102614.

McGlynn, C. and Munro, V. (eds) (2010) *Rethinking Rape Law: International and Comparative Perspectives*, London: Routledge.

McGlynn, C. and Westmarland, N. (2019) 'Kaleidoscopic justice: sexual violence and victim-survivors' perceptions of justice', *Social & Legal Studies*, 28(2): 179–201.

McGlynn, C., Westmarland, N. and Godden, N. (2012) ' "I just wanted him to hear me": sexual violence and the possibilities of restorative justice', *Journal of Law and Society*, 39(2): 213–40.

McGuire, D.L. (2011) *At the Dark End of the Street: Black Women, Rape, and Resistance – A New History of the Civil Rights Movement from Rosa Parks to the Rise of Black Power*, New York: Knopf Double Day.

McNabb, D. and Baker, D. (2021) 'Ignoring implementation: defects in Canada's "rape shield" policy cycle', *Canadian Journal of Law and Society*, 36(1): 23–46.

Ministry of Justice (2017) 'Limiting the use of complainants' sexual history in sex cases: section 41 of the Youth Justice and Criminal Evidence Act 1999 – the law on the admissibility of sexual history evidence in practice'. Available from: https://assets.publishing.service.gov.uk/government/uploads/system/uploads/attachment_data/file/667675/limiting-the-use-of-sexual_history-evidence-in-sex_cases.pdf [Accessed 31 May 2023].

Moi, T. (2004) 'From femininity to finitude: Freud, Lacan, and feminism, again', *Signs: Journal of Women in Culture and Society*, 29(3): 841–78.

Molina, J. and Poppleton, S. (2020) 'Rape survivors and the criminal justice system', Victims Commissioner, [online]. Available from: https://victimsc ommissioner.org.uk/document/rape-survivors-and-the-criminal-justice-system/ [Accessed 3 April 2023].

Moore, C.A. (1977) *Daniel, Esther, and Jeremiah: The Additions*, Garden City: Double Day.

Morgan, G. and Poynting, S. (2012) 'Introduction: the transnational folk devil', in G. Morgan and S. Poynting (eds) *Global Islamophobia: Muslims and Moral Panic in the West*, Farnham: Ashgate, 1–14.

Morris, S. (2016a) 'Social media naming of Ched Evans's accuser raises legal questions', *The Guardian*, [online] 14 October. Available from: https://www.theguardian.com/law/2016/oct/14/social-media-naming-of-ched-evans-accuser-raises-questions-law [Accessed 3 January 2023].

Morris, S. (2016b) 'Barristers say overreaction to Ched Evans case counterproductive', *The Guardian*, [online] 18 October. Available from: https://www.theguardian.com/society/2016/oct/18/criminal-bar risters-over-reaction-ched-evans-counterproductive-victims-sex-assault [Accessed 5 September 2022].

Morris, S. and Topping, A. (2016) 'Ched Evans found not guilty of rape in retrial', *The Guardian*, [online] 14 October. Available from: https://www.theguardian.com/football/2016/oct/14/footballer-ched-evans-cleared-of-in-retrial [Accessed 5 October 2022].

Mountz, A., Bonds, A., Mansfield, B., Lloyd, J., Hyndman, J., Walton-Roberts, M. et al (2015) 'For slow scholarship: a feminist politics of resistance through collective action in the neoliberal university', *ACME: An International Journal for Critical Geographies*, 14(4): 1235–59.

Murnen, S.K., Wright, C. and Kaluzny, G. (2002) 'If "boys will be boys", then girls will be victims? A meta-analytic review of the research that relates masculine ideology to sexual aggression', *Sex Roles*, 46(11): 359–75.

Naffine, N. (1994) 'Possession: erotic love in the law of rape', *Modern Law Review*, 57: 10–37.

Naffine, N. (1998) 'The legal structure of self-ownership: or the self-possessed man and the woman possessed', *Journal of Law and Society*, 25(2): 193–212.

Naffine, N. (2011) 'Women and the cast of legal persons', in J. Jones, A. Grear, R. Fenton and K. Stevenson (eds) *Gender, Sexualities and Law*, Oxford: Routledge, 24–34.

Naffine, N. (2019) *Criminal Law and the Man Problem*, Oxford: Hart Publishing.

Nagy, R. (2015) 'Combatting violence against indigenous women: reconciliation as decolonisation for Canada's stolen sisters', in A. Powell, N. Henry and A. Flynn (eds) *Rape Justice: Beyond the Criminal Law*, London: Palgrave Macmillan, 182–99.

New South Wales Law Commission (2020) 'Consent in Sexual Relationships', https://www.lawreform.justice.nsw.gov.au/Documents/Publications/Reports/Report%20148.pdf [Accessed 5 June 2023].

New Zealand Law Commission (2018) 'Issues paper: second review of the Evidence Act 2006', Wellington: New Zealand Law Commission.

New Zealand Law Commission (2019) 'Final report: second review of the Evidence Act 2006', Wellington: New Zealand Law Commission.

Nguyen, N.L. (2006) 'Roman rape: an overview of Roman rape law from the republican period to Justinian's reign', *Michigan Journal of Gender and Law*, 13(1): 75–112.

Norrie, A. (2014) *Crime, Reason and History: A Critical Introduction to Criminal Law* (3rd edn), Cambridge: Cambridge University Press.

Northern Ireland Department of Justice (2020) 'Gillen Review implementation plan' Available from: https://www.justice-ni.gov.uk/publications/gillen-review-implementation-plan [Accessed 20 March 2023].

O'Malley, T. (2020) 'Review of protection for vulnerable witnesses in the investigation and prosecution of sexual offences', Ireland: Department of Justice.

Ozkin, S. (2011) 'Balancing of interests: admissibility of prior sexual history under section 276', *Criminal Law Quarterly*, 57: 327–45.

Phipps, A. (2009) 'Rape and respectability: ideas about sexual violence and social class', *Sociology*, 43(4): 667–83.

Porter, R. (1986) 'Rape: Does it have a historical meaning?', in R. Porter and S. Tomaselli (eds) *Rape: An Historical and Cultural Enquiry*, Oxford: Blackwell, 216–30.

Powell, A., Henry, N. and Flynn, A. (eds) (2015) *Rape Justice: Beyond the Criminal Law*, London: Palgrave Macmillan.

Powell, A.J., Hlavka, H.R. and Mulla, S. (2017) 'Intersectionality and credibility in child sexual assault trials', *Gender and Society*, 31(4): 457–80.

Puar, J.K. (2007) *Terrorist Assemblages: Homonationalism in Queer Times*, Durham, NC: Duke University Press.

Puar, J.K. and Rai, A. (2002) 'Monster, terrorist, fag: the war on terrorism and the production of docile patriots', *Social Text*, 20(3): 117–48.

Raitt, F. (2013) 'Independent legal representation in rape cases: meeting the justice deficit in adversarial proceedings', *Criminal Law Review*, 9: 729–49.

Rape Crisis Network Ireland (2009) 'Rape and justice in Ireland: a national study of survivor, prosecutor and court responses to rape', Dublin: The Liffey Press.

Razack, S. (1998) *Looking White People in the Eye: Gender, Race, and Culture in Courtrooms and Classrooms*, Toronto: University of Toronto Press.

Redmayne, M. (2003) 'Myths, relationships and coincidences: the new problems of sexual history', *International Journal of Evidence and Proof*, 7: 75–100.

Redmayne, M. (2015) *Character in the Criminal Trial*, Oxford: Oxford University Press.

Robayo, L. (1994) 'The Glen Ridge trial: New Jersey's cue to amend its rape shield statute', *Seton Hall Legislative Journal*, 19: 272–321.

Roberts, P. and Zuckerman, A. (2010) *Criminal Evidence*, Oxford: Oxford University Press.

Roscoe, H. (1846) *Digest of the Laws of Evidence in Criminal Cases*, Philadelphia: T & J W Johnson.

Rumney, P.N. and Fenton, R.A. (2011) 'Judicial training and rape', *The Journal of Criminal Law*, 75(6): 473–81.

Rumney, P.N., McPhee, D., Fenton, R.A. and Williams, A. (2020) 'A police specialist rape investigation unit: a comparative analysis of performance and victim care', *Policing and Society*, 30(5): 548–68.

Russell, Y. (2013) 'Thinking sexual difference through the law of rape', *Law and Critique*, 24(3): 255–75.

Russell, Y. (2016) 'Woman's voice/law's logos: the rape trial and the limits of liberal reform', *Australian Feminist Law Journal*, 42(2): 273–96.

Russell, Y. (2021) 'Theorizing feminist antirape praxis and the problem of resistance', *Signs: Journal of Women in Culture and Society*, 46(2): 465–88.

Russell, Y. (2023) 'Toward a sexuate jurisprudence and on the "second rape" of law', in M. Rawlinson and J. Sares (eds) *What Is Sexual Difference?*, New York: Columbia University Press, 293–311.

Russo, A. (2018) *Feminist Accountability: Disrupting Violence and Transforming Power*, New York: New York University Press.

Rutherford, J. (1997) *Forever England: Reflections on Race, Masculinity and Empire*, London: Lawrence & Wishart.

Sanday, P.R. (1981) *Female Power and Male Dominance: On the Origins of Sexual Inequality*, Cambridge: Cambridge University Press.

Sanyal, M. (2019) *Rape: From Lucretia to #MeToo*, New York: Verso Books.

Saunders, C.L. (2018) 'Rape as one person's word against another's: challenging the conventional wisdom', *International Journal of Evidence and Proof*, 22: 161–81.

Schuller, R.A. and Hastings, P.A. (2002) 'Complainant sexual history evidence: its impact on mock jurors' decisions', *Psychology of Women's Quarterly*, 26(3): 252–61.

Scully, P. (1995) 'Rape, race, and colonial culture: the sexual politics of identity in the nineteenth-century Cape Colony, South Africa', *The American Historical Review*, 100(2): 335–59.

Secret Barrister (2016) 'Why the Ched Evans verdict does not set a dangerous precedent', *New Statesman*, [online] 18 October. Available from: https://www.newstatesman.com/politics/2016/10/why-ched-evans-verdict-does-not-set-dangerous-precedent [Accessed 3 April 2023].

Secret Barrister (2017) 'Harriet Harman's proposal to keep sexual histories out of court will put innocent people in prison'. Available from: https://inews.co.uk/opinion/harriet-harmans-proposal-keep-sexual-histories-court-will-put-innocent-people-prison-76934 [Accessed 5 September 2022].

Shankley, W. and Williams, P. (2020) 'Minority ethnic groups, policing and the criminal justice system in Britain', in B. Byrne, C. Alexander, O. Khan, J. Nazro and W. Shankley (eds) *Ethnicity and Race in the UK: State of the Nation*, Bristol: Policy Press, 51–72.

Sharma, K. and Gill, A.K. (2010) 'Protection for all? The failures of the domestic violence rule for (im)migrant women', in R.K Thiara and A.K. Gill (eds) *Understanding Violence against South Asian Women,* London: Jessica Kingsley Publishers, 211–36.

Sharpe, J.A. (1983) *Crime in 17th-Century England*, Cambridge: Cambridge University Press.

Sheehy, E.A., Stubbs, J. and Tolmie, J. (1992) 'Defending battered women on trial: the battered woman syndrome and its limitations', *Criminal Law Journal*, 16(6): 369–95.

Siddique, H. (2022) 'From crime to the courts: the biggest issues the UK's new PM will face', *The Guardian*, [online] 28 August. Available from: https://www.theguardian.com/uk-news/2022/aug/28/from-to-the-courts-the-biggest-issues-the-uks-new-pm-will-face [Accessed 5 September 2022].

Sidhu, J. (2022) 'Chair's final message'. Available from: https://www.criminalbar.com/resources/news/chairs-final-message-29-08-22 [Accessed 2 September 2022].

Simpson, A.E. (1984) 'Masculinities and control: the prosecution of sex offenses in eighteenth-century London', Unpublished PhD thesis, New York University. Copy on file with authors.

Simpson, A.E. (1986) 'The "blackmail myth" and the prosecution of rape and its attempt in eighteenth-century London: the creation of a legal tradition', *Journal of Criminal Law & Criminology*, 77: 101–50.

Simpson, A.E. (2004) 'Popular perceptions of rape as a capital crime in eighteenth-century England: the press and the trial of Francis Charteris in the Old Bailey, February 1730', *Law & History Review*, 22(1): 27–70.

Smart, C. (1989) *Feminism and the Power of Law*, London: Routledge.

Smart, C. (1995) *Law, Crime and Sexuality: Essays in Feminism*, London: Sage.

Smith, A. (2016) 'Representing rapists: the cruelty of cross-examination and other challenges for the criminal defense lawyer', *American Criminal Law Review*, 53: 255–309.

Smith, O. (2018) *Rape Trials in England and Wales: Observing Justice and Rethinking Rape Myths*, London: Palgrave Macmillan.

Smith, O. (2021) 'Cultural scaffolding and the long view of rape trials', in R. Killean, E. Dowds and A. McAlinden (eds) *Sexual Violence on Trial: Local and Comparative Perspectives*, London: Routledge, 241–53.

Smith, O. and Daly, E. (2020) 'Final report: evaluation of the sexual violence advocates' scheme'. Available from: https://needisclear.files.wordpress.com/2021/01/svca-evaluation-final-report-1.pdf [Accessed 20 March 2023].

Smith, O. and Skinner, T. (2015) 'IPR policy brief: court responses to rape and sexual assault in the UK', University of Bath. Available from: https://purehost.bath.ac.uk/ws/portalfiles/portal/123715444/PB_Olivia_Smith_FINAL_LKJ0902215.pdf [Accessed 31 May 2023].

Smith, O and Skinner, T. (2017) 'How rape myths are used and challenged in rape and sexual assault trials', *Social & Legal Studies*, 26(4): 441–66.

Spade, D. (2011) 'Laws as tactics', *Columbia Journal of Gender & Law*, 21: 40–72.

Spencer, J.R. (2001) ' "Rape shields" and the right to a fair trial', *Cambridge Law Journal*, 60(3): 452–55.

Srinivasan, A. (2021) *The Right to Sex*, London: Bloomsbury Publishing.

Stephen, J.F. (1948) *Digest of the Law of Evidence* (12th edn), London: Macmillan.

Stern, V. (2010) *The Stern Review*, London: Home Office.

Stevenson, K. (2000) 'Unequivocal victims: the historical roots of the mystification of the female complainant in rape cases', *Feminist Legal Studies*, 8: 343–66.

Stoler, A.L. (1995) *Race and the Education of Desire: Foucault's History of Sexuality and the Colonial Order of Things*, Durham, NC: Duke University Press.

Stoler, A.L. (2010) *Carnal Knowledge and Imperial Power: Race and the Intimate in Colonial Rule*, Berkeley: University of California Press.

Summers, H. (2022) 'UK rape victim left "feeling suicidal" after five-year wait for case to come to trial', *The Guardian*, [online] 24 July. Available from: https://www.theguardian.com/society/2022/jul/24/uk-victim-left-feeling-suicidal-after-five-year-wait-for-case-to-come-to-trial [Accessed 2 September 2022].

T.E. (1632) *The Lawes Resolutions of Womens Rights*, London: John Grove.

Temkin, J. (1993) 'Sexual history evidence: the ravishment of section 2', *Criminal Law Review* (January): 3–20.

Temkin, J. (2000) 'Prosecuting and defending rape: perspectives from the bar', *Journal of Law and Society*, 27: 219–48.

Temkin, J. (2002) *Rape and the Legal Process* (2nd edn), Oxford: Oxford University Press.

Temkin, J. (2003) 'Sexual history evidence: beware the backlash', *Criminal Law Review*, 217–42.

Temkin, J. and Krahé, B. (2008) *Sexual Assault and the Justice Gap: A Question of Attitude*, Oxford: Hart Publishing.

Temkin, J., Gray, J. and Barrett, J. (2018) 'Different functions of rape myth use in court: findings from a trial observation study', *Feminist Criminology*, 13(2): 205–26.

Thomas, C. (2020) 'The 21st century jury: contempt, bias and the impact of jury service', *Criminal Law Review*, 11: 987–1011.

Thomason, M. (2018) 'Previous sexual history evidence: a gloss on relevance and relationship evidence', *International Journal of Evidence and Proof*, 22: 342–62.

Tinsley, Y., Baylis, C. and Young, W. (2021) '"I think she's learnt her lesson": juror use of cultural misconceptions in sexual violence trials', *Victoria University Wellington Law Review*, 52: 463–86.

Tufail, W. (2015) 'Rotherham, Rochdale, and the racialised threat of the "Muslim grooming gang"', *International Journal for Crime, Justice and Social Democracy*, 4(3): 30–43.

Tufail, W. and Poynting, S. (2016) 'Muslim and dangerous: "grooming" and the politics of racialisation', in D. Pratt and R. Woodlock (eds) *Fear of Muslims?*, Cham: Springer, 79–92.

Uhrig, N. (2016) 'Black, Asian and minority ethnic disproportionality in the criminal justice system in England and Wales', Ministry of Justice. Available from: https://assets.publishing.service.gov.uk/government/uplo ads/system/uploads/attachment_data/file/639261/bame-disproportional ity-in-the-cjs.pdf [Accessed 3 April 2023].

Viner, C. (1741), *A General Abridgement of Law and Equity*. Aldershot: Printed for the author, by agreement with the law-patentees. Digital version available from: https://archive.org/details/generalabridgmen23vine/page/ n9/mode/2up [Accessed 31 May 2023].

Walker, G. (1998) 'Rereading rape and sexual violence in early modern England', *Gender and History*, 10(1): 1–25.

Walker, G. (2013a) 'Sexual violence & rape in Europe 1500–1750', in K. Fisher and S. Toulalan (eds) *Routledge History of Sex and the Body 1500–Present,* London: Routledge, 429–43.

Walker, G. (2013b) 'Everyman or monster: the rapist in early modern England', *History Workshop Journal*, 76(1): 5–31.

Walker, G. (2013c) 'Rape, acquittal and culpability in popular crime reports in England c 1670–1750', *Past & Present*, 220(1): 115–42.

Walker, S.J.L., Hester, M., McPhee, D., Patsios, D., Williams, A., Bates, L. and Rumney, P. (2021) 'Rape, inequality and the criminal justice response in England: the importance of age and gender', *Criminology & Criminal Justice*, 21(3): 297–315.

Wallach, S.L. (1997) 'Protecting the victim at the expense of the defendant's constitutional rights', *NYLS Journal of Human Rights*, 13(2): 485–521.

Wertheimer, A. (2003) *Consent to Sexual Relations*, Cambridge: Cambridge University Press.

Weiss, K.G. (2009) '"Boys will be boys" and other gendered accounts: an exploration of victims' excuses and justifications for unwanted sexual contact and coercion', *Violence Against Women*, 15(7): 810–34.

Wiener, M.J. (2004) *Men of Blood: Violence, Manliness and Criminal Justice in Victorian England*, Cambridge: Cambridge University Press.

Wiesner Hanks, M. (2008) *Women and Gender in Early Modern Europe* (3rd edn), Cambridge: Cambridge University Press.

Williams, A. (2020) 'Analysis of the cross-examination of complainants and defendants within rape trials', Unpublished PhD thesis, University of West of England. Available from: https://uwe-repository.worktribe.com/output/1491095/analysis-of-the-cross-examination-of-complainants-and-defendants-within-rape-trials [Accessed 20 March 2023].

Woodbridge, L. (1986) *Women and the English Renaissance: Literature and the Nature of Womenkind 1540–1620*, Urbana: University of Illinois Press.

Wriggins, J. (1983) 'Rape, racism and the law', *Harvard Women's Law Journal*, 6: 103–41.

Young, A. (1998) 'The waste land of the law, the wordless song of the rape victim', *Melbourne University Law Review*, 22(2): 442–65.

Zinsstag, E. and Keenan, M. (eds) (2017) *Restorative Responses to Sexual Violence: Legal, Social and Therapeutic Dimensions*, New York: Routledge.

Zydervelt, S., Zajac, R., Kaladelfos, A. and Westera, N. (2017) 'Lawyers' strategies for cross-examining rape complainants: have we moved beyond the 1950s?', *British Journal of Criminology*, 57(3): 551–69.

Index

References to footnotes show both the page number and the note number (185n1).

www.ingramcontent.com/pod-product-compliance
Lightning Source LLC
Chambersburg PA
CBHW070619030426
42337CB00020B/3851